Terror, Security, and Money

TERROR, SECURITY, AND MONEY

Balancing the Risks, Benefits, and Costs of Homeland Security

John Mueller and Mark G. Stewart

OXFORD
UNIVERSITY PRESS

OXFORD
UNIVERSITY PRESS

Oxford University Press, Inc., publishes works that further
Oxford University's objective of excellence
in research, scholarship, and education.

Oxford   New York
Auckland   Cape Town   Dar es Salaam   Hong Kong   Karachi
Kuala Lumpur   Madrid   Melbourne   Mexico   City   Nairobi
New Delhi   Shanghai   Taipei   Toronto

With offices in
Argentina   Austria   Brazil   Chile   Czech Republic   France   Greece
Guatemala   Hungary   Italy   Japan   Poland   Portugal   Singapore
South Korea   Switzerland   Thailand   Turkey   Ukraine   Vietnam

Copyright © 2011 by Oxford University Press

Published by Oxford University Press, Inc.
198 Madison Avenue, New York, New York 10016

www.oup.com

Oxford is a registered trademark of Oxford University Press

Library of Congress Cataloging-in-Publication Data
Mueller, John E.
Terror, security, and money : balancing the risks, benefits, and costs of homeland security /
John Mueller and Mark G. Stewart.
   p.   cm.
ISBN 978-0-19-979575-8 (hardcover) — ISBN 978-0-19-979576-5 (pbk.)
1. Terrorism—United States—Prevention—Cost effectiveness.
2. Terrorism—Costs. 3. National security—United States—Costs.
I. Stewart, Mark G., 1961- II. Title.
HV6432.M843   2011
363.325'170973—dc22   2011011771

9 8 7 6 5 4 3 2 1

Printed in the United States of America
on acid-free paper

To Judy and Xiaoli

CONTENTS

ACKNOWLEDGMENTS

We would like to thank the Mershon Center at Ohio State University and the Centre for Infrastructure Performance and Reliability at the University of Newcastle, Australia for travel and research support. Mark Stewart also appreciates the financial support provided by the Australian Research Council including a recent five-year ARC Professorial Fellowship which will allow this work to be continued. John Mueller appreciates the financial support from an Ohio State University Distinguished Scholar Award. A special thanks to Dr. Rick Herrmann, Director of the Mershon Center, for supporting Professor Stewart's visiting fellowships to the Mershon Center. We are grateful for helpful comments from David McBride and Judy Mueller. Thanks, too, to Jenny Wolkowicki and Ashwin Bohra for excellent work in expediting the production process.

Terror, Security, and Money

INTRODUCTION

In seeking to evaluate the effectiveness of the massive increases in homeland security expenditures since the terrorist attacks on the United States of September 1, 2001, the common and urgent query has been "are we safer?" This, however, is the wrong question. Of course, we are "safer"—the posting of a single security guard at one building's entrance enhances safety, however microscopically. The correct question is "are the gains in security worth the funds expended?" Or as this absolutely central question was posed shortly after 9/11 by risk analyst Howard Kunreuther, "How much should we be willing to pay for a small reduction in probabilities that are already extremely low?"[1]

TALLYING THE COSTS—$1 TRILLION AND COUNTING

We have, in fact, paid—or been willing to pay—a lot. In the years immediately following the terrorist attacks of September 11, 2001, on Washington and New York, it was understandable that there was a tendency to fashion policy and expend funds in haste, confusion, and maybe even hysteria on homeland security. After all, intelligence was estimating at the time that there were as many as 5,000 al-Qaeda operatives at loose in the country and, as New York Mayor Rudy Giuliani reflected later, "Anybody, any one of these security experts, including myself, would have told you on September 11, 2001, we're looking at dozens and dozens and multiyears of attacks like this."[2]

The intelligence claims and the anxieties of Giuliani and other "security experts" have clearly proved, putting it mildly, to be unjustified. In the frantic interim, however, the U.S. government massively increased its expenditures for dealing with terrorism. As we approach the tenth anniversary of 9/11, federal expenditures on domestic homeland security have increased by some $360 billion over those in place in 2001, as table I.1

Table I.1 TOTAL AND ENHANCED HOMELAND SECURITY EXPENDITURES BY THE U.S. GOVERNMENT, 2002 TO 2011, IN MILLIONS OF DOLLARS

Year	Department							Total in current dollars	Total in 2010 dollars	Enhanced expenditure since 2001 in 2010 dollars
	Homeland Security[5]	Defense[6]	Health and Human Services[7]	Justice[8]	Energy[9]	State[10]	Others[11]			
2001	-	-	-	-	-	-	-	20,100[1]	24,723	-
2002	-	-	-	-	-	-	-	32,000[2]	38,720	13,997
2003	23,063	8,442	4,144	2,349	1,408	634	2,407	42,447[3]	50,087	25,364
2004	22,923	7,024[12]	4,062	2,180	1,364	696	2,585	40,834[3]	46,959	22,236
2005	24,549	17,188	4,229	2,767	1,562	824	3,264	54,383[3]	60,909	36,186
2006	26,571	17,510	4,352	3,026	1,702	1,108	2,849	57,118[3]	61,687	36,964
2007	29,554	16,538	4,327	3,517	1,719	1,242	2,936	59,833[3]	62,825	38,102
2008	32,740	17,374	4,301	3,523	1,829	1,962	3,194	64,923[3]	65,572	40,849
2009	38,988	19,483	4,677	3,715	1,939	1,809	3,385	73,996[3]	75,476	50,753
2010	36,081	19,041	4,804	4,107	2,018	1,767	3,252	71,070[3]	71,070	46,347
2011	37,066	19,103	5,428	4,285	2,023	2,258	2,349	72,512[4]	72,512	47,789
Total in 2010 dollars	286,781	149,130	42,888	31,078	16,489	12,824	27,908	567,098	605,818	358,588

Notes for this table begin on p. 196.

demonstrates—and the vast majority of this increase, of course, has been driven by concerns over terrorism. Moreover, federal national intelligence expenditures aimed at defeating terrorists at home and abroad have gone up by $110 billion, while state, local, and private-sector expenditures have increased by $220 billion more.

Tallying all these expenditures and adding in opportunity costs—but leaving out the costs of the terrorism-related (or terrorism-determined) wars in Iraq and Afghanistan and quite a few other items that might be included—the increase in expenditures on domestic homeland security over the decade exceeds $1 trillion. The details are in table I.2. This has not been enough to move the country into bankruptcy, Osama bin Laden's stated goal after 9/11, but it clearly adds up to real money, even by Washington standards.[3] Other countries like Britain, Canada, and Australia have also dramatically increased their expenditures.[4]

EVALUATING THE EXPENDITURES

This book seeks to apply conventional cost-benefit and risk analytic approaches to this huge increase in expenditures in an effort to provide an answer to Kunreuther's exceedingly apt question. These approaches have been recommended for many years by the U.S. Office of Management and Budget, and they are routinely used by such agencies as the Nuclear Regulatory Commission, the Environmental Protection Agency, and the Federal Aviation Administration. In 2004, the 9/11 Commission specifically called on the government to apply them to assess the risks and cost-effectiveness of security measures put in place to deal with terrorism.[5] However, it appears that this simply has not been done.

Upon taking office in 2005, Department of Homeland Security (DHS) Secretary Michael Chertoff did strongly advocate a risk-based approach, insisting that the department "must base its work on priorities driven by risk."[6] Yet, a year later, when DHS expenditures had increased by some $135 billion beyond those already in place in 2001, and when the department had become the government's largest nonmilitary bureaucracy, one of its senior economists wistfully noted, "We really don't know a whole lot about the overall costs and benefits of homeland security."[7]

By 2007, RAND President James Thomson was contending that DHS leaders "manage by inbox," with the "dominant mode of DHS behavior being crisis management." Most programs are implemented, he continued, "with little or no evaluation" of their performance or effectiveness, and the

Table I.2 THE TRILLION DOLLAR TABLE: ENHANCED COSTS OF
HOMELAND SECURITY SINCE 9/11, IN BILLIONS OF 2010 DOLLARS

	2009	2002–2011
Enhanced Direct Expenditures		
Federal "homeland security" expenditures from table I.1	50	360
Federal intelligence expenditures[13]	15	110
Local and state expenditures[14]	10	110
Private-sector spending[15]	10	110
Total[16]	**85**	**690**
Opportunity Costs		
Terrorism risk insurance premiums[17]	4	40
Passenger delays caused by airport screening[18]	10	100
Increase in short-haul traffic fatalities for people avoiding airport delays[19]	3	32
Deadweight losses and losses in consumer welfare[20]	30	245
Total	**47**	**417**
TOTAL	**132**	**1107**

Relevant spending elements not included in the table

Terror-related wars in Iraq and Afghanistan[21]

Costs of crime facilitated by focus of police and FBI on, or preoccupation with, terrorism

Costs resulting from Hurricane Katrina that might have been mitigated if DHS had not been so preoccupied by terrorism

Additional post office expenditures to deal with the effects of 9/11 and the anthrax letters[22]

Effects on tourism, property and stock market values, business location decisions, and so on, though deadweight losses might capture some of these

In addition to the short-haul fatality effect included in the table, the increase in U.S. traffic fatalities of 2,300 lives to the end of 2003 due to the fear of flying and the inconvenience of extra passenger screening[23]

Extra fuel cost to airlines because of the weight of hardened (heavier) cockpit doors

Free airline seats to federal air marshals[24]

Passenger delays and inconvenience cause by false-positive identification on TSA's no-fly list

Cutbacks to Medicare, Medicaid, education, Social Security, and other government services in an effort to rein in budget deficits caused by wars in Iraq and Afghanistan and mushrooming homeland security budgets[25]

Notes for this table begin on p. 197.

agency "receives little analytical advice on issues of policy, program, and budget."[8] And analyst Jeremy Shapiro argued:

> Policy discussions of homeland security issues are driven not by rigorous analysis but by fear, perceptions of past mistakes, pork-barrel politics, and insistence on an invulnerability that cannot possibly be achieved. It's time for a more analytic, *threat-based* approach, grounded in concepts of sufficiency, prioritization, and measured effectiveness. . . . In the early days after 9/11, it made sense to take measures that responded to the circumstances of that attack and reassured a nervous public. But, five years into the apparently endless war on terrorism, homeland security should evolve from a set of emergency measures into a permanent field of important government policy that, like any other, must justify its allocation of taxpayer funds through solid analysis.[9]

Most impressively, after an exhaustive assessment, the Congressional Research Service concluded at the same time that DHS simply could not answer the "central question" about the "rate of return, as defined by quantifiable and empirical risk reductions" on its expenditure.[10]

Questions raised by private industry echo these. In a 2008 submission regarding a rule establishing security requirements for railroad operators, one carrier noted that the department's Transportation Security Administration did not "weigh the costs of the regulation against the probability of a transportation security incident," examining only the potential consequences of an incident. Since it failed "to acknowledge the relatively low probability of an attack on a rail car," it "therefore did not complete a comprehensive analysis of the rule." Another submission at the time stated that "TSA failed to provide information on the approximate percentage of total risk that would be eliminated by the rule." The agency's response was remarkably lame: it "did not attempt to quantify the benefits of overall risk reduction to the rail industry," it said, because "risk is dynamic" and "threat, vulnerability, and consequences are constantly evolving."[11] Accordingly, the agency was doing risk assessments without bothering to estimate risk.

The boilerplate emphasis on risk-informed decision making continued with the change of administrations after the 2008 elections, as Secretary Janet Napolitano insisted:

> Development and implementation of a process and methodology to assess national risk is a fundamental and critical element of an overall risk

management process, with the ultimate goal of improving the ability of decision makers to make rational judgments about tradeoffs between courses of action to manage homeland security risk.[12]

Such declarations notwithstanding, we have been able to find only *one* published reference to a numerical estimate of risk reduction after an extensive search of the agency's reports and documents.[13] Moreover, we have been able to find no reference whatever to the likelihood of a terrorist attack beyond rather vague references such as "high," "imminent," "dynamic," "persistent," and "emerging." What is needed are numbers, not adjectives—particularly ones that, without explanation, cluster entirely at the dire end of the threat spectrum. On the other hand, the publications are resplendent with menacing predictions of potential consequences and losses for various terrorist attack scenarios.

Indeed, at times DHS has ignored specific calls by other government agencies to conduct risk assessments. In 2010, the department began deploying full-body scanners at airports, a technology that will cost $1.2 billion per year. The Government Accountability Office (GAO) noted that "cost-benefit analyses are important because they help decision makers determine which . . . investments in technologies or in other security programs, will provide the greatest mitigation of risk for the resources that are available," and it then *specifically* declared that conducting a cost-benefit analysis of this new technology to be "important."[14] As far as we can see, no such study was conducted. Or there was GAO's request that DHS conduct a full cost-benefit analysis of the extremely costly process of scanning 100 percent of U.S.-bound containers. To do so would require the dedicated work of a few skilled analysts for a few months or possibly a year. Yet, DHS replied that, although it agreed that such a study would help to "frame the discussion and better inform Congress," to actually carry it out "would place significant burdens on agency resources."[15]

Clearly, DHS focuses all or almost all of its analyses on the contemplation of the consequences of a terrorist attack while substantially ignoring the equally important likelihood component of risk assessment, as well as the key issue of risk reduction. In general, risk assessment seems to be simply a process of identifying a potential source of harm and then trying to do something about it without evaluating whether the new measures reduce risk sufficiently to justify their costs.

This conclusion was strongly supported by a 2010 report of the National Research Council of the National Academies of Sciences, Engineering, and Medicine. Requested by Congress to assess the activities of the

Department of Homeland Security, a committee worked for nearly two years on the project and came up with some striking conclusions (table I.3). Except for the analysis of natural disasters, the committee "did not find any DHS risk analysis capabilities and methods that are yet adequate for supporting DHS decision making," and therefore "only low confidence should be placed in most of the risk analyses conducted by DHS." Indeed, "little effective attention was paid to the features of the risk problem that are fundamental." It also found an "absence of documentation of methods and processes," with the result that the committee sometimes had to *infer* details about DHS risk modeling. In fact, "in a number of cases examined by the committee, it is not clear what problem is being addressed." It also found "a pattern" of "trusting numbers that are highly uncertain." Concluded the committee rather glumly, "It is not yet clear that DHS is on a trajectory for development of methods and capability that is sufficient to ensure reliable risk analyses": although it found that "there are people at DHS who are aware of these current limitations," it "did not hear of efforts to remedy them."[16] This situation is particularly strange because, as the committee also notes, the risk models used in the department for *natural* hazards are "near state of the art" and "are based on extensive data, have been validated empirically, and appear well suited to near-term decision needs."[17]

We have frequently been impressed that some of the most elemental questions have only rarely been fully considered (or sometimes even asked) in the public reports by those in charge of doling out hundreds of billions of dollars in homeland security money. Nor have relevant decision makers been pointedly queried by the media. Among the questions:

- What is the probability of a terrorist attack on a prospective target?
- What are the likely (not simply the worst conceivable) consequences of such an attack, including both direct and indirect damage?
- What are the consequences of the fact that the number of potential terrorist targets is effectively infinite?
- Is it essentially impossible to adequately protect some targets (like subways) except by closing them down?
- How do the costs of protection measures compare with the costs of repair or replacement?
- What risk reduction has been achieved by homeland security spending? How many lives have been saved? What economic losses have been averted?
- What else could be done with the same money—that is, what are the trade-offs, the opportunity costs, not only to other security measures but also to the overall welfare of society?

Table I.3 CONCLUSIONS AND OBSERVATIONS FROM NATIONAL RESEARCH COUNCIL OF THE NATIONAL ACADEMIES, *REVIEW OF THE DEPARTMENT OF HOMELAND SECURITY'S APPROACH TO RISK* ANALYSIS (2010)

With the exception of risk analysis for natural disaster preparedness, the committee did not find any DHS risk analysis capabilities and methods that are yet adequate for supporting DHS decision making, because their validity and reliability are untested. Moreover, it is not yet clear that DHS is on a trajectory for development of methods and capability that is sufficient to ensure reliable risk analyses other than for natural disasters. (2–3, 80)

Assessment of individual components of risk and their integration into a measure of risk is in many cases seriously deficient and is in need of major revision. (11)

Little effective attention was paid to the features of the risk problem that are fundamental. (11)

Until these deficiencies are improved, only low confidence should be placed in most of the risk analyses conducted by DHS. (11, 98)

Most DHS risk models and analyses are quite complex and poorly documented, and thus are not transparent to decision makers or other risk analysts. Moreover, some of those models imply false precision. (7)

It is very difficult to know precisely how DHS risk analyses are being done and whether their results are reliable and useful in guiding decisions. (11)

With [one] exception, the committee was not told about or shown any document explaining the mathematics of the risk modeling or any expository write-up [explaining] exactly how the risk analyses are conducted. (42)

Because of this lack of documentation, the committee has had to infer details about DHS risk modeling. (43)

In a number of cases examined by the committee, it is not clear what problem is being addressed. (64)

It appears that the choice of weightings in these risk assessments, and the parameters in the consequence formulas, are chosen in an ad hoc fashion. (72)

The committee has not seen or heard of validation studies of any DHS risk models. (112)

DHS has frequently chosen to weight heavily its consequence analyses, where magnitudes of effects can be more easily estimated, and to reduce the weight attached to threats, where the uncertainties are large. This is not an acceptable way of dealing with uncertainty. (97)

The committee saw a pattern of DHS personnel and contractors' putting too much effort into quantification and trusting numbers that are highly uncertain. Similarly, the committee observed a tendency to make risk analyses more complex than needed or justified. (81)

DHS has a very thin base of expertise in risk analysis—many staff members are learning on the job—and a heavy reliance on external contractors. (90)

The challenges in building a risk culture in a federal agency or corporation are major, requiring a serious effort. . . . It was not clear to the committee whether DHS has any serious plan for how this will happen and any serious ongoing evaluation of progress. (106)

There are people at DHS who are aware of these current limitations, but the committee did not hear of efforts to remedy them. (65)

Source: National Research Council 2010.

- Does evidence from the fourth plane on 9/11 suggest that a direct replication of what happened to the first three has become essentially impossible because the passengers and crew will not allow the plane to be commandeered?
- Are there instances where it would be far less expensive to simply save the money intended for a security measure and use it to repair and compensate in the unlikely event of an attack?
- Is it possible to predict potential terrorist targets with any real degree of reliability and timely accuracy?
- Does protecting one potential target make other ones less safe? Does it make sense to protect one potential terrorist target if there are others of equal value nearby?
- Are there acceptable risks? If there is 1 chance in 20 million that an airplane will undergo a terrorist incident, is that safe enough? If not, what is?

Overall, it seems, security concerns that happen to rise to the top of the agenda are serviced without much in the way of full evaluation—security trumps economics, as one insider puts it—and such key issues as acceptable risk are rarely discussed, while extravagant worst-case scenario thinking dominates, and frequently savagely distorts, the discussion. In consequence, by any reasonable cost-benefit standard, a great deal of money seems to have been misspent and would have been far more productive—saved far more lives—if it had been expended in other ways.

THE PLAN OF THE BOOK

It is clearly time to examine the massive increases in homeland security expenditures in a careful and systematic way, applying the kind of analytic risk management approaches emphasizing cost-benefit analysis and determinations of acceptable and unacceptable risks that are routinely required of other governmental agencies and that have been standard coin for policy decision making for decades throughout the world when determining regulations. In the process, these approaches seek to balance the competing demands of safety and cost even in such highly charged and politicized decisions as where to situate nuclear power plants, how to dispose of toxic waste, and how to control pollution—decisions that engage the interests and passions of multiple groups. It is particularly important to do so with homeland security expenditures. They deal not with bridges to nowhere or with crop subsidies, but with public safety—or domestic tranquility—the central reason for the existence of government in the first place. It is imperative that decisions be made sensibly and responsibly in this area because human lives are at stake.

In applying standard risk and cost-benefit evaluation techniques that have been accepted and used by regulators, academics, businesses, and governments, we focus first on the cost-effectiveness of the overall enhanced expenditures on homeland security measures that have taken place since 9/11 and then on more specific measures designed to protect. We also put forward some comments about evaluating policing and intelligence matters, as well as ones concerning mitigation, resilience, and overreaction. And we include a consideration of political demands and requirements that essentially determine, and sometimes greatly distort, policy making in this area.

Chapter 1 sets out our basic approach to risk analysis, one that seeks to apply processes and procedures that have been standard for decades. In the process, it assesses the phenomena of probability neglect and cost neglect, of obsessive worst-case thinking, and of extreme risk aversion so often found in public and official discussions of the terrorism issue.

Chapter 2 deals with the nature of the challenge presented by terrorism, particularly the international or transnational terrorism that is of most concern to people in the West. It concludes that, however tragic, the amount of destruction wreaked by terrorists, and particularly the loss in human life they have been able to inflict, has been quite limited. Moreover, this condition is unlikely to worsen—indeed, the trends are substantially in the opposite direction. The chapter then places the issue in broader context, comparing the risk terrorism presents to human life with other hazards that have variously been considered acceptably or unacceptably likely. In almost all cases, annual terrorism fatality risks lie within the range generally deemed internationally to be safe or acceptable, requiring no further regulation.

Chapter 3 tallies the full costs that terrorism characteristically inflicts, not only those attending the loss of life but also the direct and indirect economic costs and the costs of reaction, including opportunity costs. To do so, it puts all the losses—including the loss of life—into economic terms. It concludes that losses due to terrorism are likely to remain rather limited except under the unlikely prospect that terrorists acquire nuclear weapons or under the more probable one in which the terrorists' victims self-destructively overreact.

Applying the material developed in chapters 2 and 3, chapter 4 takes a broad overview of the costs and benefits of increases in homeland security spending since 2001 in the United States, the United Kingdom, Canada, and Australia. It concludes that, using standard analytic risk management approaches, ones required by these governments in other circumstances, increases in American homeland security expenditures have been wildly inefficient. To be considered cost-effective in analyses that substantially bias the consideration toward the opposite conclusion, the enhanced expenditures each year would have had to have deterred, foiled, or protected against as many as 1,667 otherwise successful terrorist acts roughly like the one intended on Times Square in 2010, or more than four per day. Increases in overall security spending have been proportionately much lower in the United Kingdom, Canada, and Australia, but they still fail a cost-benefit evaluation.

Chapter 5 looks more closely at those homeland security measures specifically designed to protect people and assets from a terrorist attack, and it lays out a series of general principles or parameters that must be considered for the discussion to be sensible. These include the need to realistically seek to assess the (usually remote) likelihood of a terrorist attack on a potential target (the numbers of which are massive), the limited numbers of terrorists and the equally limited competence of most of them, the ability of terrorists to shift from one target to another if the first proves to be well protected, their method of target selection that often seems to effectively be random, the costs of repair in comparison with those of protection, the hopelessness of adequately protecting many potential targets except by closing them down, and the costs and negative consequences of protective measures. Many of these principles, however, are currently either ignored or applied in confused ways. The chapter also assesses the often-quixotic process of fabricating lists of potential terrorist targets in an effort to predict which targets are most appealing to terrorists.

Chapter 6 assesses the value of protecting specific potential infrastructure terrorist targets, particularly buildings and bridges. It concludes that, although some security measures may be cost-effective, many others currently in place, some of them remarkably expensive, fail to be so. Specifically, in analyses applying assumptions substantially biased toward the opposite conclusion, the likelihood of a successful terrorist attack on a typical office-type building for which there is no specific threat would have to be a thousand times higher than it is at present for protective security measures to be cost-effective. It also considers the built-in resilience of many potential terrorist targets.

Chapter 7 focuses on airline security, including a comparison of the risk reduction potentially supplied by such security measures as adding air marshals and hardening cockpit doors. It concludes that the air marshal service substantially fails a cost-benefit test, whereas hardened cockpit doors may well be cost-effective. It also evaluates full-body scanners, concluding it unlikely that they are cost-effective, and it assesses areas where costs on airline security could be productively cut.

Chapter 8 begins by considering some of the issues in assessing the costs and benefits of policing and intelligence. This is an area likely to be more productive in reducing risks than many protection measures, but it is an area of difficulty because of the staggering costs of accumulating and then managing a massive amount of information to deal with a limited threat, and because police measures may effectively in some instances actually invent terrorists. Also considered are the issues of mitigation, resilience, and absorption and the seemingly natural ability of people to deal with adversity. In this light, avoiding overreaction, which requires no expenditure whatever, recommends itself as by far the most cost-effective counterterrorism measure.

Chapter 9 considers the political realities and pressures that confront bureaucrats and politicians on this issue. In general, we conclude, the fact that these exist does not relieve those in charge from being responsible in the way they handle and expend public funds. In particular, they should be trying to realistically deal with terrorist fears, which can be quite harmful, instead of continually exacerbating them. Moreover, political concerns may well be overwrought. The public seems to be able to respond to adult talk about terrorism in a sensible way, and overreaction does not seem to be a political requirement: it has been avoided many times in the past. Examined as well are opportunity costs, which brings up a moral consideration: far more lives could have been saved if the funds, or even a portion of them, had been expended in other ways. For example, for a comparatively modest expenditure on shelters, the lives of many of the hundreds of Americans killed by tornadoes in 2011 could have been saved. The book concludes with a discussion of the internalization of the terrorist threat, comparing it to perceptions of the threat presented by domestic Communism during the Cold War. Excessive expenditure on counterterrorism, it appears, is likely to be around for a very long time.

CHAPTER 1

Assessing Risk

A key problem in much homeland security analysis is the tendency to take a selective approach to risk assessment, focusing almost exclusively on imagining hazard scenarios (mostly rather extreme ones) and then analyzing the prospective consequences. There is relative neglect of several steps that are crucial for risk assessment to have any real credibility:

- Establishing and trying to quantify threat likelihood
- Evaluating risks
- Setting risk acceptance criteria
- Establishing how much risk is likely to be reduced as a result of new security measures

There is also a tendency to neglect costs and to engage in conceptual clutter.

This chapter considers these issues. It then presents and explains the approach to risk analysis that we will apply throughout the book.

PROBABILITY NEGLECT

A recent book by Gregory Treverton, a risk analyst at the RAND Corporation whose work we have found highly valuable at various points in this study, contains a curious reflection:

> When I spoke about the terrorist threat, especially in the first years after 2001, I was often asked what people could do to protect their family and

home. I usually responded by giving the analyst's answer, what I labelled "the RAND answer." Anyone's probability of being killed by a terrorist today was essentially zero and would be tomorrow, barring a major discontinuity. So, they should do nothing. It is not surprising that the answer was hardly satisfying, and I did not regard it at such.

From this experience, he concluded, "People want information, but the challenge for government is to warn without terrifying."[1]

It is not clear why anyone should find his observation unsatisfying since it simply puts the terrorist threat in a general and in a personal context, suggesting that excessive alarm about the issue is scarcely called for. It is, one might suspect, exactly the kind of accurate, reassuring, adult, and unterrifying information people have been yearning for. And it deals frontally with a key issue in risk assessment: evaluating the likelihood of a terrorist attack.

Treverton's "RAND answer," calmly (and accurately) detailing the likelihood of the terrorist hazard and putting it in reasonable context, has scarcely ever been duplicated by politicians and officials in charge of providing public safety. In fact, in the ten years since 9/11, there appears to have been only one statement by a public official, a fleeting one by New York Mayor Michael Bloomberg in 2007, that has even attempted to do so.[2] Instead, the awkward problem of dealing with exceedingly low probabilities has been finessed—and questionable expenditures accordingly justified—by five stratagems that in various ways embrace a form of risk aversion that can be called "probability neglect."

Focusing on Worst-Case Scenarios

Cass Sunstein, who seems to have invented the phrase "probability neglect," assesses the version of the phenomenon that comes into being when "emotions are intensely engaged." Under that circumstance, he argues, "people's attention is focused on the bad outcome itself, and they are inattentive to the fact that it is unlikely to occur." Moreover, they are inclined to "demand a substantial governmental response—even if the magnitude of the risk does not warrant the response."[3] It may be this phenomenon that Treverton experienced.

Playing to this demand, government officials are inclined to focus on worst-case scenarios, presumably in the knowledge, following Sunstein's insight, that this can emotionally justify just about any expenditure, no matter how unlikely the prospect the dire event will actually take place. Accordingly, there is a preoccupation with "low probability/high consequence" events, such as the detonation of a sizable nuclear device in midtown Manhattan. The process could be seen in action in an article published in 2008 by Secretary of Homeland Security (DHS) Michael Chertoff. He felt called upon to respond to the observation that the number of people who die each year from international terrorism, while tragic, is actually exceedingly small. "This fails to consider," he pointed out, "the much greater loss of life that weapons of mass destruction could wreak on the American people."[4] That is, he was justifying his entire budget—only a limited portion of which is concerned with weapons of mass destruction (WMD)— by the WMD threat, even while avoiding assessing its likelihood.

It is sometimes argued that conventional risk analysis breaks down under extreme conditions because the risk is now a very large number (losses) multiplied by a very small number (attack probability). But it is not the risk analysis methodology that is at fault here, but our ability to use the information obtained from the analysis for decision making. A "high-consequence" event has been defined to be a "disaster" or "catastrophe" resulting in "great human costs in life, property, environmental damage, and future economic activity."[5] However, depending on how one weighs the words in that definition, there may have been only one terrorist event in all of history that qualifies for inclusion. Moreover, the vast bulk of homeland security expenditures is not focused on events that fit a definition like that, but rather on comparatively low-consequence ones, like explosions set off by individual amateur jihadists.

Analyst Bruce Schneier has written penetratingly of worst-case thinking. He points out that it

involves imagining the worst possible outcome and then acting as if it were a certainty. It substitutes imagination for thinking, speculation for risk analysis, and fear for reason. It fosters powerlessness and vulnerability and magnifies social paralysis. And it makes us more vulnerable to the effects of terrorism.

It leads to bad decision making because

it's only half of the cost-benefit equation. Every decision has costs and benefits, risks and rewards. By speculating about what can possibly go wrong, and then acting as if that is likely to happen, worst-case thinking focuses only on the extreme but improbable risks and does a poor job at assessing outcomes.

It also assumes "that a proponent of an action must prove that the night-mare scenario is impossible," and it "can be used to support any position or its opposite. If we build a nuclear power plant, it could melt down. If we don't build it, we will run short of power and society will collapse into anarchy." And worst, it "validates ignorance" because, "instead of focusing on what we know, it focuses on what we don't know—and what we can imagine." In the process, "risk assessment is devalued" and "probabilistic thinking is repudiated in favor of possibilistic thinking."[6]

As Schneier also notes, worst-case thinking is the driving force behind the precautionary principle, a decent working definition of which is "action should be taken to correct a problem as soon as there is evidence that harm *may* occur, not after the harm has already occurred."[7] It could be seen in action less than a week after 9/11, when President George W. Bush outlined his new national security strategy: "We cannot let our enemies strike first . . . [but must take] anticipatory action to defend ourselves, even if uncertainty remains as to the time and place of the enemy's attack. To forestall or prevent such hostile acts by our adversaries, the United States, will, if necessary, act preemptively. . . . America will act against such emerging threats before they are fully formed."[8] The 2003 invasion of Iraq, then, was justified by invoking the precautionary principle based on the worst-case scenario in which Saddam Hussein might strike. If, on the other hand, any worst-case thinking focused on the potential for the destabilizing effects a war would have on Iraq and the region, the precautionary principle would guide one to be very cautious about embarking on war. As Sunstein notes, the precautionary principle "offers no guidance—not that it is wrong, but that it forbids all courses of action, including regulation." Thus, "taken seriously, it is paralyzing, banning the very steps that it simultaneously requires."[9] It can be invoked in equal measure to act or not to act.

There are considerable dangers in applying the precautionary principle to terrorism: on the one hand, any action taken to reduce a presumed risk always poses the introduction of countervailing risks, while on the other, larger, expensive counterterrorism efforts will come accompanied by high opportunity costs.[10] Moreover, "For public officials no less than the rest of us, the probability of harm matters a great deal, and it is foolish to attend exclusively to the worst case scenario."[11]

A more rational approach to worst-case thinking is to establish the likelihood of gains and losses from various courses of action, including staying the current course.[12] This, of course, is the essence of risk assessment. What is necessary is due consideration to the spectrum of threats, not simply the worst one imaginable, in order to properly understand, and coherently deal with, the risks to people, institutions, and the economy. The relevant decision makers are professionals, and it is not unreasonable to suggest that they should do so seriously. Notwithstanding political pressures (to be discussed more in chapter 9), the fact that the public has difficulties with probabilities when emotions are involved does not relieve those in charge of the requirement, even the duty, to make decisions about the expenditures of vast quantities of public monies in a responsible manner.

Adding, Rather Than Multiplying, the Probabilities

A second stratagem for neglecting probability that is sometimes applied at DHS is to devise a rating scale where probabilities of attack are *added* to the losses. Thus, as a Congressional Research Service (CRS) analysis points out, to determine whether a potential target should be protected, DHS has frequently assessed the target's vulnerability and the consequences of an attack on it on an 80-point scale and the likelihood it will be attacked on a 20-point ranked scale. It then adds these together.[13] Thus, a vulnerable target whose destruction would be highly consequential would be protected even if the likelihood it will be attacked is zero, and a less consequential target could go unprotected even if the likelihood it will be attacked is 100 percent.

This procedure violates the principles espoused in all risk assessment techniques, such as those codified in international risk management standards supported by 26 countries, including the United States.[14] In these, risk is invariably taken to be a product in which the attack probability is *multiplied* by the losses, not added to them—a key relationship first laid out in 1711 by Abraham de Moivre, a founding father of modern statistics and a close friend of Isaac Newton.[15] Essentially, what often seems to be happening is that DHS has a pot of money to dole out, and it has worked out a method for determining which projects are worthiest while avoiding determining whether any of them are actually worth any money at all.

Assessing Relative, Rather Than Absolute, Risk

A third technique, related to the second, is, as the CRS study points out, simply to rank relative risk while neglecting to determine the actual magnitude of the risk.[16] The 2010 National Research Council study finds this approach to be wanting:

Risk management decisions seek to reduce risks in accordance with specified, absolute risk criteria for human health protection. Many of the risk analyses thus far conducted by DHS involve *risk ranking*, based on scales of presumed relative risks, and do not include attempts to provide absolute measures of risk.[17]

Following this pattern, a thoughtful study of homeland security spending by Matt Mayer contains these two consecutive sentences: "The reality is that while the risk of a terrorist attack anywhere in America exists, the probability of a terrorist attack in most of America remains very low. That said, the risk of a terrorist attack is higher in some jurisdictions in the United States." He then proceeds substantially to ignore the import of the first sentence while engaging the second with considerable imagination and intellectual gusto.[18] It may be true that New York is more likely to be struck by a terrorist than, say, Columbus, Ohio. But it is also more likely to be struck by a tsunami, and not only in Hollywood disaster thrillers. Before spending a lot of money protecting New York from a tsunami, we need to get some sort of sense about what the likelihood of that event actually is, not simply how the risk compares with that borne by other cities. And the same goes for terrorism.

The process of ranking potential targets will be discussed more fully in chapter 5. However, it is mischievous to the degree that it diverts the analyst from seeking to determine what the actual likelihood is.

Inflating the Importance of Potential Terrorist Targets

A fourth stratagem is to inflate the importance of potential terrorist targets. Thus, nearly half of American federal homeland security expenditure is devoted to protecting what the Department of Homeland Security and various presidential and congressional reports and directives rather extravagantly call "critical infrastructure" and "key resources."

Applying commonsense English about what "critical infrastructure" could be taken to mean, it should be an empty category. If any element in the infrastructure is truly "critical" to the operation of the country, steps should be taken immediately to provide redundancies or backup systems so that it is no longer so. An official definition designates "critical infrastructure" to include "the assets, systems, and networks, whether physical or virtual, so vital to the United States that their incapacitation or destruction would have a debilitating effect on security, national economic security, public health or safety, or any combination thereof."[19] Yet vast sums of money are spent under the program to protect elements of the infrastructure whose incapacitation would scarcely be debilitating and would at most impose minor inconvenience and quite limited costs.

And the same essentially holds for what DHS designates as "key resources," or formerly as "key assets." These are defined to be those that are "essential to the minimal operations of the economy or government."[20] It is difficult to imagine what a terrorist group armed with anything less than a massive thermonuclear arsenal could do to hamper such "minimal operations." The terrorist attacks of 9/11 were by far the most damaging in history, yet, even though several major commercial buildings were demolished, both the economy and government continued to function at considerably above the minimal level.

The very phrase "homeland security" contains aspects of a similar inflation in its suggestion that the essential security of the entire country is at stake. In Canada, the comparable department is labeled with more accuracy and less drama simply as "public safety." Given the actual magnitude of the terrorist hazard, an issue to be discussed much more fully in the next two chapters, the homeland is, as it happens, really quite secure, though there may be justifiable concerns about the public's safety under some conditions.

Inflating Terrorist Capacities

A final stratagem is to fail to assess, or to massively inflate, the capacities of the terrorists and therefore, by inference, both the likelihood they will attack and the consequences of that attack. This is something that should be of absolutely key importance, yet, in its big national infrastructure protection report of 2009, the DHS devoted only part of two paragraphs to describing the nature of the "terrorist adversary"—a designation that implies far more coordination among terrorists than experience suggests is valid. Moreover, none of this fleeting discussion shows any depth, and the report prefers instead to spew out adjectives like *relentless*, *patient*, and *flexible*, terms that, as will be discussed more fully in chapter 2, scarcely characterize the majority of potential terrorists.[21]

The report goes on to argue without qualification that the "terrorist adversary" not only "shows an understanding of the potential consequence of carefully planned attacks on economic, transportation, and symbolic targets" but also "seriously threatens national security, and could inflict mass casualties, weaken the economy, and damage public morale and confidence." This, too, as will be discussed in the next two chapters, is a rather extravagant exaggeration of the threat most terrorists present.

The ultimate in such thinking—common during the Bush administration and continued more sporadically in the administration of his successor, Barack Obama—is to characterize the terrorist threat as "existential." Rather amazingly, this extreme expression, which, if accepted as valid, can close off all judicious evaluation of the problem, has only rarely been called into question.

An insightful discussion seeking to put the terrorist threat into context was published in the journal *Skeptical Inquirer* a year after 9/11 by astronomers Clark Chapman and Alan Harris. They suggested that terrorism deserves exceptional attention only "if we truly think that future attacks might destroy our society." But, they overconfidently continued, "who believes that?"[22] The article triggered enormous response, and much of it, to their amazement, came from readers who believed exactly that. Those readers have had lots of company.

Thus, in 2003, the chairman of the Joint Chiefs of Staff, General Richard Myers, assured a television audience that if terrorists were able to engineer a catastrophic event that killed 10,000 people, they would successfully "do away with our way of life." And in 2004, a best-selling book by a then-anonymous former CIA official repeatedly assured us that our "survival" is at stake and that we are engaged in a "war to the death."[23]

The rhetoric of alarm has continued at a high pitch. In 2008, the *New York Times* editorial board assured its readers that "the fight against al-Qaeda is the central battle for this generation," and Republican presidential nominee John McCain more expansively, and repeatedly, labeled the struggle against radical Muslim extremism the "transcendental challenge of the 21st century," one that can affect "our very existence." In the same year, Homeland Security Secretary Michael Chertoff proclaimed the "struggle" against terrorism to be a "significant existential" one—carefully differentiating it, apparently, from all those insignificant existential struggles Americans have waged in the past.[24]

COST NEGLECT

The quest for security has not only embraced probability neglect but also more fundamentally—or at any rate more concretely—something that might be called "cost neglect." For many commentators, safety appears to be effectively an infinite good for which no cost is too high. For agencies with infinite budgets, this is, of course, no real problem. For those that inhabit the real world, by contrast, there are limits, and choices have to be made.

Thus, former CIA operations officer Charles Faddis has written a lively book in which he vividly explains over the course of 200 pages why he thinks military bases are insufficiently secure (chapter 1), rail transportation is insufficiently secure (chapter 2), malls and schools are insufficiently secure (chapter 3), chemical plants are insufficiently secure (chapter 4), the systems for storing and transporting liquid natural gas are insufficiently secure (chapter 5), dams are insufficiently secure (chapter 6), lethal pathogens are insufficiently secure (chapter 7), and nuclear power plants are insufficiently secure (chapter 8). He never bothers, however, to clutter his litany with any sort of consideration of what enhanced security measures to deal with the problems he identifies might cost and whether the measures he so passionately advocates would be worth it. One of the few times dollar signs even appear in the book is when Faddis complains about wasting money on projects like funding streetlights in a South Carolina port town for $182,080. He has difficulty imagining "what target of terrorist significance exists there."[25] But the town has a school or two and a shopping area (chapter 3) and is home to not one, but two, military installations (chapter 1). Perhaps there is even a railroad line (chapter 2) around there somewhere.

A similar process is found in the writings of Clark Kent Ervin. Once Inspector General of the DHS, he has been critical of the department's wasteful spending—nearly a half-million dollars on a lavish, self-congratulatory party for itself, for example. At the same time, he is incapable of applying such discernment to his call for spending on "backscatter machines, multi-view X-ray machines, explosive detection systems, explosive trade detection machines, radiation isotope identification devices," on "placing armed guards, bomb-sniffing dogs, surveillance cameras and sensors in subways, at rail stations, and in and around bus stations," on inspecting 100 percent of the cargo in passenger airplanes, on tripling the number of border guards, or on ending the visa-waiver program. Although he does note that such measures "all cost money," he urges that we should simply "spare no expense."[26] As is common in such books, there is no entry for *cost* in the index in his book.

The preoccupation with nuclear terrorism has led to calls for all shipping containers to be inspected, apparently under the assumptions (1) that after manufacturing their device at great expense and effort overseas, the terrorists would supply a return address and then entrust their precious product to the tender mercies of the commercial delivery system and (2) that Randall Larsen is incorrect to conclude that "anyone smart enough to obtain a nuclear device will be smart enough to put half an inch of lead around it."[27] As a result, huge amounts of money have been expended to inspect and to install radiation detectors, a preoccupation that currently triggers 500 false alarms daily at the Los Angeles–Long Beach port alone, generated by such substances as kitty litter and bananas.[28] This obsession is impressive as well because there seems to be no evidence that any terrorist has indicated any interest in, or even much knowledge about, using transnational containers to transport much of anything.[29] Seldom, however, has the cost of such an exercise entered the political debate, as Democrats and Republicans have vied to outbid each other in something of a percentage war.

As it happens, however, the inspection of all shipping containers would mean additional equipment and labor costs of upward of $320 million per year at the Port of Los Angeles alone.[30] There are also the costs of delay—a single day's delay in a shipment can add 0.5 percent of the product value to its cost, and 100 percent inspections can increase existing delays by more than an order of magnitude.[31] And even at this great cost and inconvenience, there is not 100 percent surety of detecting a nuclear or other terrorist WMD shipment.[32]

The cost-neglect process can also be seen in the periodic report cards issued by the heads of the 9/11 Commission. While insisting in their 2005 report that "Homeland security assistance should be based strictly on an assessment of risks and vulnerabilities," they scarcely apply the process—or bother to trouble themselves with considering the issue of cost—when they insist with equal fervor that more needs to be spent on improvements in airline passenger prescreening, canine teams, "biometric entry-exit" systems, advanced screening technology, new standards for birth certificates, fingerprinting passport holders, and "explosives detection trace portals."

They were particularly insistent on the expeditious installation of the last item on the list, commonly known as "puffers," to the nation's 441 commercial airports.[33] However, preliminary tests on that technology had already been conducted when the commission members sternly and urgently issued their report card, and these tests had determined that the machines might not be reliable. Nonetheless, the Transportation Security Administration deployed them widely, realizing its mistake only in 2006, as the machines clogged with dust or got confused with humidity while running up operating costs that sometimes mounted to nearly a third of their purchase price. It still had 166 in storage in 2009, though they now report that they have "since disposed of" the useless machines. The price tag for the experiment: $36 million.[34]

Ultimately, of course, a bill has to be paid and someone will have to pay it. When the paymaster runs out of funds, payment will stop. But that is scarcely the most rational process for setting up priorities.

ASSESSING RISK

In the end, one might darkly suspect, various versions of probability and cost neglect are grasped because, if realistic probabilities that a given target would be struck by terrorists were multiplied into the risk calculation and if the costs of protection from unlikely threats were sensibly calculated following standard procedures, it would be found that vast amounts of money have been misspent. It might also be concluded that if the same money, or even a portion of it, had been expended instead on methods and devices that have been demonstrated to save lives at a lower cost, a very considerable number of deaths would have been prevented.

It is true that estimating the likelihood and consequences of a terrorist attack can pose difficulties. Thus, the prominent risk analyst Kip Viscusi warily notes that unlike the risk of being in an automobile accident, we "don't have very good numbers" on what the terrorism risk is, and "if you can't assess the likelihood of a terrorist attack or how deadly it is going to be, it is really hard to say how much you should spend to try to prevent it."[35]

This concern is a sensible one. However, although measuring risk can be difficult, it is done as a matter of course in other areas, including such highly charged ones as nuclear power plant accidents (where malevolent threats are explicitly considered), aviation safety, and environmental protection. Moreover, as discussed throughout this book, there is plenty of data on how much damage terrorists have been able to do over the decades and about how frequently they attack. Seen in reasonable context, both of these numbers are exceedingly small, at least outside of war zones, though of course they could conceivably increase, should terrorists manage to become *vastly* more capable than they have thus far shown themselves to be.

The insurance industry has a distinct financial imperative to understand terrorism risks. In the immediate aftermath of the 9/11 attack in which insured losses reached $35 billion, most insurance firms placed terrorism exclusions on their policies.[36] Since then, however, the U.S. government implemented the Terrorism Risk Insurance Act to provide "a temporary window of reinsurance relief to help insurers manage the ongoing risk of terrorism."[37] With that, insurance firms reentered the terrorism insurance market, and by 2009 the median terrorism insurance premium for a $303 million property had more than halved to only $9,541 per year.[38] This represents a conservative measure of expected loss or risk, and a simple back-calculation in the risk equation suggests that the insurer estimates the likelihood of a terrorist attack on a property to be very low: less than one in 30,000 per year.[39] If the private sector can estimate terrorism risks and is willing to risk its own money on the validity of the estimate, why can't the DHS?

It is certainly true that improbable disastrous events—like the 9/11 attacks—do sometimes transpire. That is, in fact, why we call them improbable as opposed to impossible. But because improbable events sometimes do take place does not mean that all improbable events are therefore probable. To avoid or to ignore this elemental consideration is to engage in faulty, even irrational, planning and decision making.

Simply put, risk assessment is about making decisions. It is a management tool capable of being applied in a variety of situations, and it has been codified in many international conventions.[40] Risk is the expected consequences of a terrorist attack, and the accepted definition of risk, as applied in the terrorism context, is

$$\text{Risk} = (\text{probability of a successful attack}) \times$$
$$(\text{losses sustained in the successful attack})$$

Once the value of the risk—the expected consequences of a successful attack—is calculated, a decision needs to be made about whether the risk is acceptable. If not, it is then important to determine how much the risk should be reduced for it to become acceptable, balancing in the costs required to do so.

This leads to a cost-benefit analysis that compares the costs of security measures with the benefits as tallied in lives saved and damages averted. A security measure is cost-effective when the *benefit* of a security-enhancing measure outweighs the *costs* of the measure.

The *benefit of a security measure* tallies the gains—the improvement in the security situation—generated by a security measure. It is a function of three elements:

Benefit of a security measure = (probability of a successful attack) ×
(losses sustained in the successful attack) ×
(reduction in risk generated by the security measure)

The *probability of a successful attack* is the likelihood a successful terrorist attack will take place if the security measure were not in place. The *losses sustained in the successful attack* include the fatalities and other damage—both direct and indirect—that will accrue as a result of a successful terrorist attack, taking into account the value and vulnerability of people and infrastructure, as well as any psychological and political effects. The *reduction in risk generated by the security measure* is the degree to which the security measure foils, deters, disrupts, or protects against a terrorist attack.

This *benefit*, a multiplicative composite of three considerations, is then compared to the *costs* of providing the risk-reducing security necessary to attain the benefit. If the benefit of a security measure outweighs its costs, it is deemed to be cost-effective.

The interaction of these variables can perhaps be seen in an example. Suppose there is a dangerous curve on a road that results in an accident once every five years, as cars occasionally overshoot the curve and plummet down a hill. The *probability* of an accident each year under present conditions would be 20 percent, or .20. Suppose further that the accident results in one death, several injuries, and the totaling of a car, as well as some property damage. If the value of the life is taken to be, say, $4.5 million (calculations of the value of life are discussed in chapter 3), the total *losses* from the accident might sum to $5 million. The yearly *risk* of this accident would then be the losses sustained in the accident ($5 million) multiplied by the accident's yearly likelihood (.20), or $1 million.

Measures are then taken to reduce this risk. These could be ones that lower the probability of an accident by, for example, erecting warning signs, or they could be ones that reduce the losses sustained in the accident by, for example, erecting a barrier so that cars that overshoot the curve are prevented from toppling down the hill. Or they could do both: a lowered speed limit might reduce not only the likelihood of an accident but also its consequences. Suppose further that such measures result in a *reduction of risk* of 50 percent or .50. The *benefit* of the safety measures, applying the previous equation to this example, would then be $5 million x .20 x .50, or $500,000.

One would then need to compare this with the *cost* of the risk reduction measures. Included in this consideration would be not only the costs of erecting the road signs or the barrier but also indirect ones—for example, before the changes were made, the vast majority of cars were able to negotiate the curve without mishap, and to shift the speed limit on a road introduces a degree of complexity that might itself increase the danger of an accident. If the cost of the risk-reduction measures, all things considered, were less than $500,000, the benefits would outweigh the costs, and the measures would be deemed cost-effective. One might also reasonably decide to spread at least some of the costs over several years—barriers and road signs, after all, can last considerably more than a year. This would lower the yearly cost of the risk-reduction measures, making them even more cost-effective.

This standard approach to risk analysis will be applied throughout this book. It is not possible to calculate risk unless numerical values are provided for the probability of a successful attack and for the consequences or losses that would be sustained in the attack, and many risk analysts accordingly advocate the use of quantified methods for assessing terrorism risks.[41] We will seek to do exactly that.

In the process, we will also frequently make use of the break-even approach—a standard procedure for getting around the difficulties of estimating the likelihood and consequences of an undesirable event. Instead of calculating the likely destruction or the probability of an attack, we estimate how high the likelihood and/or sometimes how extensive the destruction (including indirect costs) would have to be in order for expenditures designed to reduce the risk to be cost-effective.[42] We will also incorporate sensitivity and uncertainty modeling in our analyses to test the robustness of results.

In an important sense, this book seeks to break no new ground in attempting to carry out its task. There are no fancy new models, and any innovation is in the application of standard risk-analytic and cost-benefit approaches to homeland security issues, something that clearly should have been done long ago—certainly before more than an additional trillion dollars had been expended on the problem.

We hope the book will provide a starting point for further discussion and perhaps for more detailed and complex analysis of how to manage the often conflicting societal preferences associated with assessments of risk, cost, and benefits. In the process:

- We present our analysis in a fully transparent manner: readers who wish to challenge or vary our analysis and assumptions are provided with the information and data to do so.
- In coming up with numerical estimates and calculations (some of which are rounded off for ease of presentation), we generally pick ones that bias the

consideration in favor of finding the homeland security measure under discussion to be cost-effective.

- We decidedly do *not* argue that there will be no further terrorist attacks; rather, we focus on the net benefit of security measures and apply break-even cost-benefit analyses to assess how high the likelihood of a terrorist attack must be for security measures to be cost-effective.[43]

We are aware that not every consideration can be adequately quantified—something that holds as well, of course, for other decision areas that excite political and emotional concerns. But we try, nonetheless, to keep non-quantifiable considerations in mind. We reserve the right, however, to back off when they become so overwhelming that policies effectively become absurd or when policies that could do far more good for human welfare are undercut or ignored. Assuaging emotions, we feel, is not an infinite good.

We recognize as well that risk and cost-benefit considerations should not be the sole criterion for public decision making. Nonetheless, they provide important insights into how security measures may (or may not) perform, their effect on risk reduction, and their cost-effectiveness. They can reveal wasteful expenditures and allow limited funds to be directed to where the most benefit can be attained. More important, if risk and cost-benefit advice is to be ignored, the onus is on public officials to explain why this is so and to detail the trade-offs and cuts to other programs that will inevitably ensue.

Moreover, although we understand that people are often risk averse when considering issues like terrorism, we follow the U.S. Office of Management and Budget requirement that governments expending tax money in a responsible manner need to be neutral when assessing risks, something that entails focusing primarily on mean estimates in risk and cost-benefit calculations, not primarily on worst-case or pessimistic ones.[44] This type of rational approach to risky decision making is challenging to governments that might have other priorities and political concerns. It is little surprise, then, that the level of risk averseness needed to justify current expenditures for homeland security is considerable.[45] "Policy-making is a risky business," one group of analysts has acknowledged. But they continue, "regardless of the varied desires and political pressures, we believe that it is the responsibility of analysts forcefully to advocate rational decision methods in public policy-making, especially for those with high risk."[46] Or as Elisabeth Paté-Cornell observes, if rational approaches to public policy making are not utilized, politically driven processes "may lead to raising unnecessary fears, wasting scarce resources, or ignoring important problems."[47] Important in all this, as risk analyst David Banks has suggested, is "the distinction between realistic reactions to plausible threats and hyperbolic overreaction to improbable contingencies."[48]

To present a theme that will reappear in chapter 9, to be irrational with your own money may be to be foolhardy, to give in to guilty pleasure, or to wallow in caprice. But to be irrational with other people's money, particularly where public safety is concerned, is to be irresponsible, to betray an essential trust. In the end, it becomes a dereliction of duty that cannot be justified by political pressure, bureaucratic constraints, or emotional drives.

CHAPTER 2

Terrorism as a Hazard to Human Life

In its perfunctory two paragraphs assessing "the nature of the terrorist adversary," the major 2009 Department of Homeland Security report discussed in the previous chapter projects an image of that enemy that is threatening and diabolical: one that is "relentless, patient, opportunistic, and flexible"; plots "carefully planned attacks on economic, transportation, and symbolic targets"; seriously threatens "national security"; and could inflict "mass casualties, weaken the economy, and damage public morale and confidence."[1]

That description may fit some terrorists—some of the 9/11 hijackers and planners among them—but not, it seems likely, the vast majority. This chapter and the next are devoted to evaluating the nature and capacities of the terrorist "adversary," to tallying the damage it may be able to inflict, and to assessing whether these are likely to change much in the future.

However underconsidered in such reports, this issue is absolutely key to assessing homeland security policy and expenditure, relating centrally as it does to the likelihood and potential consequences of terrorist acts in the United States and in other Western countries. That is, as set out in the previous chapter, two of the central variables that must be considered in any sensible cost-benefit analysis of counterterrorism are the likelihood of a terrorist attack and the costs such an attack might inflict.

In these two chapters, we attempt to supply a reasonably comprehensive basis for thinking about these crucial issues in order to undergird some of the more systematic analysis in later chapters. This chapter deals with the nature of the challenge presented by terrorism, particularly the international or transnational terrorism that is of most concern to people in the

West, and with the losses in human life terrorists have been able to inflict. It then places the issue in broader context, comparing the risk terrorism presents to human life with those presented by other hazards that regulatory agencies over the last decades have variously determined to be acceptably or unacceptably likely. The following chapter tallies the full costs that terrorism characteristically inflicts or might be able to inflict. These costs include not only those attending the loss of life (the primary focus of this chapter) but also the direct and indirect economic costs and the costs of reaction.

THE TRANSNATIONAL TERRORIST ADVERSARY

Middle East specialist Fawaz Gerges notes that, over time, mainstream Islamists—the vast majority within the Islamist political movement—have given up on the use of force. That is, Islamists who are still willing to apply violence constitute a tiny minority. But he also notes that the vast majority even of this small group primarily focus on various "infidel" Muslim regimes (as well as on Israel) and consider those among them who carry out violence against the "far enemy"—mainly Europe and the United States—to be irresponsible and reckless adventurers who endanger the survival of the whole movement.[2] Radical Islamists, principally al-Qaeda, who focus on the far enemy represent, then, a fringe group of a fringe group.

Counterproductive Violence

From al-Qaeda's standpoint, the 9/11 attacks, its biggest venture by far in inflicting damage on that far enemy, proved to be substantially counterproductive. Notes Patrick Porter of Britain's Joint Services Command and Staff College, the group has a "talent at self-destruction," and one disillusioned former al-Qaeda associate says, "al-Qaeda committed suicide on 9/11 and lost its equilibrium, skilled leaders, and influence." Their activities, beginning with 9/11—or even with the bombings of two American embassies in Africa in 1998—have also turned many radical Islamists against them, including some of the most prominent and respected.[3]

To begin with, the group by this action massively heightened concerns about, and outrage over, terrorism around the world. Recalls Gerges, "Less than two weeks after September 11, I traveled to the Middle East and was pleasantly surprised by the almost universal rejection—from taxi drivers and bank tellers to fruit vendors and high school teachers—of Al Qaeda's terrorism." Indeed, the key result among jihadis and religious nationalists was a vehement rejection of al-Qaeda's strategy and methods.[4]

Moreover, no matter how much they might disagree on other issues (most notably on America's war on Iraq), there is a compelling incentive for states—including Arab and Muslim ones—to cooperate to deal with any international terrorist problem emanating from groups and individuals connected to, or sympathetic with, al-Qaeda.

Important in this process was the almost immediate move, after 9/11, of the Pakistan government from support of the Taliban regime in neighboring Afghanistan to opposition. More generally, there has been a cooperative effort worldwide to deal with the terrorist problem. The FBI may not have been able to uncover all that much within the United States since 9/11, but quite a few real or apparent terrorists overseas have been rounded, or rolled, up with the aid and encouragement of the Americans. Given what seems to be the limited capacities of al-Qaeda and similar entities, these cooperative international policing efforts may not have prevented a large number of attacks, but thousands of "suspects" have been arrested around the world, and doubtless at least some of these were dangerous. Although these multilateral efforts, particularly by such Muslim states as Sudan, Syria, Libya, and even Iran, may not have received sufficient publicity, these countries have had a vital interest because they felt directly threatened by the militant network, and their diligent and aggressive efforts have led to important breakthroughs against al-Qaeda.[5]

This post-9/11 willingness of governments around the world to take on terrorists has been much reinforced and amplified as they reacted to subsequent, if sporadic, terrorist activity within their own countries. The phenomenon is hardly new: in 1997, for example, terrorists attacked Luxor Temple in Egypt, killing 68 foreigners and Egyptians, and it triggered a very substantial revulsion against the perpetrators that critically set back their cause.[6]

Following that pattern, a terrorist bombing in Bali in 2002 galvanized the Indonesian government into action and into extensive arrests and convictions. When terrorists attacked Saudis in Saudi Arabia in 2003, that country seems, very much for self-interested reasons, to have become considerably more serious about dealing with internal terrorism, including a clampdown on radical clerics and preachers. Some inept terrorist bombings in Casablanca in 2003 inspired a similar determined crackdown by Moroccan authorities. The main result of al-Qaeda-linked suicide terrorism in Jordan in 2005 was to outrage Jordanians and other Arabs against the perpetrators. Massive protests were held, and, in polls, those expressing a lot of confidence in Osama bin Laden to "do the right thing" plunged from 25 percent to less than 1 percent. In polls conducted in 35 predominantly Muslim countries, more than 90 percent condemned bin Laden's terrorism on religious grounds.[7]

If this wasn't enough, al-Qaeda has in declarations continually expanded its enemies list to the point where it has come to include not only Christians and Jews but also all Middle Eastern regimes; Muslims who don't share its views; most Western countries; the governments of India, Pakistan, Afghanistan, and Russia; most news organizations; the United Nations; and international nongovernmental organizations.[8] The group's "literalist, narrow ideology," notes Porter, "warrants aggression against anyone who fails to meet its rigid standards" with the result that, while claiming to be "the knight of Islam," it mostly "persecutes and impoverishes Muslims."[9]

In sum, with 9/11 and subsequent activity, bin Laden and gang seem mainly to have succeeded in uniting the world, including its huge Muslim portion, against their violent global jihad. In 2008, CIA director Michael Hayden was willing to go on the record to note that there had been a "significant setback for al-Qaeda globally—and here I'm going to use the word 'ideologically'—as a lot of the Islamic world pushes back from their form of Islam."[10]

The Conflicts in Iraq and Afghanistan

Al-Qaeda's seeming impact has been inflated by a tendency to conflate that organization with those fighting the American occupation in Iraq and with the destructive insurgency conducted by the Taliban in Afghanistan.

After the American invasion of Afghanistan in 2001, Abu Musab al-Zarqawi, an especially bitter and violent jihadist who sympathized with al-Qaeda's ideology and agenda, moved with 30 supporters from Afghanistan to Iraq. Pursued by Saddam Hussein's security services, this tiny band had difficulty linking up with antiregime elements. This problem was conveniently removed, of course, in 2003 by the Americans, whose war and subsequent disorder and chaos played perfectly into Zarqawi's hands. Soon he was the leader of a small army of dedicated and brutal terrorists numbering perhaps in the thousands, recruited or self-recruited from within and abroad. It was only in late 2004 that Zarqawi linked himself up with al-Qaeda (although bin Laden harbored considerable misgivings about Zarqawi's violently anti-Shiite sentiments), and this connection may have helped in attracting recruits and in generating financial and logistical support for Zarqawi's insurgents. They were further benefited by the tendency of the Americans to credit them with a far larger portion of the violence in Iraq than they probably committed, a process that also helped to burnish Zarqawi's image in much of the Muslim world as a resistance hero.[11]

Ayman Al Zawahari, then al-Qaeda's second in command, once described the war in Iraq as "the greatest battle of Islam in this era." However, whatever their connection to al-Qaeda, the mindless brutalities of his protégés—staging beheadings at mosques, bombing playgrounds, taking over hospitals, executing ordinary citizens, performing forced marriages—eventually turned the Iraqis against them, including many of those who had previously been fighting the American occupation either on their own or in connection with Zarqawi. In fact, his fighters seem to have managed to alienate the *entire* population: data from polls in Iraq in 2007 indicate that 97 percent of those surveyed opposed efforts to recruit foreigners to fight in Iraq, 98 percent opposed the militants' efforts to gain control of territory, and 100 percent considered attacks against Iraqi civilians "unacceptable." In Iraq as in other places, "al-Qaeda is its own worst enemy," notes Robert Grenier, a former top CIA counterterrorism official. "Where they have succeeded initially, they very quickly discredit themselves."[12]

For their part, the main Taliban group in Afghanistan, distinctly uncomfortable as hosts to al-Qaeda in the past, are quick to point out that they are running their own war. It seems clear that al-Qaeda plays only a limited role in their efforts. "No foreign fighter can serve as a Taliban commander," insists one Taliban leader. And, according to the American commander of U.S. detention centers in Afghanistan, less than 6 percent of his prisoners come from outside the country, and most of these are from Pakistan: "This is a very local fight," he observes. CIA Director Leon Panetta estimated in 2010 that there were "maybe 60 to 100, maybe less" al-Qaeda operatives in Afghanistan. An extensive study of the Taliban operation in Afghanistan includes al-Qaeda as part of the coalition but mentions it only very occasionally when discussing the details of the insurgency. And there are reports that the main Taliban leaders are very hostile to the foreign forces and have explicitly distanced themselves from al-Qaeda in discussions with Saudi Arabia, whose government has been repeatedly threatened by bin Laden and whose aid and good will the Taliban would desperately need were it ever to succeed in Afghanistan. Even before 9/11, the Taliban had put their troublesome "guest" under house arrest, and in an interview with the top Taliban leader at the time, veteran correspondent Arnaud de Borchgrave says he was "stunned by the hostility" expressed for bin Laden.[13]

Present Capacities

Glenn Carle, a 23-year veteran of the Central Intelligence Agency, where he was deputy national intelligence officer for transnational threats, has warned: "We must not take fright at the specter our leaders have exaggerated. In fact, we must see jihadists for the small, lethal, disjointed and miserable opponents that they are." Al-Qaeda "has only a handful of individuals capable of planning, organizing and leading a terrorist organization," and although they have threatened attacks, "its capabilities are far inferior to its desires."[14]

This is certainly the view of Michael Sheehan, New York City's former deputy director for counterterrorism, who in a 2008 book recalls a 2003 conversation in which he told his bosses, Raymond Kelly and David Cohen, "that I thought al-Qaeda was simply not very good. . . . Under the withering heat of the post-9/11 environment, they were simply not getting it done. I said what nobody else was saying: we underestimated al Qaeda's capabilities before 9/11 and we overestimated them after." Journalist Christopher Dickey describes what happened next:

> He could see that they were taken aback. It was not so much that they disagreed. . . . They all understood only too well the way the public and politicians would react if headlines started to read "Commissioner disses Qaeda." Support for counterterrorism would start to crumble. . . . And then, if the bad guys got lucky . . . Kelly, Cohen, and Sheehan agreed it would be better if Sheehan kept his estimate to himself for a while.[15]

And so, it seems, Sheehan kept his views rather quiet for several years, support for counterterrorism did not "crumble," the newspapers were kept from revealing a truth all three men agreed upon, and, had there actually been an attack in New York in the meantime, various bureaucratic backsides would have been strategically covered.

In evaluating al-Qaeda's present capacity to inflict damage and its likelihood of doing so, a good place to start is with analyses provided by Marc Sageman.[16] A former intelligence officer with experience in Afghanistan, Sageman has carefully and systematically combed through both open and classified data on jihadists and would-be jihadists around the world.

Al-Qaeda central, he concludes, consists primarily of a cluster left over from the struggles in Afghanistan against the Soviets in the 1980s. Currently, they are huddled somewhere in Pakistan and/or Afghanistan. This band, concludes Sageman, probably consists of a few dozen individuals.

Joining them in the area are perhaps a hundred fighters left over from al-Qaeda's golden days in Afghanistan in the 1990s.

These key portions of the enemy forces would total, then, less than 150 actual people. Other estimates of the size of al-Qaeda central generally come in with numbers in the same order of magnitude as those suggested by Sageman. Egyptian intelligence, for example, puts the number at less than 200, while American intelligence estimates run from 300 to upward of 500.[17]

Al-Qaeda central may operate something resembling training camps, but these appear to be quite minor affairs—in part because of the danger that they will be infiltrated by foreign agents or by sympathetic people being watched by the police who will then be arrested and productively interrogated.[18] It also seems to assist with the Taliban's distinctly separate, far larger, and very troublesome insurgency in Afghanistan and Pakistan. Overall, however, one might wonder whether al-Qaeda central has really done much of anything since 9/11 except issue threats—table 2.1 supplies a litany of these. Although the terrorist organization designed, equipped, and executed several large attacks before 9/11, every al-Qaeda-"linked" terrorist attack since seems to have been perpetrated by unaffiliated or, at best, franchised groups at least outside the Afghanistan-Pakistan area.[19] Sageman may be going too far when he argues "there is not much left of al-Qaeda except in the minds of those inside the beltway."[20] But that possibility should be included in the discussion at least as much as ones that confer on al-Qaeda capacities that are at once monumental and mounting.

THE ADVERSARY WITHIN

Beyond the tiny band that constitutes al-Qaeda central, there are, continues Sageman, thousands of sympathizers and would-be jihadists spread around the globe who mainly connect in Internet chat rooms, engage in radicalizing conversations, and variously dare each other to actually do something.[21]

All of these rather hapless—perhaps even pathetic—people should, of course, be considered to be potentially dangerous. From time to time, they may be able to coalesce enough to carry out acts of terrorist violence, and policing efforts to stop them before they can do so are certainly justified. But the notion that they present an existential threat to just about anybody seems at least as fanciful as some of their schemes.

In 2002, as noted in the preface, intelligence reports were asserting that the number of trained al-Qaeda operatives in the United States was between 2,000 and 5,000. In this spirit, FBI Director Mueller assured a

Table 2.1 THREATS TO THE UNITED STATES FROM AL-QAEDA, 2001–2010

The United States is in retreat by the grace of God Almighty and economic attrition is continuing up to today. But it needs further blows. The young men need to seek out the nodes of the American economy and strike the enemy's nodes.—Osama bin Laden, December 2001[1]

Understand the lesson of New York and Washington raids, which came in response to some of your previous crimes. . . . God is my witness, the youth of Islam are preparing things that will fill your hearts with fear. They will target key sectors of your economy until you stop your injustice and aggression or until the more short-lived of us die.—Osama bin Laden, October 2002[2]

Leave us alone, or else expect us in New York and Washington.—Osama Bin Laden, November 2002[3]

People of America, I remind you of the weighty words of our leaders, Osama bin Laden and Dr. Ayman Al Zawahiri, that what took place on September 11 was but the opening salvo of the global war on America. . . . The magnitude and ferocity of what is coming your way will make you forget about September 11. . . . The streets of America shall run red with blood . . . casualties will be too many to count and the next wave of attacks may come at any moment.—al-Qaeda spokesman Adam Gadahn, 2004[4]

As for you, the Americans, what you have seen in New York and Washington, what losses that you see in Afghanistan and Iraq, despite the media blackout, is merely the losses of the initial clashes. If you go on with the same policy of aggression against Muslims, you will see, with God's will, what will make you forget the horrible things in Vietnam and Afghanistan.—Ayman Al Zawahiri, 2005[5]

As for the delay in carrying out similar operations in America, this was not due to failure to breach your security measures. Operations are under preparation, and you will see them on your own ground once they are finished, God willing.—Osama bin Laden, January 2006[6]

God willing, our raids on you will continue as long as your support for the Israelis continues.—Osama bin Laden, January 2010[7]

---

[1]Hoffman 2006, 290.
[2]BBC News, "The New Threats from 'Bin Laden,'" October 6, 2002.
[3]"Full text: bin Laden's 'Letter to America,'" www.guardian.co.uk, November 24, 2002.
[4]www.globalsecurity.org/security/profiles/adam_gadahn_2004_video.htm.
[5]timesonline, "Extracts from the Zawahiri Tape," August 4, 2005, www.timesonline.co.uk.
[6]BBC News, "Text: Bin-Laden Tape," January 19, 2006, news.bbc.co.uk.
[7]Jason Keyser, "In Audio Message, bin Laden Says He Endorsed December 25 Airline Bomb Plot," *Washington Post*, January 25, 2010.

Senate committee on February 11, 2003, that al-Qaeda had "developed a support infrastructure" in the country and had achieved "the ability and the intent to inflict significant casualties in the US with little warning."[22] By 2005, however, after years of well-funded sleuthing, the FBI and other investigative agencies noted in a report that they had been unable to uncover a single true al-Qaeda sleeper cell anywhere in the United States, a finding (or nonfinding) publicly acknowledged two years later both in a press conference and when the officer who drafted that year's National Intelligence Estimate testified that "we do not see" al-Qaeda operatives functioning inside the United States.[23]

Indeed, they have been scarcely able to unearth anyone who might even be deemed to have a "connection" to the diabolical group. In testimony on January 11, 2007, Director Mueller, who, despite his earlier bravado, has yet to uncover a true al-Qaeda sleeper cell, suggested, "We believe al-Qaeda is still seeking to infiltrate operatives into the U.S. from overseas." But even that may not be true. Since 9/11, well over a billion foreigners have been admitted to the United States legally, even as many others have entered illegally.[24] Even if border security was so good that 90 percent of al-Qaeda's operatives were turned away or deterred from trying to enter, some should have made it in—and some of those, it seems reasonable to suggest, would have been picked up by law enforcement by now. It certainly seems either that the terrorists are far less diabolically clever and capable than usually depicted or that they are not trying very hard.

It follows that any terrorism problem in the United States and the West principally derives from rather small numbers of homegrown people, often isolated from each other, who fantasize about performing dire deeds and sometimes receive a bit of training and inspiration overseas. Indeed, in his 2007 testimony, Mueller stressed that his chief concern within the United States had become homegrown groups, a sentiment later endorsed by Obama's Homeland Security Secretary Janet Napolitano in 2009.[25] By 2010, two top terrorism analysts, Peter Bergen and Bruce Hoffman, were concluding that, although the terrorists appeared to be incapable of launching a mass-casualty attack in the United States, local terrorists would still be able to carry out "less sophisticated operations," a "trend" they somehow deemed to be "worrisome." Required to deal with this "more complex and more diverse" threat, they concluded, would be a "much greater degree of engagement of state and local public safety officials."[26] And in 2011, top officials announced that, although the "likelihood of a large-scale organized attack" had been reduced, this meant that al-Qaeda franchises were now able "to innovate on their own" (presumably developing small-scale disorganized attacks), with the result that the threat had now somehow become the highest since 9/11.[27]

Going even further, public officials have also publicly concluded that the "greatest concern" has now become the "lone wolf" terrorist. As CIA Director Leon Panetta put it, "It's the lone wolf strategy that I think we have to pay attention to as the main threat." This may be a valid concern, but it is certainly far less "worrisome" than others one might imagine. As Max Abrahms has pointed out, "lone wolves have carried out just two of the 1,900 most deadly terrorist incidents over the last four decades."[28]

Assessing the threat from homegrown Islamist terrorists, Brian Jenkins stresses that their number is "tiny," representing one of every 30,000 Muslims in the United States. This "very low level" of recruitment finds very little support in the Muslim community at large: "they are not Mao's guerrillas swimming in a friendly sea." Indeed, as will be discussed a bit more fully in chapter 8, the Muslim community has acted as an extensive antiterrorism surveillance force. Given this situation, concludes Jenkins, what is to be anticipated is "tiny conspiracies, lone gunmen, one-off attacks rather than sustained terrorist campaigns."[29] In the meantime, noted other researchers in 2010, Muslim extremists have been responsible for one fiftieth of 1 percent of the homicides committed in the United States since 9/11.[30]

Because terrorism of a considerably destructive nature can be perpetrated by a very small number of people, or even by a single individual, the fact that terrorists are few in number does not mean there is no problem, and from time to time, some of these people may actually manage to do some harm, though in most cases their capacities and schemes—or alleged schemes—seem to be far less dangerous than initial press reports suggest. Conceivably, they might even someday rise to the cleverness of the 9/11 plot. Far more likely to be representative, however, is the experience of the would-be bomber of shopping malls in Rockford, Illinois, who exchanged two used stereo speakers (he couldn't afford the opening price of $100) for a bogus handgun and four equally bogus hand grenades supplied by an FBI informant. Had the weapons been real, he might actually have managed to inflict some damage. How much is a matter of question, however. It was his idea to explode the grenades in garbage cans in order to "create shrapnel." Since grenades are essentially made of shrapnel, his approach would be comparable to shooting somebody through a wooden board in hopes they would be impaled by flying splinters. At any rate, he clearly posed no threat that was existential (significant or otherwise) to the United States, to Illinois, to Rockford, or, indeed, to the shopping mall.[31]

Or there is the case of Najibullah Zazi, arrested in September 2009. "Since the terrorist attacks of September 11, 2001," notes the *New York Times* with considerable understatement, "senior government officials have announced dozens of terrorism cases that on close examination seemed to diminish as legitimate threats." However, terrorism analysts and officials triumphantly claimed that Zazi is different and called it the "most serious" terrorism plot uncovered in the United States since 2001 and one that elevates the domestic terrorism threat to a "new magnitude." Bruce Riedel, an Obama administration terrorism adviser, proclaimed that the plot was evidence that "al-Qaeda was trying to carry out another mass-casualty attack in the United States" like 9/11 and that the group continues to pose a threat to the country that is "existential."[32]

However, the existence of the United States is unlikely to be expunged anytime soon. Recalls his step-uncle affectionately, Zazi is "a dumb kid, believe me." A high school dropout, Zazi mostly worked as a doughnut peddler in Lower Manhattan, barely making a living. Somewhere along the line, he took it into his head to set off a bomb and traveled to Pakistan, where he received extensive explosives training from al-Qaeda and copied nine pages of chemical bomb-making instructions onto his laptop. FBI Director Robert Mueller asserted in testimony on September 30, 2009, that this training gave Zazi the "capability" to set off a bomb.[33]

That, however, seems to be a substantial overstatement because, upon returning to the United States, Zazi spent the better part of a year trying to concoct the bomb he had supposedly learned how to make. In the process, he purchased bomb materials using stolen credit cards.[34] This boneheaded maneuver all but guaranteed that red flags would go up about the sale and that surveillance videos in the stores would be maintained rather than routinely erased. Moreover, even with the material at hand, Zazi *still* apparently couldn't figure it out, and he frantically contacted an unidentified person for help several times. Each of these communications was "more urgent in tone than the last," according to court documents.[35]

Clearly, if Zazi was able eventually to bring his alleged aspirations to fruition, he could have done some damage, though, given his capacities, the person most in existential danger was surely the lapsed doughnut peddler himself.

In all, as Shikha Dalmia has put it helpfully, would-be terrorists need to be "radicalized enough to die for their cause; Westernized enough to move around without raising red flags; ingenious enough to exploit loopholes in the security apparatus; meticulous enough to attend to the myriad logistical details that could torpedo the operation; self-sufficient enough to make all the preparations without enlisting outsiders who might give them away; disciplined enough to maintain complete secrecy, and—above all—psychologically tough enough to keep functioning at a high level without cracking in the face of their own impending death."[36] There don't seem to be very many such people around.

The situation seems scarcely different in Europe and other Western locations. Political scientist Michael Kenney has interviewed dozens of officials and intelligence agents and analyzed court documents. He finds that, in sharp contrast with the boilerplate characterizations favored by the Department of Homeland Security (DHS) and with the imperatives listed by Dalmia, Islamic militants there are operationally unsophisticated, short on know-how, prone to make mistakes, poor at planning, and limited in their capacity to learn.[37] Another study documents the difficulties of network coordination that continually threaten operational unity, trust, cohesion, and the ability to act collectively.[38]

In addition, the popular notion that the Internet can be effective in providing operational information seems to be severely flawed. Kenney notes that it is filled with misinformation and error and that it is no substitute for direct, on-the-ground training and experience. Anne Stenersen is similarly unimpressed: the Internet manuals she has looked at are filled with materials hastily assembled and "randomly put together" and contain information that is often "far-fetched" or "utter nonsense."[39]

Referring to the perpetrators of the only significant act of terrorism carried out in Britain since 9/11, the United Kingdom's Director of Public Prosecutions Sir Ken Macdonald characterized the internal enemy in vivid terms: "Those innocents who were murdered on July 7, 2005 were not victims of war. And the men who killed them were not, as in their vanity they claimed on their ludicrous videos, 'soldiers'. They were deluded, narcissistic inadequates. They were criminals. They were fantasists."[40]

THE EXTENT OF TERRORIST VIOLENCE: DEATHS

The most noteworthy consequence of terrorism, of course, is the destruction of human life. There are a number of ways to estimate and evaluate the extent of violence terrorists have been able to perpetrate against people thus far in the history of terrorism.

For several decades, the U.S. State Department collected data on international or transnational terrorism, defining the act as premeditated, politically motivated violence perpetrated by subnational groups or clandestine agents against noncombatant targets (civilians and military personnel who at the time of the incident are unarmed or not on duty) that involve citizens or the territory of more than one country. The data so accumulated over the period 1975 to 2003 are arrayed in Figure 2.1.[41] As can be seen in the figure, the number of people worldwide who died during the period as a result of all forms of transnational terrorism (Islamist or other) by this definition is 482 a year. Another study using comparable data for the longer period from 1968 to 2006 arrives at an average of 420 per year.[42] The yearly probability of being killed in a transnational terrorist attack—the annual fatality risk—is thus the number of fatalities divided by the world's population of 6.8 billion. It comes to be about 1 in 14 million.

It can also be seen from the figure that, outside of 2001, far fewer Americans were killed in any grouping of years by all forms of transnational terrorism than were killed by lightning. Moreover, virtually none of these terrorist deaths occurred within the United States itself: the upward blip for 1983 is due to a terrorist bombing of an American barracks in Lebanon, and the one for 1988 is due to the bombing of an American airliner over Lockerbie, Scotland. Even with the September 11 attacks included in the count, the number of Americans killed by international terrorism over the period is not a great deal more than the number killed by accident-causing deer or by severe allergic reactions to peanuts over the same period.[43]

Astronomer Alan Harris also has assessed the likelihood of being killed by a terrorist. He begins with these State Department figures for transnational terrorism and then doubles the yearly count to 1,000 under the assumption there would be another 9/11 somewhere in the world every several years. Over an 80-year period under those conditions, some 80,000

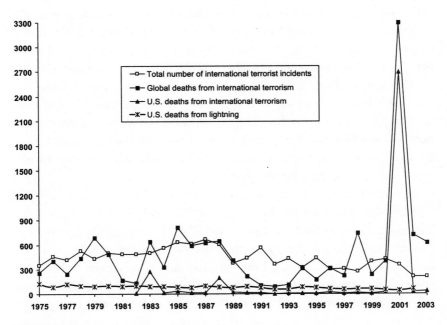

Figure 2.1
International Terrorism and Lightning, 1975–2003.

deaths would occur, which would mean that the lifetime probability that a resident of the globe will die at the hands of international terrorists is about one in 85,000 (80,000 divided by 6.8 billion). If there are no repeats of 9/11, the lifetime probability of being killed by an international terrorist becomes about one in 130,000. This, he points out, is about the same likelihood that one would die over the same interval from the impact on the earth of an especially ill-directed asteroid or comet.[44]

Another approach is to focus on the kind of terrorism that really concerns people in the developed world by restricting the consideration to violence committed by Muslim extremists outside of war zones, whether that violence be perpetrated by domestic Islamist terrorists or by ones with international connections. Included in the count would be terrorism of the much-publicized sort that occurred in Bali in 2002 and 2005; in Saudi Arabia, Morocco, and Turkey in 2003; in the Philippines, Madrid, and Egypt in 2004; and in London and Jordan in 2005. Three publications from think tanks have independently provided lists or tallies of such violence committed in the several years after the 9/11 attacks.[45] The lists include not only attacks by al-Qaeda but also those by its imitators, enthusiasts, lookalikes, and wannabes, as well as ones by groups with no apparent connection to it whatever. Although these tallies make for grim reading, the total number of people killed in the years after 9/11 by Muslim extremists outside of war zones comes to some 200 to 300 per year. That, of course, is 200 to 300 too many, but it hardly suggests that the destructive capacities of the terrorists are monumental. For comparison, during the same period more people—320 per year—drowned in bathtubs in the United States alone.[46] Or there is another, rather unpleasant comparison noted in table I.2. Increased delays and added costs at U.S. airports due to new security procedures provide incentive for many short-haul passengers to drive to their destination rather than flying, and, since driving is far riskier than air travel, the extra automobile traffic generated has been estimated to result in 500 or more extra road fatalities per year.[47]

Also useful for assessing this issue is the Global Terrorism Database (GTD), developed by the U.S. National Consortium for the Study of Terrorism and Responses to Terrorism (START). It contains country-by-country information for more that 80,000 terrorist incidents—both domestic and transnational, both Islamist and non-Islamist—that have taken place throughout the world between 1970 and 2007. Its definition of terrorism is "the threatened or actual use of illegal force and violence by a nonstate actor to attain a political, economic, religious, or social goal through fear, coercion, or intimidation" and includes many incidents of terrorism committed by such nonmurderous groups as the Animal Liberation Front, incidents that in many cases might more comfortably be designated as vandalism.

A country-by-country summary of fatalities from this source for the United States, the United Kingdom, Canada, and Australia is shown in table 2.2.[48] There were 3,292 fatalities from terrorist incidents within the United States during that 38-year period. However, the 9/11 attacks in 2001 represented almost all of these and most of the rest come from the attack by a domestic (and non-Islamic) terrorist, Timothy McVeigh, on a federal building in Oklahoma City in 1995: 3,140 in total. In all, this generates an annual fatality risk for the period of 1 in 3.5 million. If we limit our analysis to the New York metropolitan area on the assumption that this is the region with the highest threat, the annual fatality risk is 1 in 260,000.[49]

One might also look at the potential consequences of the set of Islamic terrorist attacks authorities claim to have foiled between 2001 and 2007 in the United States. Table 2.3 lists these, and for each we have provided an estimate of the number of lives saved for each foiled plot.[50] While it can be argued that some estimates of lives saved could be higher, not all of these threats would have caused maximum (worst-case) fatalities, and many might never have been carried out at all—when rolled up, most were far more nearly aspirational than operational.[51] Nonetheless, table 2.3 shows that the total estimated lives saved as a result of thwarting these planned terrorist attacks over the years (assuming each had been successfully consummated) is 1,700, approximately half of the deaths inflicted by the 9/11 attacks and some 250 per year.[52]

The highest overall terrorism fatality risk in any of the four countries has been suffered in the United Kingdom, where 2,196 perished during the period from terrorism. The sectarian strife in Northern Ireland between republican and loyalist paramilitaries represents the overwhelming majority—nearly all, in fact—of the terrorist incidents and fatalities. Yet even this fatality risk is less than one in a million. Considering only Great Britain (England, Scotland and Wales), there were 438 fatalities per year (including the 1988 Lockerbie bombing) over 38 years, resulting in an annual fatality risk of 1 in 5.2 million. The annual fatality risk in Northern Ireland alone for the period is very high, at 1 in 43,000. Yet even at the height of violence, terrorism in this troubled region did not result in the mass casualties we are conditioned to fear today—only five attacks killed more than 10 people, the worst being 28 fatalities from the 1998 Omagh bombing in Northern Ireland. Most fatalities were the result of assassinations of individuals with pistols or other firearms.

Table 2.2 TERRORISM FATALITIES AND ANNUAL FATALITY RISKS, 1970–2007

		Year	Fatalities	Annual Fatality Risk
United States				
LaGuardia Airport Bombing	New York	1975	11	
Murrah Federal Building	Oklahoma City	1995	165	
9/11: World Trade Center	New York	2001	2,751	
9/11: Pentagon	Washington	2001	184	
9/11: UA Flight 93	Pennsylvania	2001	40	
Others			141	
TOTAL			3,292	1 in 3,500,000
TOTAL (1970–2000)			309	1 in 30,000,000
TOTAL (2001)			2,982	1 in 101,000
TOTAL (2002–2007)			1	1 in 1.8 billion
United Kingdom				
Pub bombings	Birmingham	1974	21	
Omagh bombing	Omagh	1998	28	
Pan Am Flight 103	Lockerbie	1988	270	
Kings Cross Station	London	2005	26	
Tavistock Square (bus)	London	2005	13	
Aldgate Station	London	2005	7	
Edgeware Road Station	London	2005	6	
Others (Northern Ireland)			1,723	
Others (Great Britain)			102	
TOTAL for the UK			2,196	1 in 1,100,000
TOTAL for Northern Ireland			1,758	1 in 43,000
TOTAL for Great Britain			438	1 in 5,200,000
Canada				
Air India Flight 182	Atlantic	1985	329	
Others			7	
TOTAL			336	1 in 3,800,000
Australia				
TOTAL			25	1 in 33,300,000
TOTAL including Bali bombings			117	1 in 7,100,000

Sources: Global Terrorism Database.
Population data: U.S. (308 million), U.K. (62 million), Northern Ireland (2 million), Canada (34 million), Australia (22 million).

The Canadian annual fatality risk is comparable to the U.S. risk, but as with the United States, this is attributable nearly entirely to a single event—the 1985 mid-Atlantic bombing of an Air India Flight 182 by Sikh terrorists that departed from Montreal, a tragedy that, until 2001, stood as the most destructive terrorist act in history.

Australia has the lowest fatality rate—there has been no significant terrorist incident there at all. However, bombings in Bali killed 88 Australians in 2002 and another 4 in 2005. Australian Prime Minister John Howard expressed the sentiment of many Australians when he said that the 2002 Bali bombing "shocked our nation to the core," while New Zealand's Prime Minister Helen Clark referred to the 2002 attack as "Australia's September 11."[53] Therefore, although these attacks occurred outside of Australia, they were viewed (rather expansively) as being in its backyard. If these deaths are included in the count, the Australian annual fatality risk for the 1970–2007 period becomes 1 in 7.1 million.

ACCEPTABLE RISK

Is the likelihood of being killed by terrorists unacceptably high, or is it something that is negligible and that we in society are willing to accept? That is, just how safe is safe enough? When does a risk become acceptable?

Tolerating Risk

This is a tricky consideration, and an illustration may be instructive. Suppose an engineering firm tomorrow came up with an amazing new form of transportation that people would find convenient and economical to use. They would step inside a booth, dial a location, and then be taken apart atom by atom and transmitted over wires to the desired location, where they would be reassembled. After thoroughly testing the new device for safety, the firm has concluded that the overwhelming majority of trips would be utterly without incident—one could easily emerge from a lifetime of use without a scratch. Unfortunately, in a very tiny percentage of trips, things would go wrong, and the traveler would never rematerialize. Injuries, from minor contusions to paralysis, would also occasionally occur. The total for the United States: probably not much more per year than 40,000 deaths and 2 million or so disabling injuries, concentrated, for some odd reason, not among the weak and infirm, but among healthy

Table 2.3 TERRORIST PLOTS THAT UNITED STATES AUTHORITIES CLAIM
THEY HAVE FOILED AND THE EXPECTED LIVES SAVED, 2001–2007

Date	Description	Estimate of lives saved	Comments
Dec 2001	"Shoe bomber" Richard Reid foiled as a suicide bomber on an American Airlines flight from Paris to Miami.	200	Prompt action by flight attendants and passengers averted the plot, not the security services.
May 2003	Iyman Faris convicted of planning to destroy the Brooklyn Bridge.	200	Many people on a bridge survive its collapse, as evidenced by the Minneapolis 10-lane I35W bridge collapse in 2007, containing 111 vehicles with only 13 fatalities.
Aug 2004	Two men convicted of plotting to attack the New York Stock Exchange and other financial institutions in New York.	200	Truck bomb attack on Federal building in Oklahoma City in 1995 killed 165 people; 1993 bombing of WTC killed 6.
Aug 2004	Two men convicted of plotting to blow up a subway station in New York.	100	London underground bombings killed 39 subway commuters in 2005.
Aug 2005	Four men indicted for allegedly conspiring to attack Los Angeles–area military targets.	100	High level of armed security at U.S. military bases.
June 2006	Seven men indicted for allegedly plotting to blow up the Sears Tower.	200	Truck bomb attack on Federal Building in Oklahoma City in 1995 killed 165 people; 1993 bombing of WTC killed 6.
July 2006	One man arrested for allegedly plotting to bomb New York City train tunnels and flood the financial district.	100	London underground bombings killed 39 commuters in 2005; flooding unlikely to cause mass casualties.
May 2007	Six men were charged with plotting the shooting of U.S. soldiers in an armed assault on Fort Dix.	100	High level of armed security at U.S. military bases.
June 2007	Four men planned to destroy JFK international airport by blowing up jet fuel lines.	500	Mass casualties very unlikely as jet fuel is flammable, not explosive in nature.
TOTAL		1,700	

List of plots: "Plots since 9/11," wcbstv.com, June 3, 2007.

young adults. There would also be considerable death and illness because of atmospheric pollution.

The United States has installed a system with costs like that: the private passenger automobile.[54] We often say that there is nothing more important than the value of human life. Yet, obviously, we don't really believe this: Americans are clearly willing to sacrifice tens of thousands of lives per year to have the automobile. It is, of course, quite possible to move people without killing them. Engineers have also invented devices for doing that. Large commercial airlines have gone entire years without fatalities; passengers killed on railroads in a year can often be numbered on the fingers of one hand; the New York subway system, regularly maligned for filth, inefficiency, noise, and other indignities, moves millions of people every day and sometimes goes *decades* without a fatality caused by subway system defects or misjudgments.[55]

Thus in cases like this, the risks with their well-known costs have effectively been accepted, or tolerated, because the benefits appear to exceed the risk. We might well conclude, for example, that 40,000 lives and 2 million disabling injuries per year (plus pollution) is a small price to pay for the blessings of the automobile—the pleasure, the convenience, the personal mobility, the economic benefit, the aesthetic charm, the macho gratification.[56]

Many other social policies involve the same sort of consideration. To take an extreme example, every year a few thousand people in the United States die in falls from buildings that are more than one story high. Those lives could be saved by closing off all buildings at the second floor. To reject such a policy is to say tall buildings are worth that cost in lives. As a society, we regularly and inescapably adopt policies in which human lives are part of the price, yet we often casually gloss over the issue.

But if this risk with its attendant cost in lives is essentially deemed acceptable, it should also be explicitly acknowledged. And sometimes that happens: in the United Kingdom, the Health and Safety Executive puts it this way: "Tolerability does not mean acceptance. It refers to the willingness to live with a risk to secure certain benefits and in the confidence that it (risk) is being properly controlled. To tolerate a risk means that we do not regard it as negligible or something we might ignore, but rather as something we need to keep under review and reduce still further if and as we can."[57]

Thus there is continuing demand for automobile travel to be safer, as evidenced by the sales appeal of cars with safety features like air bags and antilock brake systems, by the construction of improved roads, and by the acceptance of more stringent enforcement of speed and alcohol limits. Traffic fatalities in the United States decreased from 52,627 to 37,261 between 1970 to 2008, equivalent to a 55 percent reduction in fatalities for every 100,000 people.[58] And deaths per vehicle mile declined by 90 percent over the course of the twentieth century. This is an impressive reduction in risk, and still cars are cheaper in real terms than ever before. Thus the system has been subjected to a coherent cost-benefit analysis that has delivered improved safety at acceptable cost. For example, the U.S. National Highway Traffic Safety Administration regularly performs cost-benefit analyses of proposed car safety regulations. One of their findings is that safety belt use prevented 11,900 fatalities, 325,000 serious injuries, and $50 billion in injury-related costs in 2002.[59] Since installing seat belts and air bags is not terribly expensive, it is understandable that their use could be very cost-effective. In the case of automobiles, societies have obviously been willing to accept risk and to bear cost because of the benefits—even while working and spending to reduce the risk.

The willingness to accept risk is influenced by a variety of psychological, social, cultural, and institutional processes depending on such qualities as the uncontrollability of the risks; the dread (or fear) they inspire; their involuntary nature or catastrophic potential; whether they can be preventively controlled, are certain to be fatal, can easily be reduced, result in an inequitable distribution of risk, threaten future generations, or affect one personally; whether they are increasing or not observable, unknown to those exposed, new or unfamiliar, and unknown to science; and whether they have immediate effect or affect a large number of people.[60]

Calibrating Acceptable and Unacceptable Risks

Despite this array of considerations and complications, deliberations, many of them very contentious, about acceptable and unacceptable risk have been conducted throughout the world for several decades over a wide range of issues, such as pesticide use, pollution, and sites for nuclear power plants. For example, in an important 1980 case, Justice John Paul Stevens of the U.S. Supreme Court set out the basic parameters of consideration in his statement announcing the judgment of the court: "Some risks are plainly acceptable and others are plainly unacceptable. If for example, the odds are one in a billion that a person will die from cancer by taking a drink of chlorinated water, the risk clearly could not be considered significant. On the other hand, if the odds are one in a thousand that regular inhalation of gasoline vapors that are 2 percent benzene will be fatal, a reasonable person might well consider the risk significant and take the appropriate steps to decrease or eliminate it."[61]

In the process of such deliberations, a substantial consensus has been reached, resulting in a fair degree of agreement about risk acceptability.

Unacceptable risk is often denominated *de manifestis* risk, literally meaning a risk of obvious or evident concern, a risk so high that no reasonable person would deem it acceptable.[62] A widely cited *de manifestis* risk assessment comes from that 1980 Supreme Court decision. It ruled on the efforts of the Occupational Safety and Health Administration (OSHA) to establish risk criteria for worker inhalation of gasoline vapors containing benzene. Applying the thinking process that Stevens laid out, it concluded that an annual fatality risk of one in 40,000 is unacceptable. This reasoning is in line with practice that has become standard in the regulatory world. Given the contentious nature of risk acceptability and the many jurisdictions in which it operates, there is no single or universally agreed risk threshold that defines unacceptable risk. There is consensus, though, that risks considered unacceptable are those found likely to kill more than 1 in 100,000 per year or sometimes 1 in 10,000.

At the other end of the spectrum are risks that are considered acceptable, and there is a fair degree of agreement about that range of risk as well. For example, after extensive research and public consultation, the U.S. Nuclear Regulatory Commission (NRC) has concluded that the annual fatality risk should not exceed 1 in 2 million per year for risks resulting from accidents, and 1 in 500,000 per year for risks from nuclear power plant operations.[63]

In Britain, the Health and Safety Executive came to a similar conclusion in 2006, when it set about establishing safety policy for nuclear facilities, concluding that the individual risk of death to a person off the site should not exceed 1 in 1 million to 10 million per year.[64] At the same time, the Nuclear Safety Commission of Japan established safety targets mandating that the annual fatality risk resulting from an accident of a nuclear installation to individuals of the public should not exceed 1 in 1 million per year.[65] And in Australia, potentially hazardous industries are permitted in the state of New South Wales only if they present an annual fatality risk of less than 1 in 1 million for residential areas.[66]

In addition, a review of 132 U.S. federal government regulatory decisions associated with public exposure to environmental carcinogens found that regulatory action never occurred if the individual annual fatality risk was lower than 1 in 700,000.[67] Perhaps the most surprising aspect of this study was the consistency among OSHA, the Environmental Protection Agency, the Consumer Product Safety Commission, and six other federal agencies when they sought to determine the acceptable level of risk.

Established regulatory practices in several developed countries suggest, then, that risks are deemed unacceptable if the annual fatality risk is higher than 1 in 10,000 or perhaps higher than 1 in 100,000. Risks are deemed acceptable if the annual fatality risk is lower than 1 in 700,000 or perhaps 1 in 1 million or one in 2 million. Between these two ranges is an area that might be considered tolerable risk.

These considerations, substantially accepted for years, even decades, by public regulatory agencies after extensive evaluation and considerable debate and public discussion, are designed to provide a viable, if somewhat rough, guideline for public policy. As noted by Richard Meserve, chairman of the NRC when it established its safety goals, the commission was seeking "to provide guidance as to the level of public protection which nuclear plant designers and operators should strive to achieve" and to "provide guidance to the NRC staff to use in the regulatory decision-making process."[68]

Clearly, hazards that fall in the unacceptable range (traffic accidents, for example) should generally command the most attention and the most resources. Those in the tolerable range may also be worthy of consideration, though obviously the urgency is less, and only relatively inexpensive measures to further reduce the risk should be pursued. Those hazards in the acceptable range (drowning in bathtubs, for example) would generally be deemed of little or even negligible concern—they are risks we can live with—and further precautions would scarcely be worth pursuing unless they are quite remarkably inexpensive.

In all cases, measures to reduce risk must satisfy essential cost-benefit considerations. If a risky activity produces benefits that are taken to outweigh the costs, as in the case of automobiles, society would be willing to tolerate such risks. Required here would be hard evidence demonstrating that there is societal benefit in accepting the risk, and if none can be provided, society should not accept the activity that is generating the risk. But since funds are not infinite, choices must be made. A medical procedure capable of reducing deaths from cancer by 10 percent in the developed world for an expenditure of $5 billion is far superior to one that would reduce deaths from a rare disease by 10 percent for the same price.

In summary, although the boundaries are not hard-and-fast, there is broad consensus almost irrespective of the hazard being considered that the following quantitative safety targets should be used for judging the acceptability of risks to the public:

- annual fatality risks that exceed one in ten thousand, or perhaps one in 100 thousand, are generally deemed to be unacceptable, and regulation or strenuous efforts to reduce the fatality rate is considered mandatory;
- annual fatality risks between one in ten thousand, or perhaps one in 100 thousand, and one in a million are considered tolerable if the benefits outweigh the risks; and
- annual fatality risks smaller than one in a million are broadly acceptable as long as precautions are maintained, and further improvements are not required if these involve much in the way of a cost.[69]

These safety goals or targets have been developed to provide overall guidance to operators and regulators, but any specific decision will necessarily involve other criteria as well, much of it nonquantifiable and/or emotional, that may also be important in balancing the preferences of interested parties. Overall, however, it is clear that governments and their regulators have been able to set, and agree upon, risk acceptance criteria for use in decision making for a wide variety of hazards, including ones that are highly controversial and emotive such as pollution, nuclear and chemical power plant accidents, and public exposure to nuclear radiation and environmental carcinogens.

TERRORISM AS AN ACCEPTABLE RISK

If the Department of Homeland Security wants to apply a risk-based approach to decision making, as it claims frequently, risk acceptance criteria developed for other hazards provide appropriate context for such considerations. Terrorism has elements of dread and the unknown that cause many people to perceive the risk to be higher than it actually is.[70] But the same can be said for other hazards, particularly those dealing with radiation and pollution, and debates over such issues have been around for decades, have aroused heated passions from concerned citizens, and have polarized communities and governments.

To this end, table 2.4 supplies the annual fatality risks for a wide variety of hazards, including terrorism as variously gauged. As can be seen, almost all annual terrorism fatality risks are less than one in a million and therefore generally lie within the range deemed by regulators internationally to be safe or acceptable—that is, they scarcely require further regulation.[71] In this, they are similar to the risks of using home appliances (200 deaths per year in the United States) or commercial aviation (130 deaths per year in

Table 2.4 COMPARISON OF ANNUAL FATALITY RISKS

Hazard	Territory	Period	Total Fatalities for the Period	Annual Fatality Risk
World War II	Worldwide	1939–1945	61,000,000	1 in 221
Cancers	US	2009	560,000	1 in 540
War (civilians)	Iraq	2003–2008	113,616	1 in 1,150
All accidents	US	2007	119,000	1 in 2,500
Traffic accidents	US	2008	37,261	1 in 8,200
Traffic accidents	Canada	2008	2,431	1 in 13,500
Traffic accidents	Australia	2008	1,466	1 in 15,000
Homicide	US	2006	14,180	1 in 22,000
Traffic accidents	UK	2008	2,538	1 in 23,000
Terrorism	No. Ireland	1970–2007	1,758	1 in 43,000
Industrial accidents	US	2007	5,657	1 in 53,000
Homicide	Canada	2008	611	1 in 55,000
Intifada	Israel	2000–2006	553	1 in 72,000
Homicide	Great Britain	2008	887	1 in 67,000
Homicide	Australia	2008	290	1 in 76,000
Terrorism	US	2001	2,982	1 in 101,000
Terrorism	New York area[1]	1970–2007	2,795	1 in 260,000
Natural disasters	US	1999–2008	6,294	1 in 480,000
Drowning in bathtub	US	2003	320	1 in 950,000
Terrorism	UK	1970–2007	2,196	1 in 1,100,000
Home appliances	US	yearly average	200	1 in 1,500,000
Deer accidents	US	2006	150	1 in 2,000,000
Commercial aviation	US	yearly average	130	1 in 2,300,000
Terrorism	US	1970–2007	3,292	1 in 3,500,000
Terrorism	Canada	1970–2007	336	1 in 3,800,000
Terrorism	Great Britain	1970–2007	438	1 in 5,200,000
Peanut allergies	US	yearly average	50–100	1 in 6,000,000
Lightning	US	1999–2008	424	1 in 7,000,000
Terrorism	Australia incl. Bali attack	1970–2007	117	1 in 7,100,000
Transnational Terrorism	World outside war zones	1975–2003	13,971	1 in 12,500,000
Terrorism by al-Qaeda types	World outside war zones[2]	2002-mid-2007	1,632	1 in 22,200,000

[1]See note 73 on p. 214.
[2]See note 45 on p. 211.

the United States).[72] Even when we restrict our analysis to the New York metropolitan area, the annual fatality risk from terrorism (dominated, of course, by 9/11) is considerably lower than an unacceptable risk of 1 in 100,000.[73]

It is abundantly clear from this comparison that the hazard presented to human life by terrorism outside of war zones under present conditions is very low—at least half the risk of being killed in a natural disaster and nearly a thousand times less than being killed in an accident. Thus, applying conventional standards, terrorism currently presents a threat to human life outside of war zones that is acceptable, and efforts, particularly expensive ones, to further reduce its likelihood or consequences are scarcely justified.

GAUGING THE IMPACT OF COUNTERTERRORISM MEASURES ON THE HAZARD

We have assessed the hazard terrorism poses to human life under present conditions—which include, of course, the existence of counterterrorism measures specifically designed to reduce that hazard. The analysis suggests that additional efforts to reduce its likelihood are scarcely justified.

It is possible that any relaxation in these measures will increase the terrorism hazard, that the counterterrorism effort is the reason for the low hazard terrorism currently presents. However, for the terrorism risk to border on becoming unacceptable by established risk conventions—that is, to reach an annual fatality rate of 1 in 100,000—the number of fatalities from all forms of terrorism in the United States and Canada would have to increase 35-fold, in Britain (excluding Northern Ireland) more than 50-fold, and in Australia more than 70-fold.

Thus, to justify current counterterrorism efforts in this manner, one would need to establish, in the case of the United States, that the measures have successfully deterred, derailed, disrupted, or protected against attacks that would otherwise have resulted in the deaths of more than 3,000 people in the country every year, equivalent to experiencing attacks as devastating as those on 9/11 at least once a year or 18 Oklahoma City bombings every year. As indicated in table 2.3, even if all the (mostly embryonic and in many cases moronic) terrorist plots exposed since 9/11 in the United States had been successfully carried out, their likely consequences would have been much lower. Indeed, as the earlier discussion indicates, the number of people killed by terrorists throughout the world outside (and

sometimes within) war zones both before and after 2001 generally regis-
ters at far below that number.

A FUTURE INCREASE?

We have been using historical data here, and there is, of course, no guaran-
tee that the terrorism frequencies of the past will necessarily persist into
the future. However, there seems to be little evidence terrorists are becoming any more destructive, particularly in the West. In fact, if anything,
there seems to be a diminishing, not expanding, level of terrorist activity
and destruction at least outside of war zones. As Andrew Mack concludes,
there is "no evidence of any substantial increase in the fatality toll since
data on both domestic and international terrorism began to be collected in
1998." Indeed, the two data sets he examines that have statistics going back
to that year both "reveal a decline in deaths from terrorism."[74]

Moreover, according both to official government and to prominent academic accounts as discussed earlier, the levels of violence likely to be committed by Islamic extremists within Western countries seem, if anything, to
be in decline. Fears about large, sophisticated attacks have been replaced
by ones concerning tiny conspiracies, lone wolves, and one-off attackers.
As noted, the DHS description of the "adversary" as "relentless, patient,
opportunistic, and flexible" seems excessive, as does the notion that it is
carefully planning attacks on important targets, that it seriously threatens
national security, and that it could inflict "mass casualties, weaken the
economy, and damage public morale and confidence."

Those who wish to discount such arguments and projections need to
demonstrate why they think terrorists will suddenly get their act together
and inflict massively increased violence, visiting savage discontinuities on
the historical data series (the potential for atomic terrorism is addressed in
the next chapter). Moreover, they should also restrain themselves from
using historical data themselves to explain, for example, why attacks on
New York are more likely than ones on Xenia, Ohio, or Perth, Australia.

Actually, a most common misjudgment has been to embrace extreme
events as harbingers presaging a dire departure from historical patterns. In
the months and then years after 9/11, as noted at this book's outset, it was
almost universally assumed that the terrorist event was a harbinger rather
than an aberration.[75] There were similar reactions to Timothy McVeigh's
1995 truck bomb attack in Oklahoma City, as concerns about a repetition
soared. And in 1996, shortly after the terrorist group Aum Shinrikyo set off

deadly gas in a Tokyo subway station, one of terrorism studies' top gurus, Walter Laqueur, assured the world that some terrorist groups "almost certainly" will use weapons of mass destruction "in the foreseeable future."[76] Presumably any future foreseeable in 1996 is now history, and Laqueur's near certainty has yet to occur.

CHAPTER 3

The Full Costs of Terrorism

The discussion in chapter 2 focused on deaths caused by terrorism, the issue of greatest concern to most people. However, terrorism inflicts other costs as well. To obtain a full appreciation for terrorist damage, these other costs must be considered, and the most comprehensive way to do this is to put all the losses—including the loss of life—into economic terms.

THE VALUE OF HUMAN LIFE

While it can be a morally difficult consideration, there is a long history of placing a monetary value on human life. The calculation is often referred to as the value of a statistical life (VSL), and table 3.1 supplies estimates of how much has been spent to save a single human life as the consequence of dozens of government regulations.

The results are anything but tidy, and they often reflect psychological and political aspects of risk perception or electoral and lobbyist pressure.[1] However, some general tendencies and limits have been established over time. Thus, looking over such data, Elizabeth Paté-Cornell suggests that a VSL ceiling of $3 million, inflation adjusted to 2010 dollars, seems roughly appropriate in current practice—though there are clearly quite a few entries in the table that are substantially, even spectacularly, higher.[2] But regulators and administrators seem generally rather unwilling to spend more to save a life, implying that they value life at about that amount. For

Table 3.1 REGULATORY EXPENDITURE PER LIFE SAVED

Regulation	Year	Agency	Cost per Life Saved in 2010 Dollars
Steering column protection standards	1967	NHTSA	140,000
Ban on unvented space heaters	1980	CPSC	140,000
Seat belt/air bag	1984	NHTSA	140,000
Aircraft cabin fire protection standard	1985	FAA	140,000
Underground construction standards	1989	OSHA	140,000
Auto fuel system integrity	1975	NHTSA	710,000
Trihalomethane in drinking water	1979	EPA	850,000
Aircraft seat cushion flammability	1984	FAA	850,000
Alcohol and drug controls	1985	FRA	850,000
Aircraft floor emergency lighting	1984	FAA	990,000
Concrete and masonry construction	1988	OSHA	990,000
Passive restraints for trucks and buses	1989	NHTSA	1,100,000
Children's sleepwear flammability ban	1973	CPSC	1,400,000
Auto side impact standards	1990	NHTSA	1,400,000
Metal mine electrical equipment standards	1970	MSHA	2,400,000
Trenching and evacuation standards	1989	OSHA	2,600,000
Hazard communication standard	1983	OSHA	2,700,000
Trucks, buses and MPV side impact	1989	NHTSA	3,700,000
Grain dust explosion prevention	1987	OSHA	4,700,000
Rear lap/shoulder belts for autos	1989	NHTSA	5,400,000
Standards for radionuclides in uranium mines	1984	EPA	5,800,000
Ethylene dibromide in drinking water	1991	EPA	9,700,000
Asbestos occupational exposure limit	1972	OSHA	14,000,000
Benzene occupational exposure limit	1987	OSHA	15,000,000
Electrical equipment in coal mines	1970	MSHA	15,800,000
Arsenic emission standards for glass plants	1986	EPA	22,900,000
Cover/move uranium mill tailings	1983	EPA	76,100,000
Acrylonitrate occupational exposure limit	1978	OSHA	87,000,000
Coke ovens occupational exposure limit	1976	OSHA	107,400,000
Arsenic occupational exposure limit	1978	OSHA	180,800,000
Ban on asbestos	1989	EPA	187,200,000
1,2-Dechloropropane in drinking water	1991	EPA	1,103,900,000
Hazardous waste land disposal ban	1988	EPA	7,084,000,000
Municipal solid waste landfills	1988	EPA	32,300,000,000

continued

Table 3.1 CONTINUED

Regulation	Year	Agency	Cost per Life Saved in 2010 Dollars
Formaldehyde occupational exposure limit	1987	OSHA	145,723,000,000
Hazardous waste listing for wood-preserving chemicals	1990	EPA	9,635,870,000,000

Adapted from Viscusi 2000.

its purposes, the U.S. Department of Transportation adopts a figure of $4.4 million.[3]

The concept can be, and has been, expanded to embrace security concerns. For example, Robert Hahn assessed the cost of heightened airport security measures implemented soon after the midair explosion and crash of a TWA flight in 1996 (the probable cause later turned out not to be terrorism related). He notes that the cost per life saved was $200–$300 million—well in excess, obviously, of most regulatory safety goals.[4]

Following the widely applied VSL approach, a report for the Department of Homeland Security (DHS) by Lisa Robinson concludes that the best estimate for homeland security analysis is about $6.5 million in 2010 dollars.[5] This suggests, for example, that if a terrorism security measure can be shown to have saved ten lives at a total cost of no more than $65 million, it would be considered a worthy expenditure of funds.

Characteristically, court awards or compensation payouts are considerably lower. In the case of the 9/11 attacks, there was compensation of $3.1 million per victim, but much of this came from generous payments by governments and donations by the public generated by the shock of the event and the enormity of the sympathy to the victims and their families. Payments like that are by no means typical in terrorist attacks: for example, the victims of the dramatic Oklahoma City bombing of 1995 received little or no federal assistance at all. Moreover, the average life insurance payout to 9/11 victims was $350,000, and workers' compensation was $400,000. Court awards may be higher than this, but not always. A 1988 study of aviation fatality compensation payments found that the average compensation for cases that went to trial was approximately $1.2 million with a maximum of $10 million; however, half of all payouts, including those settled before trials began, were less than $350,000. Payments to the families of soldiers killed in the Iraq War total $500,000, up from $112,240 before that conflict.[6]

Court awards are geared toward providing compensation to meet the needs of the survivors and, in some cases, to provide deterrence by awarding punitive damages against the defendants. On the other hand, value of statistical life measures, as Kip Viscusi points out, are used by regulators to "establish sufficient incentives for safety for deterrence and accident prevention" and seem to better represent the public's willingness to pay for greater safety.[7] Accordingly, the DHS recommended value of statistical life of $6.5 million seems appropriate for our cost-benefit analyses.

Most VSL studies focus on relatively common risks (e.g., workplace or motor vehicle accidents), and Robinson suggests that "more involuntary, uncontrollable, and dread risks may be assigned a value that is perhaps twice that of more familiar risks," a process that essentially adds into the analysis much of the substantial indirect and ancillary costs associated with a terrorist event. Our analysis uses the lower figure of $6.5 million per life saved and then adds the other costs to it. However, her basic point, that people often effectively place a higher value on a life lost to terrorism than on one lost to more mundane and less sensational hazards, should be kept in mind.

AGGREGATING THE COSTS: CONVENTIONAL ATTACKS

To establish something of an upper bound for the costs inflicted by conventional terrorist attacks, it may be best to begin with an estimate of the aggregate costs, as expressed in economic terms, inflicted by the terrorist attack that has been by far the most destructive in history, that of September 11, 2001.

That attack directly resulted in the deaths of nearly 3,000 people. With a VSL of $6.5 million, the associated loss is approximately $20 billion. In addition, 9/11 caused, of course, great direct physical damage, amounting to approximately $30 billion in 2010 dollars, including rescue and cleanup costs.[8] Indirect costs were even more substantial. Thus, the International Monetary Fund estimates that the 9/11 attacks cost the U.S. economy up to 0.7 percent in lost GDP ($100 billion in 2010 dollars, adjusting for inflation) in that year alone,[9] while others estimate that associated business costs and loss of tourism cost the U.S. economy $190 billion over three years.[10] A comprehensive 2009 study by the National Center for Risk and Economic Analysis of Terrorist Events found that the impact on the U.S. economy of the 9/11 attacks ranges from $40 to $140 billion of GDP, or 0.3 to 1.0 percent of annual GDP.[11]

The magnitude of the effects of terrorism on GDP is highly variable, but as economist Paul Krugman suggests, "on an economy-wide basis—except for small economies like that of Israel—the costs of behavioral responses to terrorism at current levels are probably fairly small, almost surely less than 1 percent of GDP." Financial markets are popularly viewed as very fragile and jittery about news of terrorist attacks. After 9/11, the New York Stock Exchange was closed for several days, and the Standard & Poor's 500-stock index plummeted 4.9 percent on the next day of trading. However, these losses were recovered over the next two months of trading. *Business Week's* David Wyss notes that after the 9/11 attacks, "the economy—measured by real GDP—dropped only in the third quarter (and September 11 was pretty much the end of the third quarter anyway), was up a modest 1.6% in the fourth, and saw an increase of 2.5% a year later" and concludes that the "financial consequences of these one-time events tend to be small and fleeting."[12]

An exhaustive review of international terrorism losses by Todd Sandler and Walter Enders concludes that "for most economies, the economic consequences of terrorism are generally very modest and of a short-term nature" and "large diversified economies are able to withstand terrorism and do not display adverse macroeconomic influences. Recovery is rapid even from a large-scale terrorist attack." In part, this is because "developed countries can use monetary and fiscal policies to offset adverse economic impacts of large-scale attacks. Well-developed institutions also cushion the consequences." Additionally, "the immediate costs of most terrorist attacks are localized, thereby causing a substitution of economic activity away from a vulnerable sector to relatively safe areas. Prices can then reallocate capital and labor quickly."[13]

This last point is a telling one. When expenditures are either transferred somewhere else or deferred temporarily, money will still be spent one way or the other. There will be loss of economic activity to the affected areas, but other areas or sectors of the economy will benefit with increased economic activity. For example, after 9/11, Hawaii experienced a boom in domestic visitors, generating an extra $550 million in 2004 alone because more Americans decided to take vacations closer to home than travel internationally.[14] If there is an attack on a subway, more people will catch a bus or take a taxi. So there will be winners and losers, not just losers, as we often assume when discussing economic losses from terrorism. None of this is to dismiss the tragic and life-changing losses faced by the victims and their families. But when we step back and look at the bigger picture, the overall losses and damages to society may not be as great as they first appear.

The total costs inflicted by the terrorists on September 11, 2001, far the worst terrorist attack in history, can then be summed. If the loss of life from the 9/11 attacks is valued at $20 billion based on VSL measures, direct physical damage at $30 billion, and loss of GDP at $70 to $140 billion (equivalent to 0.5 to 1 percent of GDP), the total losses come to approximately $120 to $190 billion. One might also include the value of lives lost by those who, in the first months and years after 9/11, avoided airlines and drove in more dangerous automobiles instead. Various estimates put this loss at 2,300 lives,[15] for a total VSL of $15 billion. To account for these and other indirect losses like social disruption, we will err on the conservative (or high) side and adopt $200 billion as the full cost of losses experienced from the 9/11 attacks.[16]

The 2005 attacks on underground trains and a bus in London that killed 52 people and injured many hundreds of commuters and passersby can be evaluated in a similar way. The loss of lives is valued at near $350 million based on VSL measures. In addition, the repair costs to the London Underground and London buses is estimated at $100 million,[17] and losses from ticket sales on the London Underground (£11 million), restaurants (£40 million), tourism (£450 million), and retailers (£1.6 billion) sum to £2.1 billion or $3.2 billion.[18] And there are estimates that lost tourism and transport revenues could exceed £600 million or roughly $1 billion.[19]

The effects on financial markets were even more short-lived than those for 9/11, with the FTSE 100 Index closing only 1.4 percent lower on the day of the bombing from the previous day's close. The following day, the FTSE 100 Index had recovered from this loss, most likely when the markets became aware that the damage of the bombings was less than initially feared. And despite significant disruption to London's transport network, the London Chamber of Commerce reported that in "every case businesses had resumed normal operation within two working days" and that "because there was little disruption to the supply chain, there was little evidence of the knock-on effect that the business community had feared in the worst case scenario."[20] An essential factor in the business rebound was that bus services resumed service on the same day as the attacks and most underground services reopened the following day. If the government had reacted by closing all London transport for an extended period of time to assess and reduce vulnerabilities, the social and economic consequences would have been much larger. After the London attacks, there was the expected drop in foreign visitors to London, which was offset partly by increases in visitors to other British regions, and overall visitor numbers to the United Kingdom by the end of 2005 had increased by 6 percent over 2004, and by another 9.2 percent in 2006.[21] In total, then, the losses from the London attacks sum to upward of $3 to $4 billion.

The next largest terrorist attack in Britain was in 1993, when the Irish Republican Army detonated a 1,100-pound truck bomb in the financial district of London, killing 1 person, injuring 40 others, and damaging about 72 buildings. The total damage cost is estimated at £1 billion, with building reconstruction costs estimated at £350 million.[22] The London Chamber of Commerce reported an insured loss of $907 million.[23] The losses from this attack in 2010 dollars total, then, around $2 billion.

The bombing of commuter trains in Madrid on March 11, 2004, was far more devastating in lives lost than the 2005 transit attacks in London: 191 commuters were killed and more than 1,800 injured. This has been characterized as "the worst Islamic terrorist attack in European history," a characterization that still holds.[24] The direct losses totaled €212 million ($282 million), including €4 million for repair to the trains and rail infrastructure and the cost of the human lives lost and of the injuries inflicted.[25] Tourism in Madrid took a short-term hit, with business down by 10 percent, but by the end of 2004, Madrid's foreign tourist figures were 10.9 percent higher than the previous year, suggesting "that the terrorist attacks in Spain did not have any significant impacts on tourism."[26] As a London Chamber of Commerce study notes, "The example of the 2004 Madrid bombings shows that a city can swiftly bounce back from attacks on a similar scale to 7/7 and that the economic cost can be relatively short-term, even in the terrorism-sensitive tourism sector."[27] The losses from this attack total several billion dollars.[28]

Bali, the scene of a major terrorist attack in 2002 that killed more than 200 people, most of them foreign tourists, also has shown a resilient tourism sector. While foreign visitor numbers dropped by nearly 300,000 in the year following the 2002 attack, by 2008 foreign arrivals were 46 percent higher than in 2001.[29] The total losses from this attack also run to no more than several billion dollars.[30]

Other studies have attempted to assess the direct and indirect costs of other extreme terrorist attacks with conventional weapons. A 2002 Brookings report analyzes scenarios in which a set of bombings and bomb scares kills several hundred people and effectively shuts down several major cities for a day at a cost, including loss of life, of $10 billion. A larger attack, one that "exposes a finite and repairable vulnerability (like 9/11)," causing substantial but temporary weakening of the economy, would cost $100 billion. Their worst-case conventional attack scenario has potential losses of $250 billion caused by "widespread terror against key elements of public economy across a nation (mall, restaurants, movie theatres, etc.)."[31]

A RAND study developed a "moderate" case in which a terrorist attack on the United States results in 1,175 deaths and 8,700 injuries costing $6.1 billion. To this is added $1.6 billion in property damage and $6.1 billion in reduced GDP, for a total loss of $13.8 billion in direct and indirect damage in 2010 dollars.[32] And an Australian study commissioned by the Australian Federal Police investigated the economic effects of a terrorist attack similar in scope to the July 2005 London bombings, concluding that the total loss would range from $1 to $5 billion.[33]

It is important to stress, however, that very few terrorist attacks exact damage on the scale of these.

Thus, an analysis of the Global Terrorism Database (GTD) shows that, of 219 terrorist incidents in the United Kingdom involving explosives, only two inflicted damage that the GTD considered "catastrophic"—a bombing in London that killed three people in 1992 and the 1993 London financial area bombing, each causing damage of $1 to 2 billion. Sixteen others inflicted major damage (from $1 million to $1 billion), and 202 caused damage of less than $1 million.[34]

The overwhelming majority of domestic and transnational terrorist attacks kill very few, if any, people. Further applying the GTD, table 3.2 shows that few terrorist attacks within the United States kill anyone and that very few kill more than two people. Terrorism statistics for the United Kingdom find a slightly higher frequency of terrorist attacks that inflict multiple fatalities.

Even in that most permissive of terrorist environments, Iraq, fatalities from truck and car bombs against buildings and infrastructure have exceeded 50 people in fewer than 1 of every 200 attacks. The deadliest bombings target markets and other open-air congregations of civilians. These caused the vast majority of mass casualties, but none inflicted more than 250 fatalities.[35]

Similarly, data arrayed in figure 3.1 show that property damage is generally less than $1 million for the average terrorist attack—often *much* less—while catastrophic damage in excess of $1 billion is limited to a few isolated instances. The typical terrorist act results in no fatalities whatever. And while any death is regrettable, the most likely outcome from a deadly terrorist attack is one or perhaps two fatalities, inflicting damage that is

Table 3.2 FREQUENCY OF FATALITIES PER TERRORIST ATTACK,
1970–2007

Number of Fatalities from a Single Terrorist Attack	Frequency	
	U.S.	U.K.
0	1,129	1,615
1	94	1,220
2	15	124
3	0	41
4	3	10
5	1	10
6	0	7
7	0	3
8	0	1
9	0	1
10	0	1
11	1	1
12	0	0
13	0	1
14	0	1
15	0	1
16	0	1
17	0	0
18	0	0
19	0	0
20	0	0
21	0	1
22	0	0
23	0	0
24	0	0
25	0	0
26	0	1
27	0	0
28	0	1
29	0	0
30	0	0
40	1	0
165	1	0
184	1	0
270	0	1
1375	2	0

Source: Global Terrorism Database. Includes both domestic and transnational terrorism in all forms. The GTD defines a single terrorist attack as one occurring in the same geographic area and at the same point in time. Hence the 9/11 attacks are regarded as four incidents, as are the 2005 London attacks.

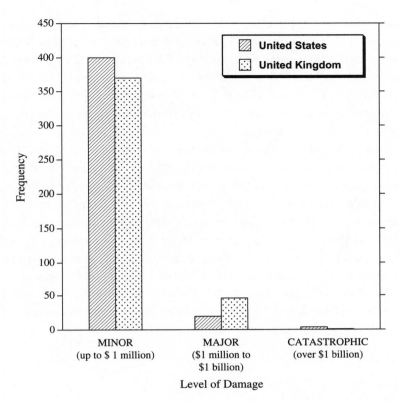

Figure 3.1
Direct Economic Damage Resulting from Terrorist Attacks Excluding the Costs of Loss of Life, 1970–2007.
Source: Global Terrorism Database.

limited, even minor. A monetary value placed on such attacks (including the costs of the loss of life) would run into the tens of millions of dollars per attack, and not much more.

EXPANDING TERRORIST DESTRUCTION?

In the history of terrorism, then, 9/11 stands out as extreme in terms of the human and economic destruction it wreaked: there has been nothing similar, ever. It may be too early to conclude that 9/11 was an aberration rather than a harbinger. However, even assuming the latter—that terrorists might be able to commit mayhem on the scale of 9/11 from time to time—the overall conclusions about terrorism as a hazard to human life and about its aggregate consequences do not alter all that much. Indeed, even if "another 9/11" were to occur in the United States every three months for the next five years, an American's chance of being killed in one of them is two one-hundredths of 1 percent: the posited attacks would kill 60,000 in total, which is about 0.02 percent of the U.S. population of 308 million.[36] This would be, of course, an extended and major tragedy, but an individual's chances of being killed, while no longer microscopic, would remain small even under this extreme—even, one hopes, ridiculous—scenario.

Nonetheless, argue many, just because something even worse hasn't happened before doesn't mean it can't happen in the future. However, for damage to be inflicted by terrorists that is radically worse than in the past, they would have to become *vastly* more capable of inflicting damage than they have so far shown themselves to be. And as suggested at the end of chapter 2, there seems to be little evidence they are becoming any more destructive, particularly in the West. In fact, if anything, there may be a diminishing, not expanding, level of terrorist activity and destruction at least outside of war zones, as concern shifts from the dangers presented by large, sophisticated, conventional attacks to amateurish ones perpetrated by tiny cells or lone operators.

Atomic Terrorism

Actually, to substantially outdo the damage inflicted on 9/11, terrorists would pretty much need to acquire an atomic arsenal and the capacity to deploy and detonate it, a prospect that continues to excite great alarm. In a major speech on April 11, 2010, President Barack Obama proclaimed it to be "the single biggest threat to U.S. security." Others, like Indiana Senator Richard Lugar, consider that terrorists armed with weapons of mass destruction present an "existential" threat to the United States or even, in columnist Charles Krauthammer's view, to "civilization itself." Graham Allison, too, thinks nuclear terrorists could "destroy civilization as we know it," while Joshua Goldstein is convinced they could "destroy our society" and that a single small nuclear detonation in Manhattan would "overwhelm the nation." And Michael Ignatieff warns that "a group of only a few individuals equipped with lethal technologies" threaten "the ascendancy of the modern state."[37]

The possibility that small groups could set off nuclear weapons has repeatedly raised alarms at least since 1946, when atomic bomb maker J. Robert Oppenheimer warned that if three or four men could smuggle in units for an atomic bomb, they could "blow up New York." And over the course of the ensuing decades, there have been many predictions that a terrorist bomb explosion would transpire fairly soon.[38]

The 9/11 experience ought, it would seem, to be taken to suggest that the scenario most to be feared is one in which terrorists are once again able, through skill, careful planning, suicidal dedication, and great luck, to massively destroy with ordinary, extant devices. In addition, the potential for destruction on that magnitude is hardly new: a tiny band of fanatical, well-trained, and lucky terrorists could have sunk or scuttled a large passenger ship like the *Titanic* and killed many hundreds or even thousands.[39] However, concerns about a terrorist atomic bomb and about the imminence of an explosion escalated greatly after the September 11 attacks, even though the terrorists used weapons no more sophisticated than box cutters on that terrible day.[40] Brian Jenkins has run an Internet search to discover how often variants of the term *al-Qaeda* appeared within ten words of *nuclear*. There were only 7 hits in 1999 and 11 in 2000, but this soared to 1,742 in 2001 and to 2,931 in 2002.[41] By 2008, Defense Secretary Robert Gates was assuring a congressional committee that what keeps every senior government leader awake at night is "the thought of a terrorist ending up with a weapon of mass destruction, especially nuclear."[42]

Nuclear weapons are clearly the most destructive weapons ever invented, but there has been a tendency for decades to exaggerate that capacity, however awesome. For example, Oppenheimer casually inflated the destructiveness of the kind of bomb terrorists might have been able to set off in 1946 by a factor of 100: a ground-burst Hiroshima-size bomb would have "blown up" about 1 percent of New York, not all of it. And in a book published 61 years later, former CIA Director George Tenet extravagantly proclaims that a single "mushroom cloud" would "destroy our economy."[43] On the same page for his April 11, 2010, address, Obama insisted that if a terrorist organization were able to obtain a nuclear weapon, that "could change the security landscape of this country and around the world for years to come."[44]

A rather more careful, responsible, and specific effort to assess the effects of atomic terrorism is included in a 2006 RAND study evaluating the detonation of a ten-kiloton (that is, Hiroshima-size) nuclear device at the Port of Long Beach in California. It concludes that total losses of $1 trillion could be expected.[45] The bulk of the economic costs in this study arise from the assumption that wide areas would have to be evacuated because they would become contaminated by radioactivity under current standards.[46]

Another study assesses the effects of the detonation of a ten-kiloton nuclear device at New York's Grand Central Terminal on a busy day. This might conceivably kill hundreds of thousands of people, inflict immediate property damage in the tens of billions, and cause radioactive contamination that would cost hundreds of billions in lost economic activity, property damage, and long-term health effects. With loss of life and both direct and indirect consequences, including disruption of the U.S. economy, this nightmare scenario, the study concludes, could cost up to $5 trillion.[47]

In our analysis, we will use the figures generated by these studies to establish upper-bound cost estimates for the consequences of an atomic explosion set off by terrorists. While dire, however, these are not necessarily the most probable atomic scenarios. As terrorists have typically inflicted only limited, if nonetheless significant, destruction with conventional explosives, atomic terrorists are not particularly likely to be able to deliver their ordnance in the most effective manner and on the most consequential of targets—and there are few potential target areas in the West that are so densely populated as Grand Central.

It should also be noted that terrorist groups thus far seem to have exhibited only limited desire and even less progress in going atomic. This may be because, after brief exploration of the possible routes, they, unlike generations of alarmists, have discovered that the tremendous effort required is scarcely likely to be successful.[48]

A common concern envisions a newly nuclear country palming off a bomb or two to friendly terrorists for delivery abroad. However, there would be too much risk, even for a country led by extremists, that the ultimate source of the weapon would be discovered before or after detonation or that it would be exploded in a manner and on a target the donor would not approve—including on the donor itself. In addition, al-Qaeda is unlikely to be trusted by just about anyone: as noted in chapter 2, its explicit enemies list includes all Middle Eastern regimes, as well as the governments of India, Pakistan, Afghanistan, and Russia.

Nor is it likely that a working nuclear device could be stolen and detonated. "A theft," point out physicists Christoph Wirz and Emmanuel Egger, "would involve many risks and great efforts in terms of personnel, finances, and organization," while safety and security systems on the weapons "ensure that the successful use of a stolen weapon would be very unlikely."[49] Bombs can be kept disassembled, with the component parts stored in separate high-security vaults, and things can be organized so that two people and multiple codes are required not only to use the bomb but also to store, maintain, and deploy it. If the terrorists seek to enlist (or force) the services of someone who already knows how to set off the bomb, they would find, as Stephen Younger, former research director at

Los Alamos, stresses, that "only a few people in the world have the knowledge to cause an unauthorized detonation of a nuclear weapon." Weapons designers know *how* a weapon works, he explains, but not the multiple types of signals necessary to set it off, and maintenance personnel are trained only in a limited set of functions.[50]

Most analysts consider a terrorist group's most promising route would be to attempt to make a bomb using purloined fissile material—plutonium or highly enriched uranium.[51] However, this remains an extraordinarily difficult task. As the Gilmore Commission, a special advisory panel to the president and Congress, stresses, building a nuclear device capable of producing mass destruction presents "Herculean challenges." The process requires a lengthy sequence of steps, and if each is not fully met, the result is not simply a less powerful weapon, but one that can't produce any significant nuclear yield at all or can't be delivered.[52]

First, the terrorists would need to steal or illicitly purchase the crucial plutonium or highly enriched uranium necessary. This probably would require the corruption of a host of greedy confederates, including brokers and money transmitters, any one of whom could turn on them or, out of either guile or incompetence, furnish them with material that is useless.[53] The theft would also be likely to trigger an international policing effort.

Then, to manufacture a bomb, the terrorists would need to set up a large and well-equipped machine shop somewhere and populate it with a very select team of highly skilled scientists, technicians, machinists, and managers. The group would have to be assembled and retained for the monumental task while no consequential suspicions are generated among friends, family, and police about their sudden and lengthy absence from normal pursuits back home. Members of the bomb-building team would also have to be utterly devoted to the cause and willing to put their lives, and certainly their careers, at high risk because after their bomb was discovered or exploded, they would be likely to become the targets in an intense worldwide dragnet operation facilitated by the fact that their skills would not be common ones.

After assessing the terrorists' task in detail, Wirz and Egger conclude that fabricating a nuclear weapon "could hardly be accomplished by a subnational group" because of "the difficulty of acquiring the necessary expertise, the technical requirements (which in several fields verge on the unfeasible), the lack of available materials and the lack of experience in working with these."[54] Younger has made a similar argument, stressing the "daunting problems associated with material purity, machining, and a host of other issues" and concluding, "to think that a terrorist group, working in isolation with an unreliable supply of electricity and little access to tools and supplies" could fabricate an atomic bomb or device "is far-fetched at best."[55]

Under the best of circumstances for the would-be bomb makers, the process could take months or even a year or more, and it would all, of course, have to be carried out in utter secrecy, even while local and international security police are likely to be on the intense prowl. In addition, people in the area, as well as local criminal gangs, may observe with increasing curiosity and puzzlement the constant comings and goings of technicians unlikely to be locals.

The process of fabricating a nuclear weapon requires, then, the effective recruitment of people who at once have great technical skills and complete devotion to the cause. In addition, a host of corrupted coconspirators, many of them foreign, must remain utterly reliable, international and local security services must be kept perpetually in the dark, and no curious outsider must get consequential wind of the project over the months or even years it takes to pull off.

Finally, the resulting weapon, apt to weigh a ton or more, would have to be moved to a target site in a manner that did not arouse suspicion. And then, at the target site, a crew, presumably suicidal, would have to set off its improvised and untested nuclear device, one that even the alarmed Graham Allison acknowledges would probably be "large, cumbersome, unsafe, unreliable, unpredictable, and inefficient."[56] While doing this, they would have to hope and fervently pray that the machine shop work has been perfect, that there were no significant shake-ups in the treacherous process of transportation, and that the thing, after all this effort, doesn't prove to be a dud.

The financial costs of the extended operation in its cumulating entirety could easily become monumental. There would be expensive equipment to buy, smuggle, and set up and people to pay—or pay off. Any criminals competent and capable enough to be effective allies in the project are likely as well to be not only smart enough to see boundless opportunities for extortion but also psychologically equipped by their profession to be willing to exploit them.[57]

Terrorists with Other "Weapons of Mass Destruction"

Chemical, biological, and radiological weapons have commonly been bracketed with nuclear ones, particularly over the last two decades, into a category known as weapons of mass destruction, but the identification is highly questionable.[58] Although they can cause problems, kill people, and inflict damage, they can scarcely do so on a large scale.

Chemical arms may have the potential, under appropriate circumstances, for panicking people; killing masses of them in open areas, however, is beyond their modest capabilities. Although they obviously can be hugely lethal when released in gas chambers, their effectiveness as weapons has been singularly unimpressive—they accounted for less that one percent of the battle deaths in the First World War. Biologist Matthew Meselson calculates that it would take fully a ton of nerve gas or five tons of mustard gas to produce heavy casualties among unprotected people in an open area one kilometer square. Or as the Gilmore Commission calculates, it would take a full ton of sarin gas released under favorable weather conditions for the destructive effects to become distinctly greater than could be achieved by conventional explosives.[59]

Properly developed and deployed, biological weapons could potentially, if thus far only in theory, kill hundreds of thousands, perhaps even millions, of people. The discussion remains theoretical because biological weapons have scarcely ever been used. For the most destructive results, they need to be dispersed in very low-altitude aerosol clouds. Moreover, 90 percent of the microorganisms are likely to die during the process of aerosolization, while their effectiveness could be reduced still further by sunlight, smog, humidity, and temperature changes. Explosive methods of dispersion may destroy the organisms, and, except for anthrax spores, long-term storage of lethal organisms in bombs or warheads is difficult. In the summary judgment of two careful analysts, delivering microbes and toxins over a wide area in the form most suitable for inflicting mass casualties—as an aerosol that could be inhaled—requires a delivery system of enormous sophistication, and even then effective dispersal could easily be disrupted by unfavorable environmental and meteorological conditions.[60]

Radiological weapons or "dirty bombs," in which radioactive materials are sprayed over an area by a conventional explosion, are incapable of inflicting much immediate damage at all. In fact, it would be almost impossible to disperse radioactive material from a dirty bomb explosion so that victims would absorb a lethal dose before being able to leave the area, and it is likely that few, if any, in the target area would be killed directly, become ill, or even have a measurably increased risk of cancer.[61] The costs of disruption and cleanup could, however, be considerable. Moreover, although a dirty bomb would be easier to assemble than a nuclear weapon, the construction and deployment of one is difficult and requires considerable skill.[62]

In addition, the degree to which al-Qaeda has pursued or even has much interest in any sort of WMD may have been exaggerated. Norwegian analyst Anne Stenersen concludes, after an exhaustive study of available materials, that although "it is likely that al-Qaeda central has considered the option of using non-conventional weapons," there "is little evidence that such ideas ever developed into actual plans." Indeed, an al-Qaeda computer left behind in Afghanistan in 2001 when the group beat a hasty retreat indicates that only some $2,000 to $4,000 was earmarked for WMD research and that was mainly for very crude work on chemical weapons.[63] And evidence seized after bin Laden's death in 2011 suggests his group was cash-strapped and preoccupied with dodging U.S. drone attacks.

In effect, terrorists seem to be heeding the advice found in a memo on an al-Qaeda laptop seized in Pakistan in 2004: "Make use of that which is available . . . rather than waste valuable time becoming despondent over that which is not within your reach."[64] Or as another put it, "a hand grenade that explodes in one of New York's streets, is better than a nuclear bomb capable of destroying half of New York that does not explode!"[65] That is, keep it simple, stupid. As concern shifts to the amateur or minimally trained homegrown perpetrator, it seems officials are increasingly accepting this view of the terrorist threat.

Opportunity Costs and the Costs of Extreme Reaction

The analysis here has thus far assessed and aggregated the cost, rendered in economic terms, both of the direct damage inflicted by terrorists and of the reaction (or overreaction) as seen in reductions in GDP and other indirect costs—which in many cases, including even 9/11, can be much larger than the costs directly inflicted by the terrorists themselves.[66] Most important for present purposes, however, are the costs of extreme reaction. In particular, the 9/11 attacks made the wars in Iraq and Afghanistan politically possible, and by 2010 these conflicts had claimed nearly 6,000 U.S. military fatalities while exacting a cost in treasure to the United States variously estimated at multiple hundreds of billions to a few trillion dollars.

Such extreme reactions are, of course, highly contingent on a large number of other considerations and are rare: few terrorist events trigger full-blown wars, though it could be argued that World War I was caused, or at least triggered, by a terrorist event, an assassination, that directly took only two lives.[67] However, the wars were far from a necessary result of the terrorist event: the terrorists did not directly cause these ventures, but rather facilitated them by shifting the emotional or political situation, potentially making possible a policy some political actors desired for other reasons. Thus, many people in the Bush administration had long been yearning for a war to depose Saddam Hussein in Iraq, and many of them immediately moved into operation after 9/11 in the belief, correct it now seems, that that dramatic event, even though it had nothing to do with Iraq, might well have shifted the political environment sufficiently to allow them to carry out the policy they had been longing for.[68]

Sometimes states massively overreact to terrorist events not so much to carry out a preexisting agenda as simply out of rage, fear, or a desire to exact revenge. In 1999, for example, responding to several vicious acts of terrorism apparently perpetrated by Chechens, the Russian government reinstituted a war against the breakaway republic that resulted in far more destruction of Russian (and, of course, Chechen) lives and property than the terrorists ever brought about. And when two American embassies in Africa were bombed in 1998, killing more than 200 (including a few Americans), President Bill Clinton retaliated by bombing some of Osama bin Laden's terrorist training camps in Afghanistan, which caused the Afghan government, the Taliban, to renege on pledges to extradite the troublesome and egoistic bin Laden to Saudi Arabia, made him into an international celebrity, essentially created his al-Qaeda organization by turning it into a magnet for funds and recruits, and converted the Taliban from reluctant hosts to allies and partners.[69] Outraged by a series of terrorist attacks and shellings perpetrated by Palestinian forces based in bordering Lebanon, the Israelis moved in with massive force in 1982. By the time Israeli forces were withdrawn in 2000, vastly more Israelis among the occupying forces had been killed by harassing Arab attacks than had been killed by terrorists before 1982.

In this vein, many commentators in the United States warn that in the event of substantial additional terrorism in the country, the government and people would respond by going on a rampage of self-destruction. For example, Michael Ignatieff explains in some detail how Americans will destroy themselves in response to the next attack. Although Americans did allow their leaders one fatal mistake in September 2001, they simply "will not forgive another one." If there are several large-scale attacks, he confidently predicts, the trust that binds the people to its leadership and to each other will crumble, and the "cowed populace" will demand that tyranny be imposed upon it and quite possibly break itself into a collection of rampaging lynch mobs devoted to killing "former neighbors" and "onetime friends."[70]

Actually, it is not at all clear that even another 9/11 would trigger the extreme reaction engendered by the original intensely shocking event. And that experience suggests that, far from engendering panicky behavior, the most likely response would be to pull together to confront the threat.[71] Moreover, although there is often a political imperative that public officials "do something" when a dramatic terrorist event takes place, history clearly demonstrates that massive overreaction is not necessarily inevitable, nor is it even very common. Sometimes, in fact, leaders have been able to restrain their instinct to overreact—the restraint of the Indian government to the dramatic, outrage-producing Mumbai attacks that had been directed from neighboring Pakistan is very much a case in point.[72] This phenomenon will be discussed more fully in chapter 9.

Whatever such considerations, if counterterrorism measures manage to prevent terrorist attacks that would necessarily lead to severe reactions, the measures would be, to say the least, of great value. They would be so not by preventing destruction inflicted by the terrorists as much as by preventing the danger of massively self-destructive reactions by the terrorists' victims.

THE COSTS AND LIKELIHOOD OF TERRORIST ATTACKS

It is important—indeed, crucial—in current policy discussions about terrorism to keep the adversary's capacity in mind: as discussed in chapter 2, although al-Qaeda certainly does not wish us well, its ability to carry out attacks in the United States and the West is constrained. That chapter attempted to assess terrorism as a hazard to human life, concluding that, compared with a wide variety of other hazards, its record at killing people is rather limited. In fact, under present conditions, terrorism is an "acceptable risk"—the likelihood any person living outside a war zone will be killed by a terrorist is so low that the risk can, applying accepted conventional standards, be considered minimal.

This chapter has sought to aggregate the total costs inflicted by terrorism—not only the loss of life but also the direct and indirect economic costs. These, too, are typically—although not always, of course—quite limited.

These conclusions are based on historical records of the amount of damage terrorism has been able to inflict. However, it certainly seems likely that few, if any, future attacks are going to be of a massively greater destructive magnitude. On the contrary, they are likely to be rare and mostly of comparatively limited (though still tragic) consequence.

There are serious analysts, however, who strongly disagree. When 85 foreign policy experts were polled by Senator Richard Lugar in 2004 and 2005, they concluded on average that there was a 29 percent likelihood a nuclear explosion would occur somewhere in the world within the next ten years, and they overwhelmingly anticipated that it would be carried out by terrorists, not by a government.[73] In an influential 2004 book, Graham Allison relayed his "considered judgment" that "on the current path, a nuclear terrorist attack on America in the decade ahead is more likely than not"—that is, more than 6.6 percent per year.[74] And in 2007, physicist Richard Garwin assessed the likelihood of a nuclear explosion on an American or European city by terrorist or other means to be 20 percent per year, which would work out to 89 percent over a ten-year period.[75]

There is also the potential for the victim country to greatly enhance the negative effects of terrorism by massive overreaction. Ignatieff is not alone in arguing that Americans will respond to another major attack by committing societal suicide. And although lashing out in rage or seizing the opportunity afforded by a terrorist act to initiate wars and other destructive activity is not common, it clearly can happen.

Since both of these dire scenarios—atomic terrorism and massive overreaction—are taken very seriously by many observers, they will be included in later analyses.

Chapter 2, then, has supplied background thinking for the likelihood of a terrorist attack, and this chapter has added in other considerations to develop a range of expectations about the extent of damage terrorism can inflict. The next chapter combines these considerations with others to develop a full cost-benefit analysis of homeland security counterterrorism expenditures.

CHAPTER 4

Evaluating Increases in Homeland Security Spending

A cost-benefit analysis for homeland security spending is well overdue, one that allows the decision maker to make a risk-informed decision about whether counterterrorism expenditures are excessive or a productive and sensible use of society's resources.

This chapter sets out some basic and rather broad-scaled thinking about how such a process might be carried out to evaluate expenditures on terrorism. It applies established risk assessment and cost-benefit techniques to determine the overall value of increases in homeland security expenditures since 2001.[1] We look first at the increased expenditures for the United States and then compare these with those for the United Kingdom, Canada, and Australia.

COST-BENEFIT ASSESSMENT

As outlined in chapter 1, a conventional approach to cost-effectiveness compares the costs of security measures with the benefits, as tallied in lives saved and damages averted.

A security measure is cost-effective when the benefit of the measure outweighs the costs of providing the security measures. The *benefit of a security measure* is a function of three elements:

Benefit = (probability of a successful attack) × (losses sustained
in the successful attack) × (reduction in risk)

The *probability of a successful attack* is the likelihood a successful terrorist attack will take place if the security measure were not in place. The *losses sustained in the successful attack* include the fatalities and other damage—both direct and indirect—that will accrue as a result of a successful terrorist attack, taking into account the value and vulnerability of people and infrastructure as well as any psychological and political effects. The *reduction in risk* is the degree to which the security measure foils, deters, disrupts, or protects against a terrorist attack. This *benefit*, a multiplicative composite of three considerations, is then compared with the *costs* of providing the risk-reducing security that are required to attain the benefit.

If the benefit of the security measure outweighs its cost, it is deemed to be cost-effective.

Application to Terrorism: Benefit

In the matter at hand, where we are concerned with the cost-effectiveness of enhanced (post-9/11) security expenditures, the *probability of a successful attack* is the likelihood a successful terrorist attack will take place if no new security measures were put into place. As discussed at length in chapter 2, terrorism, at least outside war zones, is very infrequent: it is a low-probability event.

The *losses sustained in the successful attack* include the fatalities and other damage—both direct and indirect—caused by the terrorist attack, taking into account the value and vulnerability of people and infrastructure, as well as any psychological and political effects. Chapter 3 reviewed the full losses sustained in terrorist attacks and showed that a successful terrorist attack, on average, can inflict costs in the tens of millions of dollars. Exceptional attacks, like the one on 9/11, can cost $200 billion, and losses could conceivably reach $5 trillion for the nightmare scenario of the detonation of a sizable nuclear device in a densely populated area of a city.

The third and final consideration in calculating the benefit of the security expenditures is the *reduction in risk*, which in this case concerns the effectiveness of enhanced security measures to foil, deter, disrupt, or protect against a terrorist attack.[2] That is, it is the degree to which new security measures reduce the likelihood of a successful terrorist attack and/or the losses sustained in such an attack.

In assessing risk reduction, it is important first to look at the effectiveness of homeland security measures that were in place before 9/11 in reducing risk. The 9/11 Commission's report points to a number of failures, but it acknowledges as well that terrorism was already a high priority of the U.S. government before 9/11, pointing out that a 1998 presidential decision directive "reiterated that terrorism was a national security problem, not just a law enforcement issue."[3] Moreover, it notes that the efforts of the National Security Council, State Department, Pentagon, CIA, and Justice Department "were sometimes energetic and sometimes effective. Terrorist plots were disrupted and individual terrorists were captured."[4] In a review of 20 studies, statisticians Frederick Mosteller and Cleo Youtz find that the expression "sometimes" corresponds to a probability of 19 to 38 percent.[5] The 9/11 Commission Report's observation that pre-9/11 security was "sometimes effective" could quite reasonably be said to translate into a risk reduction in that range.

More pointed is an observation from Michael Sheehan, former New York City deputy commissioner for counterterrorism:

> The most important work in protecting our country since 9/11 has been accomplished with the capacity that was in place when the event happened, not with any of the new capability bought since 9/11. I firmly believe that those huge budget increases have not significantly contributed to our post-9/11 security. . . . The big wins had little to do with the new programs.[6]

As this suggests, police and domestic intelligence agencies have long had in place procedures, techniques, trained personnel, and action plans to deal with bombs and shootings and those who plot them.

Nor is violent terrorism a new concern for them. It may be useful in this regard to quote Brian Jenkins at some length. Noting that the scale of the September 11, 2001, attacks has "tended to obliterate America's memory of pre-9/11 terrorism," he points out that

> measured by the number of terrorist attacks, the volume of domestic terrorist activity was much greater in the 1970s. That tumultuous decade saw 60 to 70 terrorist incidents, mostly bombings, on U.S. soil every year—a level of terrorist activity 15 to 20 times that seen in the years since 9/11, even when foiled plots are counted as incidents. And in the nine-year period from 1970 to 1978, 72 people died in terrorist incidents, more than five times the number killed by jihadist terrorists in the United States in the almost nine years since 9/11.
>
> In the 1970s, terrorists, on behalf of a variety of causes, hijacked airliners; held hostages in Washington, New York, Chicago, and San Francisco; bombed embassies, corporate headquarters, and government buildings; robbed banks; murdered diplomats; and blew up power transformers, causing widespread blackouts. These were not one-off attacks but sustained

campaigns by terrorist gangs that were able to avoid capture for years. The Weather Underground was responsible for 45 bombings between 1970 and 1977, the date of its last action, while the New World Liberation Front claimed responsibility for approximately 70 bombings in the San Francisco Bay area between 1974 and 1978 and was believed to be responsible for another 26 bombings in other Northern California cities. Anti-Castro Cuban exile groups claimed responsibility for nearly 100 bombings. Continuing an armed campaign that dated back to the 1930s, Puerto Rican separatists, reorganized in 1974 as the Armed Front for National Liberation (FALN), claimed credit for more than 60 bombings. The Jewish Defense League and similar groups protesting the plight of Jews in the Soviet Union claimed responsibility for more than 50 bombings during the decade. Croatian and Serbian émigrés also carried out sporadic terrorist attacks in the United States, as did remnants of the Ku Klux Klan.[7]

And according to 9/11's chief planner, Khalid Sheikh Mohammed, the greatest difficulty the plotters faced was getting their band of terrorists into the United States. Such a task may be even more difficult now, but the strictures before already presented a considerable hurdle.[8]

The Department of Homeland Security (DHS) and the Transportation Security Administration (TSA) provide possibly the best yardstick of what risk reductions are possible. In a 2008 press release, they were proud to announce that regulations associated with rail transportation of toxic inhalation hazards aimed to reduce risk by 50 percent and actually achieved an overall risk reduction of more than 60 percent.[9] These agencies are not known for underselling their achievements. If they can trumpet that their target risk reduction is 50 percent (to be achieved by developing "sound security measures without excessively burdening owners and operators"), this can only be viewed as a target they are eager to endorse. A target or aim is something that is ambitious in nature, and the fact that the TSA was aiming for a risk reduction of 50 percent, and not a more newsworthy 80 or 90 or 99 percent, is an excellent indicator of the kind of risk reduction they believe can be achieved at reasonable cost.

There is another consideration. The tragic events of 9/11 massively heightened the awareness of the public to the threat of terrorism, resulting in extra vigilance that has often resulted in the arrest of terrorists or the foiling of terrorist attempts. Most dramatically, because airplane passengers have become much more attuned to suspicious or dodgy behavior of their fellow passengers, two terrorist attempts to blow up airliners have been foiled: the shoe bombing effort of 2001 and the underwear effort of 2009. Both were detected and restrained by crews and passengers, not by the many costly enhanced security measures put into place by the TSA. The same holds for the peddler in New York who reported the smoking vehicle bomb in Times Square in 2010. And tip-offs have been key to prosecutions in many of the terrorism cases in the United States since 9/11.

In our analysis, we will assume that risk reduction caused by the security measures in place before 9/11 and by the extra vigilance of the public after that event reduced risk by 50 percent. This is an exceedingly conservative estimate not only because of Sheehan's observation but also because security measures that are at once effective and relatively inexpensive are generally the first to be implemented—for example, one erects warning signs on a potentially dangerous curve in the road before rebuilding the highway. Thus, a 2006 RAND study on reducing terrorism risks at shopping centers found that the least costly measures, suspicious package reporting, reduced risk by 60 percent, but the costly and inconvenient searching of bags at entrances achieved only 15 percent risk reduction. Overall, in fact, the cheapest six security measures reduced risk by 70 percent, and the remaining 12 costlier security measures reduced risks by only another 25 percent.[10] Furthermore, as suggested in chapters 2 and 3, most terrorists (or would-be terrorists) do not show much intelligence, cleverness, resourcefulness, or initiative, and therefore measures to deal with them are relatively inexpensive and are likely to be instituted first. Dealing with the smarter and more capable terrorists is more difficult and expensive, but such people represent, it certainly appears, a decided minority among terrorists.

In addition, we will assume that the increase in U.S. expenditures on homeland security since 2001 has been dramatically effective, reducing the remaining risk: total risk reduction is assumed to be 95 percent, with the preexisting measures and the extra public vigilance responsible for 50 percent and the enhanced expenditures responsible for the remaining 45 percent. This assumption is very generous to the security measures since a risk reduction of 95 percent is extremely challenging to achieve: given the ease with which a bomb can be set off or a bullet fired, no set of security measures is guaranteed to foil or protect against nearly every terrorist attack.

Application to Terrorism: Costs

As indicated, benefits are a multiplicative composite of three considerations: the probability of a successful attack, the losses sustained in a successful attack, and the reduction in risk furnished by security measures.

This product, the benefit, is then compared with the costs of the security measures instituted to attain the benefit.[11]

For the purposes of this analysis, we assess only the costs of *increased* government expenditures on homeland security after the 9/11 attacks. That is, we assume homeland security measures in place before the attacks continue, and we evaluate the additional funds that have been allocated to homeland security, almost all of it designed, of course, to deal with terrorism, the only hazard that notably inspired increased alarm after the attacks.

RESULTS FOR THE UNITED STATES

To conduct a cost-benefit analysis of enhanced homeland security expenditures for the United States, we need first to estimate how much those expenditures have increased since 2001. The Office of Management and Budget (OMB) defines "homeland security activities" as "activities that focus on combating and protecting against terrorism, and that occur within the U.S. and its territories,"[12] and its data show that U.S. federal government spending on such activities increased from $20.1 billion in 2001[13] to $75 billion in 2009.[14] Returning to table I.1, it can be seen that homeland security expenditures increased steadily in real terms since 2001, a pattern that is likely to continue. Some 44 percent of this expenditure is devoted to preventing and disrupting terrorist attacks through policing and intelligence efforts,[15] and another 46 percent to protecting the American people, critical infrastructure, and key resources,[16] while 9 percent is devoted to responding to and recovering from incidents.[17] Funding goes to DHS, the Department of Defense, the Department of Justice, the Department of Health and Human Services, the Department of Energy, and 26 other federal agencies as arrayed in table I.1. In all, federal government spending on homeland security for 2009 was $75 billion, or $50 billion more in 2010 dollars than in 2001, adjusting for inflation.[18]

To limit our focus to increases in expenditures by the federal government would be a considerable restriction that ignores the recently declassified national intelligence costs, as well as state and local government outlays on homeland security. The budget for U.S. intelligence operations was $75 billion in 2009,[19] and a core function is "protecting against the threat of international terrorism in the United States."[20] As shown in table I.2, the "Trillion Dollar Table," we conservatively estimate enhanced intelligence expenditures since 9/11 devoted to domestic homeland security to be

$15 billion in 2009. As the table also indicates, enhanced outlays for state and local homeland security spending are approximately $10 billion per year.

The increase in annual federal government outlays, then, is $50 billion per year, and the addition of national intelligence and state and local homeland security outlays of $25 billion gives a total of $75 billion per year. We will use this figure, although it is a very conservative measure of the degree to which homeland security expenditures have risen since 9/11 because we do not include several other items totaling (far) more than $200 billion per year, as also indicated at the bottom of table I.2 and in its notes. These include (1) private-sector expenditures on homeland-security-related measures costing $10 billion per year; (2) terrorism risk insurance premiums of nearly $4 billion per year; (3) hidden and indirect costs or deadweight losses of implementing security-related regulations that amounted to at least $30 billion in lost output per year; (4) various opportunity costs, including those attendant on the increase of 500 traffic fatalities per year due to increased delays and added costs at airports diverting many short-haul passengers to their cars instead, valued at $3.2 billion a year, as well as other opportunity costs; and (5) the costs of the terror-related wars in Iraq and Afghanistan, which reached $150 billion for the year of 2009.

To summarize, our analysis for the United States applies these estimates and assumptions:

1. We assume those security measures in place before 9/11 continue and that these, combined with the extra public vigilance induced by 9/11, reduce the likelihood of a successful terrorist attack or reduce the losses sustained in such an attack by 50 percent.
2. We assume the enhanced security expenditures since 9/11 have successfully reduced the likelihood of a successful terrorist attack or have reduced the losses sustained in such an attack by a further 45 percent, leading to an overall risk reduction of 95 percent.
3. We include in our cost measure only enhanced local, state, and federal security expenditures and enhanced intelligence costs since 9/11 (totaling $75 billion per year), leaving out many other expenditures including those incurred by the private sector, opportunity costs, and the costs of the terror-related wars in Iraq and Afghanistan.

Table 4.1 puts this all together. It displays the benefit generated by enhanced security measures if they have been able to prevent or protect against an otherwise successful attack for a range of losses from a successful attack and for a range of annual attack probabilities.

Table 4.1 NET BENEFIT IN BILLIONS OF DOLLARS FOR U.S. ENHANCED HOMELAND SECURITY EXPENDITURES OF $75 BILLION PER YEAR, ASSUMING THESE HAVE REDUCED RISKS BY 45 PERCENT

Annual probability of a successful attack in the absence of security expenditures	Losses from a Successful Terrorist Attack						
	$100 million	$1 billion	$5 billion London bombing	$100 billion	$200 billion 9/11	$1 trillion Nuclear port	$5 trillion Nuclear Grand Central
0.1 percent	-75	-75	-75	-75	-75	-75	-73
1 percent	-75	-75	-75	-75	-74	-71	-53
5 percent	-75	-75	-75	-73	-71	-53	38
10 percent	-75	-75	-75	-71	-66	-30	150
25 percent	-75	-75	-74	-64	-53	38	488
50 percent	-75	-75	-74	-53	-30	150	1,050
100 percent[1]	-75	-75	-73	-30	15	375	2,175

Each entry represents the benefit-minus-cost result for each loss and for each attack probability. Entries that are positive would be considered to be cost-effective. A value of -75 denotes no benefit.

Break-Even Analysis

The number of otherwise successful attacks averted by security expenditures required for enhanced expenditures to be cost-effective at several levels of loss — that is, for the security benefit of the expenditures to equal their costs

1,667 per year	167 per year	33 per year	2 per year	1 per year	1 every 6 years	1 every 30 years

[1] One per year.

As discussed in chapter 3, in the years since 2001 (or, for that matter, in those previous to it), al-Qaeda-like terrorists operating outside war zones have generally inflicted less than $1 million in property damage and a limited number of fatalities in a successful attack. A monetary value of the destruction wreaked in attacks like that would be tens of millions of dollars. Of late, as discussed in chapter 2, a number of analysts and policy makers have suggested that these are the kind of attacks that are by far the most likely. A high estimate for small successful attacks would be $100 million. This would be the amount of damage the Times Square bomber of 2010 might have been able to inflict if he had killed about a dozen people, destroyed some property, and caused some disarray in tourism and economic activity for a while (higher estimates are also possible in that case). Table 4.1 indicates in the first column that, even if the likelihood of such an attack were 100 percent per year without security measures, the money spent to prevent or protect against the attack would not be worth it: the costs of security would outweigh the benefit of the security.

There is another way to look at this. If

$$\text{Benefit} = (\text{probability of a successful attack}) \times (\text{losses sustained in the successful attack}) \times (\text{reduction in risk})$$

the same equation can be used in a break-even analysis to calculate how many attacks would have to take place to justify the expenditure. That is, thinking of the "benefit" as the cost of the security measure:

$$(\text{probability of a successful attack}) = \text{security cost}/\left[(\text{losses sustained in the successful attack}) \times (\text{reduction in risk})\right]$$

Thus for a successful attack in which the enhanced security cost is $75 billion, losses sustained are a very high $100 million, and the reduction in risk is .45, the probability of a successful attack would need to be at least

$$(\text{probability of a successful attack}) > \$75 \text{ billion}/$$
$$[\$100 \text{ million} \times .45] = 1{,}667 \text{ attacks per year}$$

That is, for enhanced U.S. expenditures on homeland security to be deemed cost-effective under our approach—which substantially biases the consideration toward the opposite conclusion—they would have to deter, prevent, foil, or protect against as many as 1,667 otherwise successful attacks roughly like the one on Times Square per year, or more than four per day. The array of numbers at the bottom on table 4.1 gives this quantity for a variety of loss levels.

As discussed in chapter 3, the losses from attacks like those of July 2005 in London would not exceed $5 billion. For enhanced security measures to be cost-effective for attacks of that magnitude, their rate of occurrence without security measures would have had to exceed 30 per year.[21] If we posit that such an attack is thwarted once per year, a conservative threat likelihood by any measure, the ratio of benefit to cost is a meager 0.03 meaning that spending $1 buys only 3 cents of benefits.[22]

For a terrorist attack, or set of attacks, that, like those of September 11, 2001, caused $200 billion dollars of destruction (something that has occurred only once in all of history), enhanced expenditures would be cost-effective only if that sort of attack would have occurred more than once a year without them. Moreover, as suggested in chapter 3, it is not clear that other 9/11-like attacks would trigger the extreme economic reaction engendered by the original intensely shocking event—that is, the full costs of another 9/11 might not reach those sustained in the original event.

An extreme upper bound would be the detonation of a ten-kiloton nuclear device at New York's Grand Central Terminal on a busy day, a nightmare scenario that, as discussed in chapter 3, might exact losses of up to $5 trillion. Enhanced homeland security expenditures would be cost-effective in this case only if, without them, such an extreme attack would have successfully been executed once every 30 years. The same, roughly, would hold for the other extreme scenario in which the terrorist attack triggers an expensive war like the one in Iraq.[23]

We can look at this in yet another way. If we take increased expenditures on homeland security in the United States for a given year to be $75 billion (a number likely to be a considerable underestimate), if we take $6.5 million to be the value of each saved life, and if we assume that all the lives saved have been *solely* the result of enhanced homeland security measures, approximately 11,500 lives would have to have been saved in that year for the increased homeland security expenditure to be cost-effective.[24] The same general conclusion holds, of course, when the calculation is reversed. If there is a likelihood of one in a hundred that a terrorist attack similar to 9/11 will occur this year, the cost per life saved, if enhanced security measures were entirely responsible for saving the lives, would be $2.5 billion.[25] If the likelihood of such an attack is 50 percent, the cost per saved life is $50 million. In either case, the cost per life saved is greatly in excess of the regulatory safety goal, as set out in a DHS study, of $6.5 million per life saved and hugely excessive in comparison with most of the items detailed in table 3.1.

If the risk reduction of those security measures in place before 9/11 and extra public vigilance induced by 9/11 seem overly optimistic, and risk reductions due to enhanced security measures seem too pessimistic, we can drastically change them and, for example, assume

1. that those security measures in place before 9/11 continue, and that these, combined with the extra public vigilance induced by 9/11, result in a risk reduction of only 25 percent (not 50 percent) and
2. that enhanced security expenditures since 9/11 further reduce the risk by a high 74.9 percent, leading to an impressive, if unrealistic, overall risk reduction of 99.9 percent.

Table 4.2 arrays the revised break-even calculations for this upscaled risk reduction of 74.9 percent. While the frequency of attacks needed for the security benefit of the expenditures to equal their cost is reduced somewhat, the general conclusion that the likelihood of a successful terrorist attack absent security measures needs to be fantastically high for the enhanced security measures to be cost-effective still holds.[26] This type of sensitivity analysis shows our findings to be robust even when we make assumptions that bias the calculations even more in favor of finding $75 billion of enhanced expenditures to be cost-effective.

There are extreme scenarios that can be taken to suggest that enhanced U.S. security expenditures could be cost-effective—the nightmare nuclear

Table 4.2 SENSITIVITY AND BREAK-EVEN ANALYSIS FOR U.S. ENHANCED HOMELAND SECURITY EXPENDITURES OF $75 BILLION PER YEAR, ASSUMING THESE HAVE REDUCED RISKS BY AN IMPRESSIVE 74.9 PERCENT

Losses from a Successful Terrorist Attack						
$100 million	$1 billion	$5 billion London bombing	$100 billion	$200 billion 9/11	$1 trillion Nuclear port	$5 trillion Nuclear Grand Central

The number of otherwise successful attacks averted by security expenditures required for enhanced expenditures to be cost-effective at several levels of loss—that is, for the security benefit of the expenditures to equal their costs

| 1,001 per year | 100 per year | 20 per year | 1 per year | 1 every 2 years | 1 every 10 years | 1 every 50 years |

vision, as well as the costly overreaction scenario discussed in chapter 3. However, for those who find such outcomes dangerously likely, the policy response would logically be to spend on reducing the risk of nuclear terrorism in the one case and to develop strictures to overreaction in the other. The logical policy response would not be, for example, to spend tens of billions of dollars each year on protection measures.

In virtually all contexts, then, overall enhanced expenditures on homeland security in the United States fail to be cost-effective—spectacularly so, in most instances—even in an analysis that very substantially biases the calculations in favor of the opposite conclusion.

RESULTS FOR THE UNITED KINGDOM

In its 2007 spending review, the government of the United Kingdom contends that it faces a "real and unprecedented threat of terrorism" and that the "threat to the UK from terrorist attack remains high."[27] There is good cause for such concern, evidenced by the attacks on buses and on underground trains in London in 2005, an unsuccessful attempt at a repeat two weeks later, and other terrorist activity and incidents. There is also, of course, the ongoing (albeit much reduced) threat from Irish republican and loyalist paramilitaries. No wonder, then, that some security analysts label the United Kingdom as "another frontline state in the campaign against terrorism."[28] Assessing U.K. security expenditure will help place the U.S. expenditure in some sort of context.

As figure 4.1 indicates, dedicated spending on counterterrorism, intelligence, and resilience in the United Kingdom steadily increased from £923 million in 2001–2002 to £2.5 billion in 2007–2008 and will increase to £3.5 billion by 2010/11.[29] Expenditures in 2010–2011 will increase by approximately £2.6 billion, which is more than triple the pre-9/11 levels. The U.K. government labels this as the "security budget" aimed at "protecting the nation from external and internal threats."[30] It includes funding to the police, security services, and Home Office, as well as to other relevant government agencies like the Centre for the Protection of National Infrastructure, which includes the government's counterterrorism strategy CONTEST, divided into four main categories: pursue, protect, prepare, and prevent. The British prefer the term "counterterrorism, intelligence, and resilience," but there is no doubt that these expenditures are directly comparable to what the Americans call homeland security.

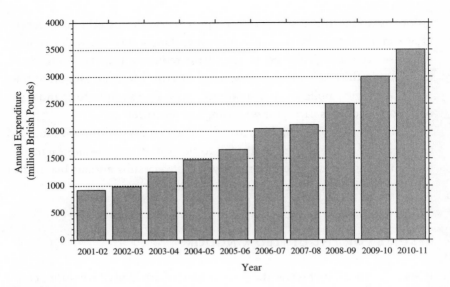

Figure 4.1
United Kingdom Counterterrorism/Resilience Spending since 2001–2002.
Source: HM Treasury, *2004 Spending Review*, 76, Lords Hansard, Written Answers, 2 December 2009.

It is unclear whether counterterrorism capabilities within the British military are included in the government's security budget. However, Jonathan Stevenson surmises that, with the exception of Northern Ireland, the British military has a limited or supportive role in counterterrorism. Specifically, he notes that critical infrastructure protection is primarily the responsibility of civilian authorities and private owners, that the military "has little direct military involvement in territorial border security," and that the "key agencies" in border control "are all civilian." The same applies for transportation security. Overall, notes Stevenson, the armed forces have essentially played a police support role in countering terrorism, which the British government has treated since 1976 as a criminal problem.[31] Ministry of Defence expenditure on counterterrorism clearly has been substantial because of the large numbers of military personnel deployed to Northern Ireland for the past few decades. Most relevant to our analysis, however, is that its expenditures on counterterrorism are unlikely to have risen dramatically after September 2001 because the country had already been engaged in domestic counterinsurgency and counterterrorism for many years prior to 2001. This situation is in stark contrast to the United States, where $19.4 billion was earmarked within the Department of Defense budget in 2009 for homeland security, comprising 26.2 percent of the entire federal outlay on homeland security.

As with the United States, it is unlikely that the governments would want to downplay the value of homeland security and counterterrorism resources and efforts: any official would surely prefer to say that his or her government has increased homeland security fivefold, rather than three-fold, because the latter implies a reduced level of safety. So we take at face value, as others have, that the highly publicized U.K. "security budget" is an accurate measure of the country's homeland security expenditure. Unlike the United States, the United Kingdom has centralized homeland security responsibilities and budgets: whereas the United States has nearly 20,000 law enforcement jurisdictions at the state and local level, the United Kingdom has 43 regional police forces, while the overwhelming bulk of counterterrorism funding goes to national security agencies like the Metropolitan Police (Scotland Yard), MI5, and MI6. The large degree of centralization means that the U.K. security budget is comparable to the combined U.S. federal, state, and local expenditures.

Because 2010–2011 expenditures will increase by approximately $4.1 billion from 2001 levels (adjusting for inflation),[32] it seems safe to surmise that the increase in annual outlays on homeland security in the United Kingdom since 2001 has reached $4.1 billion per year. We will round this up to $5 billion per year to allow for county expenditures on counterterrorism that are likely, however, to be rather small.[33] As with the American case, we do not include British military operations in the wars in Iraq and Afghanistan that cost more than £4.5 billion in 2008–2009.[34]

An enhanced British expenditure of $5 billion is equivalent to $80 per capita or 0.23 percent of GDP.[35] Enhanced expenditures for the United States, at $244 per capita or 0.53 percent of GDP,[36] are more than twice those of the United Kingdom.[37]

Table 4.3 gives the benefit or loss for a range of annual attack probabilities and losses when these estimates and assumptions are applied. As table 4.1 demonstrates, for enhanced U.S. homeland security expenditure to be cost-effective when a loss of $200 billion would otherwise have been suffered, the yearly probability of a successful terrorist attack needs to be higher than 100 percent, or more than once per year. For the United Kingdom, the yearly attack probability in that case needs only to be a bit higher than 5 percent, or once every 20 years. There are clearly more benefit (positive) values in table 4.3 than there are for the United States in table 4.1, and this means that the U.K. enhanced expenditure is much more likely to be cost-effective than U.S. expenditure under comparable assumptions— indeed, the minimum attack probability for U.K. expenditure to be cost-effective is 15 times lower than for the United States overall.[38] For U.S.

Table 4.3 NET BENEFIT IN BILLIONS OF DOLLARS FOR U.K. ENHANCED HOMELAND SECURITY EXPENDITURES OF $5 BILLION PER YEAR, ASSUMING THESE HAVE REDUCED RISKS BY 45 PERCENT

Annual probability of a successful attack in the absence of security expenditures	Losses from a successful terrorist attack						
	$100 million	$1 Billion	$5 Billion	$100 billion	$200 billion	$1 trillion	$5 Trillion
0.1 percent	-5.0	-5.0	-5.0	-5.0	-4.9	-4.6	-2.8
1 percent	-5.0	-5.0	-5.0	-4.6	-4.1	-0.5	17.5
5 percent	-5.0	-5.0	-4.9	-2.8	-0.5	17.5	107.5
10 percent	-5.0	-5.0	-4.8	-0.5	4.0	40.0	220.0
25 percent	-5.0	-4.9	-4.4	6.3	17.5	107.5	557.5
50 percent	-5.0	-4.8	-3.9	17.5	40.0	220.0	1120.0
100 percent	-5.0	-4.6	-2.8	40.0	85.0	445.0	2245.0

Each entry represents the benefit-minus-cost result for each loss and for each attack probability. Entries that are positive would be considered to be cost-effective. A value of -5.0 denotes no benefit.

Break-Even Analysis

The number of otherwise successful attacks averted by security expenditures required for enhanced expenditures to be cost-effective at several levels of loss—that is, for the security benefit of the expenditures to equal their costs

111 per year	11 per year	2 per year	1 every 10 years	1 every 20 years	1 every 100 years	1 every 500 years

enhanced security measures to be cost-effective, losses from large, but feasible, terrorist attacks, like the 2005 London bombings that caused, by some estimates, close to $5 billion in damage, would need to exceed 30 per year. For the United Kingdom, there would need to have been more than two such attacks per year.

However, even these lower attack frequencies are not credible. The United Kingdom has scarcely had two attacks—or potential attacks or imagined attacks—that caused, or had the potential to cause or might conceivably have had the potential to cause, losses of roughly this magnitude over the last decade, much less each year.

RESULTS FOR CANADA AND AUSTRALIA

Homeland security budgets for Canada and Australia are quite opaque when compared with the United States and the United Kingdom.[39] However, the sums of money are clearly considerably smaller. As with the analysis of the United States and Britain, expenditures on military operations in Iraq and Afghanistan, which run into the billions of dollars for both countries, are omitted from this analysis.

Eric Lerhe, a fellow of the Canadian Defence and Foreign Affairs Institute, after an examination of his country's budget, reveals that in the seven years after 2001, successive budgets raised total antiterrorist spending to C$9.5 billion.[40] This is a *cumulative* expenditure over the seven years from 2002 to 2008, not an annual one. A year-by-year breakdown of expenditure is not available, but if we assume that expenditure has incrementally increased equally every year for eight years, the yearly increase in expenditure in 2010 came to approximately C$2.1 billion, or US$1.9 billion.[41]

The Australian situation is similar. In 2008, cumulative enhanced expenditure on domestic elements of national security activities from 2002–2003 to 2011–2012 was expected to be A$8.03 billion, according to Athol Yates, executive director of the Australian Homeland Security Research Centre.[42] When we apply the same accounting assumptions as for the Canadian budget, the yearly increase in expenditure has been has been approximately A$1.3 billion, or US$1.1 billion.[43]

Expenditures on homeland security in Canada and Australia, then, have increased by only one or two billion dollars per year, equivalent to 0.14 percent for Canada and 0.12 percent of GDP for Australia.[44] These expenditures, expressed in relation either to GDP or to population size, are less that those of the United Kingdom and less than a quarter of what the United States spends on homeland security.[45]

A cost-benefit analysis comparable with the ones detailed in tables 4.1 and 4.3 for these two countries shows that the likelihood of a successful terrorist attack inflicting $200 billion in losses needs to be higher than 2.1 percent and 1.2 percent per year for Canadian and Australian homeland security expenditure to be cost-effective, respectively. For losses of $5 billion, the probability of a successful attack needs to be higher than 84 percent for Canada and 49 percent for Australia—that is, more than one attack every one to two years would have had to be foiled by enhanced security measures for them to be cost-effective. For the far more realistic attack losses of $100 million, however, there would have had to be more than 25 such attacks every year for Canadian and Australian homeland security expenditures to be cost-effective. This scarcely seems plausible, but then again, the comparatively modest expenditure on counterterrorism in the two countries is perhaps prudent in times of threat uncertainty.

EVALUATIONS OF COST-EFFECTIVENESS

A risk-based model that assesses the cost-effectiveness of increased U.S. homeland security expenditures since 9/11 found that increased expenditures on homeland security begin to be cost-effective only if, for example, the consequences of a terrorist attack are $100 billion and attacks of that magnitude would have occurred nearly twice a year without security measures. Even in the dire scenario of the detonation of a ten-kiloton nuclear device at the Port of Long Beach causing a trillion dollars damage, the attack probability would need to exceed 17 percent per year, or an 85 percent chance over ten years.[46]

The analyses for the United Kingdom, Canada, and Australia revealed homeland security spending to be considerably less than half of that of the United States in proportion to GDP or population. Even for these more modest expenditures, attack probabilities in the order of 2 to 10 percent are required for homeland security to be cost-effective in the case of a very expensive terrorist attack imposing a cost of $100 billion. This also is not cost-effective.

The lack of cost-effectiveness reaches ridiculous proportions when a far more likely attack is considered, one causing property damage and death or injury to a few people and inflicting losses of $100 million, something like the attempt at Times Square in 2010. In this case, 1,667 such attacks would need to be thwarted annually in the United States by enhanced homeland security expenditures for them to be cost-effective. Under the same conditions, enhanced homeland security expenditures would be cost-effective only if they could plausibly be held to have thwarted 111 terrorist attacks each year in the United Kingdom, 42 in Canada, and 29 in Australia. Attack frequencies of that magnitude are scarcely found anywhere outside war zones like Iraq or Afghanistan.

Those are rather extreme numbers perhaps. But those who distrust the analysis are free to do their own calculation to check the robustness of our findings. What is important is that such considerations be done in a transparent manner. The analysis applied here should provide a starting point for discussion and for more detailed and complex analysis—something that should have happened, one might think, *before* deciding to increase expenditures on homeland security by more than a trillion dollars.

As we discuss more fully in the concluding chapter, diverting even a few billion dollars from the $75 billion annual homeland security budget to smoke alarms, tornado shelters, car safety, and other effective lifesaving measures would save hundreds of lives, far more than the mammoth homeland security expenditures, with their limited lifesaving benefit.

However, our findings dealing with the total enhanced homeland security expenditures should not be taken to suggest that all specific security measures necessarily fail to be cost-effective: there may be some measures that are so. This issue is explored in subsequent chapters.

CHAPTER 5

Protecting the Homeland

Some Parameters

To this point, we have evaluated the overall cost-effectiveness of homeland security expenditures. We now focus somewhat more narrowly on a substantial subset of these outlays: those devoted to making potential targets notably less vulnerable to terrorist attack—to protecting what the Department of Homeland Security (DHS) and various presidential and congressional reports and directives in the United States call "critical infrastructure" and "key assets" or "key resources." Such protection measures cost $34 billion in 2009 and were some 46 percent of the total of all American federal homeland security expenditures.[1]

As noted in the preface, it is not entirely clear what these terms mean, and "protection" has been applied to many elements that seem to be far from critical or key. Thus the Army has extrapolated grandly from 9/11 to conclude that "it is unsafe to have employees in urban office buildings." To protect them, it decided to move tens of thousands of people in its more obscure agencies out of the Washington, D.C., area to the distant Fort Belvoir.[2] How the "incapacitation" of these people "would have a debilitating effect on security" or on "national economic security" ("critical") or how they are "essential to the minimal operations of the economy and government" ("key") is not at all clear.

However that may be, this chapter puts forward a set of general parameters for coming to grips with this homeland security concern in order to provide a framework for analysis. It also addresses some specific issues in the quest to prioritize protection, to imagine what cities and specific targets terrorists would be most interested in attacking. The following two chapters apply some of these considerations, evaluating the cost-effectiveness of specific protective measures in more focused and systematic detail. In the process, we seek to forge something of an assessment of which targets it may make sense to protect and which ones might best be left unprotected.

The concern in these three chapters, then, is with *protection*—measures constituting what military people might call passive defense, such as posting security guards, hardening targets against explosions, screening people entering an area, setting up barriers, and installing security cameras.[3] We do not deal with *policing*, including intelligence gathering and other active defense measures—efforts to hunt down and detain terrorists after they have committed violent acts or (preferably, of course) before they have done so. Nor are we concerned with *mitigation*—measures that seek to reduce the consequences of a terrorist attack after it happens, such as the establishment of emergency procedures for evacuation, measures that might contain the damage, or facilities to provide medical treatment to the injured. Nor is there an assessment of the promotion of *resilience*—the ability to absorb, and sensibly respond to, a terrorist attack.[4] The costs and benefits of policing, mitigation, and resilience promotion can be subjected to a similar analysis, and chapter 8 supplies some assessments along that line. But except incidentally, that is not the focus in these chapters.

POLICY CONSIDERATIONS: PREMISES

There seem to be at least eight premises (or in some cases conundrums) that should be taken into consideration in formulating policy for protecting the homeland and seeking to reduce its vulnerability.

1. The Number of Potential Terrorist Targets Is Essentially Infinite

Terrorists seek to kill people and/or destroy property in pursuit of a political goal.[5] They may exercise some discrimination in selecting targets, but because people and vulnerable property are readily at hand everywhere, they have a wealth of potential targets—in the United States, there are something like 5 million commercial buildings alone, for example.[6] Nothing can be done to change this fundamental condition. Indeed, it is difficult to think of something that *couldn't* be a target. Even a tree in the woods, after all, could be ignited to start a forest fire.

2. The Number of Terrorists Appears to Be Exceedingly Small and Their Efforts and Competence Rather Limited

The competence and size of the terrorist adversary was assessed at some length in chapters 2 and 3. As noted there, because terrorism of a considerably destructive nature can be perpetrated by a very small number of people, or even by a single individual, the facts that terrorists are few in number and that most are not terribly competent does not mean there is no problem. However, many homeland security policies were put in place when the threat seemed far larger and the terrorists' capacity to do destruction seemed far greater than it has since so far proven to be, and those early perceptions may still be fueling, and possibly distorting, current policy.

3. In Many Cases, Target Selection Is Effectively a Random Process

It is true, of course, that some terrorist attacks are carefully planned, and there is no reason to suspect that terrorists flip coins or consult tables of random numbers when selecting targets. The difficulty for those who seek to predict potential terrorist targets, however, is that much, quite possibly most, terrorist target selection *effectively* becomes something like a random process. In most cases, it seems, the only way one could predict what will actually be attacked is to be inside the minds of the perpetrators.

As Max Abrahms has pointed out, the internal motivating mechanism for terrorist groups often is group cohesion and conspiratorial camaraderie, not grand planning. Characteristically, terrorists have difficulty explaining why they are doing what they are doing and have little in the way of long-term planning.[7] This is likely to be true for many homegrown terrorists, and, as has increasingly been accepted, they seem to be the most likely prospective perpetrators of terrorism.

In consequence, targets are likely to be selected almost capriciously and often simply for their convenience. Thus, one would-be bomber discussed in chapter 2 targeted a mall in Rockford, Illinois, because it was nearby. Similarly, the two men in 2007 who sought to ram a car loaded with explosives into the airport in Glasgow, Scotland, presumably selected that target because they happened to live near it.

Although they never actually carried out any attacks, terrorist plotters in Los Angeles in 2005 drew up a target list that may not have been random in their minds but would essentially be so in the minds of people trying specifically to anticipate their next move. The targets, all within a 20-mile radius of their shared apartment, included an El Al ticket counter at Los Angeles Airport, the Israeli Consulate, 16 U.S. Army recruitment centers and offices, and a U.S. military base in the tiny, laid-back suburb of Manhattan Beach.[8] (According to the city clerk, Manhattan Beach does not have a military base within its four-square-mile compass, though there is a State Army National Guard armory there.) Or there was the terrorist who conducted Google map searches related to "Jewish entities," a Baptist church, Times Square, a child care facility, a U.S. post office, and military recruiting centers in six different cities.[9] In 2009, he decided to kill rabbis in Little Rock, Arkansas, and in Memphis and Nashville, Tennessee, after which he planned to attack army recruitment centers in several cities. But when he tried to kill the Nashville rabbi with a Molotov cocktail, the explosive bounced off the rabbi's window and, regardless, failed to explode; moreover, the terrorist had the wrong house. He then decided to shoot up a military recruitment center in Florence, Kentucky (chosen because "it was near an interstate highway and bordered Ohio"), only to find out that the office was closed. Finally, he went home to Little Rock and, with no plan at all, shot at a recruiting center three miles from his apartment, killing one.[10] Or there is the neo-Nazi terrorist in Norway who, on his way to bomb a synagogue, took a tram going the wrong way and ended up dynamiting a mosque instead.[11]

This sort of caprice—or effective caprice from the standpoint of the people trying to predict terrorist actions—can be found in the deliberations even of terrorists who very carefully plan their actions. Thus, in 1995 Timothy McVeigh scouted in five states before settling on a government building in Oklahoma City as his target. However, he says he "messed up" and would have diverted to a different target if he had known there was a day care facility inside that building.[12] In the event, even *he* probably didn't know the absence of such a facility would be relevant to his selection process. He would have realized it was important to him only if and when the information came to his attention.

4. The Probability That Any Specific Target Will Be Attacked Is Extremely Small in Almost All Cases

As discussed in chapter 3, terrorism, despite the attention it garners, is a rather rare occurrence comprised of incidental, isolated acts of mayhem perpetrated by individuals or by small groups, violence that generally does a comparatively limited amount of damage. Even under quite dire scenarios, the chance an individual target will be hit, particularly in a country outside a war zone, is very small.

Given that it can be carried out by a single individual or by a very small group, terrorism, like crime, can never be fully extinguished. Therefore, it is, of course, essentially certain that *some* target *somewhere* will be struck by terrorists. However, the chance any individual target will be attacked is exceedingly low, perhaps even vanishingly so in almost all cases. Protection measures may effectively reduce this likelihood further by deterring the terrorists or by reducing the target's vulnerability to attack. But for the overwhelmingly vast number of targets, they do so by nudging that likelihood from near zero to even more nearly zero.

5. If One Potential Target Happens to Enjoy a Degree of Protection, the Agile Terrorist Generally Can Readily Move on to Another One: The Maginot Problem

There is also a displacement effect, a transfer of risk. Terrorists can choose, and change, their targets, depending on local and immediate circumstances. This process, of course, does not hold in the case of natural disasters: a tornado bearing down on Kansas does not decide to divert to Oklahoma if it finds Kansans too well protected. In stark contrast, if the protection of one target merely causes the terrorist to seek out another from among the near-infinite set at hand, it is not clear how society has gained by expending effort and treasure to protect the first. The people who were saved in the first locale are gainers, of course, but their grief is simply transferred to others.

For example, there have been instances in Israel in which suicide bombers, seeing their primary targets, shopping malls, rather well protected, blew themselves up instead on the street.[13] The Israelis count this as something of a gain since they claim that fewer people died as a consequence, something likely to be of rather small comfort to the victims' families. Actually, however, if the goal of terrorists is to kill, shopping malls do not generally make all that attractive a target because people tend to be fairly widely dispersed in them, something that is often less true on the sidewalks.[14] The 2011 suicide bombing at Moscow's Domodedovo airport took place in the arrivals area, well away from the passenger security screening. Accordingly, any risk reduction passengers gained by being in the secure zone of the airport was simply transferred to those outside, as the attackers targeted a place of public assembly for which there are few countermeasures.

As James Lewis points out arrestingly, there may be parallels in homeland protection measures with the experience with the Maginot Line—a symbol for a "mindless defense mentality," as he puts it—that shows that "an inventive opponent will simply go around a massive defense."[15] The experience in Israel and Russia suggests that the opponent need not necessarily be all that inventive to make use of the effect.

Because of the massive number of lucrative targets presented by any one country, it also seems essentially impossible—indeed, quixotic—to protect them enough so that international terrorists are directed in frustration to visit their violence on other countries. Measures that make it sufficiently difficult for outside terrorists to get into the country may conceivably do so, as may policing and intelligence measures within it, but not ones devoted to protection.

6. To the Degree Protection Measures Make One Target Safer, They Make Other Ones Less Safe

An inference deriving from the displacement or risk transfer effect should be specifically pointed out and considered. Building hurricane shelters in one area does not increase the likelihood another place will be struck by the hurricane, but in the case of terrorism, the displacement effect essentially means that any effort to protect or to deter a terrorist attack on a specific potential target means that other targets become more at risk.[16] Obviously, this would be of no concern if all potential targets could be protected, but that is clearly impossible. Protection policy therefore necessarily requires making choices about what to protect, and this, equally necessarily, means that targets left off the protection list become more attractive to the terrorist.

A DHS report does acknowledge this issue. But it fails really to explore its implications. Instead, it simply suggests rather opaquely that the problem "underscores the necessity for a balanced, comparative approach that focuses on managing risk commensurately across all sectors and scenarios of concern."[17]

For example, there is a program to protect bridges in the United States, and a list of something like 200 of the most important bridges has been drawn up. There seems to be no evidence terrorists have any particular desire to blow up a bridge, due in part, perhaps, to the facts that it is an exceedingly difficult task under the best of circumstances and that the number of casualties is likely to be much lower than for many other targets.

The apparent hope of the protectors in this case is that, after security is improved for all these targets, any terrorists who happen to have bridges on their hit list will become disillusioned. If so, however, they might become inclined to move on to the 201st bridge or, more likely perhaps, to another kind of bridge: the highway overpass, of which there are some 600,000 in the United States.[18] If the terrorists' attention is drawn, further, to any one of a wide array of multiple overpass bridge networks, they might be inclined to destroy one of those. The financial and human consequence, not to mention the devastating traffic inconvenience, that could result from such an explosion might well surpass the destructive consequences of one directed at one of those 200 bridges. The issue, then, is: how has society been benefited by the protection of the bridges? The cost-effectiveness of bridge protection is discussed more fully in chapter 6.

Or there is the case of the installation of sensors to measure chemical, biological, or radiological levels in New York. Presumably, any terrorists clever enough to engineer the relevant weapons (perhaps an empty set) are likely to be able to learn where the sensors have been put in place, and there is no gain to society if they simply choose to move to Newark or Washington or Columbus. However, this elemental consideration does not appear to have been part of the decision process.[19]

7. Most Targets Are Vulnerable in the Sense That It Is Not Very Difficult to Damage Them but Invulnerable in That They Can Be Rebuilt in Fairly Short Order and at Tolerable Expense

On the one hand, most, probably almost all, potential terrorist targets are vulnerable in the sense that they can be damaged, in many cases badly, even by a simple explosion. On the other hand, if a damaged target can be readily repaired or replaced at an acceptable cost in time and money, including rea-sonable compensation to any victims—that is, if the effect of the violence can be readily absorbed—there is a sense in which it could be said that the target is not vulnerable. (This discussion focuses entirely on material tar-gets; people are also highly vulnerable and, if killed, cannot, of course, be repaired.) For example, the considerable damage inflicted on 9/11 on part of the Pentagon was repaired within one year,[20] and the Marriott and Ritz-Carlton hotels in Jakarta were reopened within two weeks of the 2009 bomb attacks that killed seven people.[21] And of course, very few terrorist strikes cause nearly as much damage as was suffered in those attacks. In the case of 9/11, it makes sense to use words like *destroy, demolish,* and *annihilate* for the destruction wreaked on the World Trade Center. Those terms are utterly inappropriate, however, for the attack on the Pentagon.[22]

8. It Is Essentially Impossible to Adequately Protect a Very Wide Variety of Potential Terrorist Targets Except by Completely Closing Them Down

Veronique de Rugy has drawn an important lesson from Britain's experience with terrorism during the July 2005 attacks on the London Underground.[23] In part because of previous experience with Irish Republican Army terrorism in the city, the London Underground is normally fairly well policed. Then, after the terrorist attacks of July 7, 2005, these prevention and protection measures were vastly enhanced. Yet, despite this, terrorists successfully infiltrated more bombs into the underground a mere two weeks after the first attack. As it happened, the bombs did no damage because they were poorly constructed and did not actually explode, but this fortunate result, of course, stems entirely from terrorist incompetence, not from protective measures.

As she concludes, this experience strongly suggests that the quest to make targets like that adequately secure is essentially hopeless. Protective measures may complicate the situation for the terrorist somewhat, but generally only marginally so. Short of completely closing down such potential targets, their essential vulnerability will always remain, and we should be realistic about it.

POLICY CONSIDERATIONS: IMPLICATIONS

Several policy conclusions or implications can be derived at least in part from these premises.

1. Any Protective Policy Should Be Compared with a Null Case: Do Nothing, and Use the Money Saved to Rebuild and to Compensate Any Victims or Their Families

Working from the premises previously outlined, any policy that seeks to protect potential targets—to make them less vulnerable to terrorist attack—should routinely be compared in cost-effectiveness to a null alternative. This would hold that, given the (exceedingly) low probability that any individual target will be hit, given the essentially random nature of much target selection, given the ability of terrorists to redirect their focus from one of a huge number of potential targets to another, and given the often rather modest costs of rebuilding an attacked target, it is incumbent on the policy maker to consider whether the proposed protection policy is more cost-effective than refraining from spending anything at all on a particular target or set of targets and then using the money saved to rebuild, repair, and compensate in the unlikely event that an attack actually happens to take place.[24] Included in the calculation should be a consideration of the emotional and psychological costs potentially inflicted by the terrorist act, as well as its indirect economic costs.

Scott Hook assesses the full costs inflicted by, and stemming from, a terrorist attack on a major metropolitan area in Australia on the scale of the London bombings of 2005. He calculates that the costs of the damage would be about what Australia had spent over a few years on counterterrorism. He concludes from this observation that perhaps Australia "does not appear to be spending too much on counter-terrorism." Similarly, in the United States, economist Benjamin Zycher estimates how much damage a terrorist attack might inflict and compares this with the homeland security expenditures designed to prevent or deal with such an attack. He concludes from the comparison that the United States does not appear to be spending too much.[25] Both analysts, however, are engaging in a form of probability neglect—they leave out of consideration the likelihood of a terrorist attack. Unless it can be shown that the costly attacks they envision are essentially certain to be prevented or effectively dealt with by the security measures, a question arises. Given the apparent low likelihood of such a terrorist attack (and in the Australian scenario given that an attack like the London bombings is almost impossible to protect against), would it not potentially be wise—that is, more productive and less expensive—for the countries to hang on to their counterterrorism funds, expending them to rebuild and compensate if and when a terrorist attack actually occurred? The answer to this question is not necessarily either affirmative or obvious, but the question should be asked.

2. Consider the Negative Effects of Protection Measures: Not Only Direct Cost but Also Inconvenience, Enhancement of Fear, Negative Economic Impacts, and Reduction of Liberties

As discussed in chapter 3, terrorism inflicts not only direct costs but also indirect ones—and often the indirect costs considerably outweigh the direct ones. In like manner, it is elemental that any sensible antiterrorism policy proposal must include a consideration of both the direct and indirect costs that might flow from the policy.

Clearly, there are sizable direct economic costs to seeking to protect the homeland. Some of these are sustained in direct protective expenditures—for example, to deal with the extremely unlikely event of an exact replication of the anthrax attacks of 2001, the post office has spent some $1 billion for each fatality suffered in those attacks.[26] But they can also accrue in indirect ones, such as deterring inconvenienced customers from entering protected shopping centers.[27]

Sometimes security measures can even cost lives. As noted earlier, they have caused many short-haul passengers to drive instead of flying, and this appears to have resulted in 500 or more extra road fatalities per year.[28]

Moreover, as Frank Furedi notes, such a "vulnerability-led response" can "foster a climate that intensifies people's feeling of insecurity and fear," and this in turn "invariably leads to the discovery of weaknesses that have the potential to turn virtually any institution in any place into a terrorist target."[29]

Policies that enhance fear and anxiety can in time have negative health consequences, a concern to be addressed in chapter 9, and exercises in security theater can have counterproductive effects in the case of terrorism. One preliminary study finds that visible security elements like armed guards, high walls, and barbed wire made people feel less vulnerable to crime. However, when these same devices are instituted in the context of dealing with the threat of terrorism, their effect is to make people feel tense, suspicious, and fearful, apparently because they implicitly suggest that the place under visible protection is potentially a terrorist target.[30] In other words, the protective measures supplied exactly the negative emotional effect terrorists hope to induce themselves.

By the same token, however, security measures that *do* manage to reduce fear may be beneficial even if they don't actually enhance security. As Cass Sunstein puts it, "The reduction of even baseless fear is a social good."[31] Thus over the course of the 1990s, New Yorkers became less fearful of crime in their city in part because graffiti was washed away, the homeless were moved out of sight, and panhandlers were policed out of business—theatrical measures that scarcely affected the actual incidence of crime. This issue is assessed by Jeffrey Rosen:

> The best argument for DHS is that the illusion of safety may itself provide tangible psychological and economic benefits: If people feel less afraid, they may be more likely to fly on planes. But even if conceived on these terms—as a more-than-$40-billion-dollar-a-year-pacifier—the department is hard

to defend, since there's no good evidence that it has, in fact, calmed Americans down rather than making us more nervous.[32]

A systematic cost-benefit assessment would still need to be done in this case, however. It would have to evaluate the costs of the security theater measures, balancing that against prospective benefits from any reduction in fear and perceived risk. In particular, one would be on the lookout for cost-effective measures that compellingly convince people that risk has been reduced. Unfortunately, as discussed at some length in chapter 9, public pronouncements on terrorism have rather consistently exacerbated fears of terrorism and enhanced the public's propensity to be more afraid than they should be. They have been, therefore, exercises in what might be called "insecurity theater."

3. Consider the Opportunity Costs, the Trade-Offs, of Protection Measures

Any sensible policy analysis must include a consideration of what else could have been done with the effort and money being expended on the policy proposed.[33] As discussed more fully in chapter 9, it is highly likely that far more lives would have been saved if homeland security money (or even a portion of it) had been invested instead in a wide range of more cost-effective risk mitigation programs. Any analysis that leaves out such considerations is profoundly faulty, even immoral.

IMAGINING TERRORIST TARGETS

Probably impelled by the 9/11 Commission's conclusion that there was a "lack of imagination" before 2001, homeland security and terrorism-combating agencies have devoted considerable effort over the course of the ensuing decade to imagination sharpening. Much of this has been focused on seeking to envision which targets terrorists might prefer to attack.[34] Out of concern that they need help in this quest, they have even enlisted the aid of Hollywood scriptwriters.[35]

Listing Cities

Since international terrorists active in the United States—thus far at least—have concentrated on buildings in major cities, many think it reasonable to suggest that protective efforts should disproportionately focus on major cities. Thoughtful and presumably well-paid planners had by 2003 come up with a terrorist hit list of seven: New York, Washington, Chicago, San Francisco, Seattle, Houston, and Los Angeles. This exercise in metropolitan chauvinism, however, proved to be notably unpopular in places like, for example, Columbus, Ohio—not to mention Oklahoma City, kept off the list presumably because, although it suffered more deaths from terrorism than all but two of the cities on the list combined, it had been the target merely of a domestic terrorist. Accordingly, the list was quickly expanded to 30 and, by 2005, to 73 (including Oklahoma City).[36]

In the end, it is difficult to see a plausible way to adequately adjudicate this debate. It is true that cities like New York, London, Madrid, and Washington have been attacked by terrorists in recent years, but so have Glasgow, Scotland, and Little Rock, Arkansas, as well as resort areas in Egypt and Indonesia that are far from major cities. And plotters and suspects apprehended within the United States have variously been accused of planning to inflict (or at least of vaguely thinking about inflicting) mayhem not only on targets in New York but also on ones in such places as Baltimore, Washington, Portland (Oregon), Boston, Chicago, Minneapolis, Dallas, Little Rock, Columbus, Miami, upstate New York, Los Angeles, and Rockford and Springfield, Illinois, as well as at military bases in New Jersey, Texas, and Virginia.[37]

Actually, it is entirely possible that international terrorists might one day come to realize there is more payoff for them in hitting more ordinary and typical targets because that would scare more people. Of particular appeal to terrorists, perhaps, would be towns that tend to be synonymous with ordinary America, in part because they have peculiar or amusing names, like Peoria, Illinois; Sheboygan, Wisconsin; Pocatello, Idaho; Azusa, California; or Xenia, Ohio. After all, if a bomb goes off in one of those, it can go off anywhere.

Finally, it is not at all clear how one can even *begin* to protect large (or even not-so-large) cities against random acts of terror that can be carried out by a single individual with a bomb or pistol in a backpack. Even Maginot, one suspects, would have thrown up his hands.

Listing Targets

Beyond dreaming about protecting whole cities from acts of violence, homeland security officials have tried to imagine which specific targets within those cities (or outside them) might appeal to the adversary.

Accordingly, it has set about creating the National Asset Database, an inventory of assets from which the most critical targets can be drawn. By 2004, the inventory included no fewer than 30,000 items, to the apparent dismay of the department's director at the time, Tom Ridge. Dismay was premature: within a year, the list had been expanded to 80,000.[38]

Although the list has remained secret, there have been a number of leaks indicating that miniature golf courses are included, as well as Weeki Wachee Springs, a roadside waterpark in Florida.[39] This massive database, noted the DHS Office of Inspector General in 2006, contains a "large number of out-of-place assets" whose "criticality is not readily apparent." It supplies such examples as a Mule Day Parade, a casket company, a petting zoo, a flea market, a groundhog zoo, and some, but not all, Wal-Marts. Although there is a process by which "assets" of "extreme insignificance" can be removed from the list, it found that most of the removals were because the assets "were determined not to exist." Only in "rare instances" were some eliminated because they were deemed to have "negligible value."[40] More recently, this list has been vastly expanded by incorporating other compilations, and it now reportedly runs into the hundreds of thousands, becoming in the process even more of an exercise in self-parody.

The Pork Barrel

Once a list is established—whether of cities or of specific targets—the logic of protection can become overtaken by the effusive, self-generating, and self-perpetuating reality of the pork barrel. Because essentially anything can be a target, those seeking funds can easily imagine themselves on the list in a determined pursuit of shares of the largesse. Thus, in 2004 Democratic Senator Pat Leahy of a mostly rural state, Vermont, complained that the Bush administration wanted "to shortchange rural states," even as Democratic Senator Hillary Clinton of urbanized New York faulted that same administration for the opposite perceived defect: "The reality is that they don't have a constituency in big cities," she claimed.[41]

Pork barrelers from rural areas can (and indeed have) come up with observations like these as reported by *Time*'s Amanda Ripley:

- We realize North Dakota may not be first on Osama bin Laden's list. But we have some significant infrastructure, we have big buildings you can put a lot of people in at one time, we have the border (with Canada).

- Yes, New York's more target rich. But there's been a lot of added security there. If you're a terrorist, you may say, Why waste your time in New York City when you can make a hell of mess in Maryland or Delaware or, God forbid, Portsmouth, New Hampshire?
- We have two major interstate highways, and a significant proportion of the traffic is hazardous materials. We have two major railroads. Also, Wyoming has major mining, major electrical generating plants and coal-bed methane. Any one of those becomes a vulnerability for a terrorist.
- We don't have crystal balls. We just believe that we're as important as anyone else.
- No one can say Caspar, Wyoming, can't be a terrorist target.
- In an era of satellite television, attacking a rural target may actually instill more fear by delivering the message that no one is safe.

To this, their big city counterparts energetically respond:

- Blowing off New York and L.A. so that you can make sure Wyoming is safe makes no sense.
- We have some cities in there that don't even have minor-league baseball teams.

And in a 2007 New York newspaper story entitled, "Waking Up to Terror: City Counterterror Chief Says Each Day He Expects Subway Attack Because Feds Fail to Protect Rails," said chief observes that the federal government spends $9 on security per airline passenger but less than half a penny on each mass transit rider. "There is something wrong with this," he concluded. And then, grandly extrapolated from an exceedingly low number of cases, he asserted, "Terrorists are attacking the subway system worldwide."[42]

Compiling Lists and Doing Cost-Benefit Analysis

In many respects, the list makers are engaging in a form of probability neglect as outlined in chapter 1. It is true that not every potential material terrorist target is equally valuable, equally vulnerable, or equally costly to protect or repair or replace. But as noted there, given that risk is the probability of an attack on a specific target multiplied by the losses sustained in that attack, risks begin to look much alike when losses are multiplied by probabilities very close to zero.

Because of the multiplicity of targets (especially if killing people is the terrorists' goal), because of the exceedingly low likelihood any particular target will be struck, because inconvenienced terrorists can shift (or drift) from one potential target to another, and because of the semirandom and perhaps quite limited nature of the terrorism enterprise, the process of target identification can quickly become one of obsessive, worst-case scenario thinking.

And indeed, in developing terrorist risk assessment scenarios for fixed targets, the DHS applies what it calls "reasonable worst-case conditions." Although it sensibly warns against compounding "numerous unlikely conditions" into such thinking, that process can become almost inevitable.[43] Given the limited nature of the terrorist enterprise and the multiplicity of potential targets, the likelihood a specific target will be hit is breathtakingly small. And given the quite modest capacities of most terrorists, the likelihood is also extremely low that any strike will even remotely correspond to "reasonable worst-case" possibilities, such as a duplication of the 1995 Oklahoma City attack, when a vehicle-borne device delivered an explosion equivalent to 4,000 pounds of TNT. In addition, since funds are limited, it is not at all clear that protecting a relatively small number of potential targets from extreme (if perhaps "reasonable") attacks makes more sense than protecting a much larger number against lesser (and more likely) attacks.

Evaluating protection measures and policies in a responsible manner does not involve simply ranking targets by their vulnerabilities, by the consequences of an attack on them, or by the likelihood they will be attacked. Rather, it requires a composite cost-benefit assessment in which the costs of protection are systematically blended with the consequences of an attack on a target, with the (often exceedingly small) likelihood the target will be attacked, and with the degree to which protection reduces the consequences and/or the likelihood of an attack, keeping in mind in the process issues like the potential for displacement or risk transfer. That is the central task of the next two chapters, as specific protection measures are evaluated.

CHAPTER 6

Homeland Protection

Infrastructure

Following the discussion of general parameters concerning protection as set out in chapter 5, we begin in this chapter an effort to generate some specific policy recommendations about situations and conditions under which it may be sensible—that is, cost-effective—to seek to protect potential terrorist targets, as well as ones under which it may not be. The following chapter focuses on the special and important issue of protecting commercial passenger airliners.

As suggested in chapter 5, protection is a questionable use of resources for many potential terrorist targets and unlikely to be cost-effective. For a few, however, protection may make sense, particularly when protection is feasible for an entire class of potential targets and the destruction of something in that target set would have quite large physical, economic, psychological, and/or political consequences.

Protection of a potential terrorist target may also become advisable if the target is vulnerable as well to higher probability hazards, such as lightning, storms, earthquakes, and perhaps sabotage, and if the combined probability, with terrorism added, now becomes high enough to justify the costs of protection. In general, of course, quite apart from terrorism concerns, there would be value in any effort that, seeking to discover terrorism vulnerabilities, happens instead to uncover a significant and previously unrecognized vulnerability to higher probability hazards.

An interesting and important difference here is with protection against crime. Although many efforts designed to protect people from crime may well fail to be cost-effective, protection policy in this area at least has some hope of success because crime is vastly more common and, in particular, because it is comparatively easy to designate high-crime areas and to ascertain what criminals are generally after: loot. Because of these circumstances, protective measures can often make a potential target less vulnerable to crime, in some cases even effectively invulnerable—though there would still be a displacement or risk transfer problem. Specifically, if there is nothing valuable at the target or if any valuables there cannot be lifted at acceptable cost and risk, and if criminals know this, the target becomes distinctly (and predictably) unattractive to them. For example, an entire class of targets—municipal buses—were removed from the criminal target list when exact fare procedures were put into effect, which meant that any significant amount of money on the bus was now encased in a hardened lockbox rather than in a cash drawer used by the driver to collect fares and make change.[1]

In contrast, terrorism is much less like crime than like vandalism. It comes close effectively (and seemingly) to being a random occurrence, and the potential targets of the perpetrators are exceedingly difficult to predict. Although New York seems to have been able to get graffiti under control on the subways, this was accomplished not by making the subways invulnerable—by adequately protecting them from vandalism—but rather by continually cleaning up the graffiti, thus reducing the graffiti artistes' incentive to decorate. Ultimately, one cannot readily become invulnerable to vandalism, though displacement may be possible in some cases.

Many reports and studies have highlighted the vulnerability of critical infrastructure to terrorism.[2] The list of potential targets is extensive and typically includes buildings, bridges, airports, dams, pipelines, ports, and nuclear facilities. In our analysis, we focus on office-type buildings and on bridges, with some additional consideration of other infrastructure elements.

We mostly ignore attacks by weapons of mass destruction in this discussion. It is difficult to imagine protecting a potential target against an atomic explosion because of the bomb's destructive capacity and because an atomic terrorist can choose where to set off the device. Moreover, not many people like to live or work in a bunker. For attacks with chemical, biological, and radiological weapons, the chief victims would be people, not structures, and protection measures are unlikely to be feasible— indeed, nearly impossible.[3] Accordingly, policy in this area would sensibly focus on prevention and policing, and also perhaps on mitigation efforts, concerns to be discussed in chapter 8.

PROTECTING OFFICE-TYPE BUILDINGS

David Lakamp and Gill McCarthy conducted a cost-benefit assessment of campus security at the U.S. Naval Postgraduate School and concluded that "the school is receiving a tiny benefit, at a very high cost."[4] An economic analysis of the issue by Richard Little has shown that unless the probability of attack against a specific building is high, the expected benefits are unlikely to offset the cost of protecting multiple structures.[5] We expand these considerations here and mostly arrive at the same conclusions.

The Record

Attacks on buildings can employ explosives ranging from small improvised explosive devices (IEDs) of several pounds to vehicle borne improvised explosive devices (VBIEDs), truck bombs carrying thousands of pounds of explosives.

One of the largest VBIED attacks was on the U.S. Marines barracks in Beirut, Lebanon, in 1983, when a suicide bomber detonated a truck bomb containing more than 12,000 pounds of explosives, killing 241 U.S. military personnel while wounding more than 100 others. According to a Department of Defense report, "The force of the explosion ripped the building from its foundation. The building then imploded upon itself. Almost all the occupants were crushed or trapped inside the wreckage."[6] That blast, asserts CBS News, was "the largest non-nuclear explosion that had ever been detonated on the face of the Earth."[7] And indeed, only the 22,000-pound Grand Slam or Earthquake bomb the British used in World War II was bigger, although the mining and construction industries have routinely used hundreds of tons of explosives in their work, and accidental gas and other explosions have exceeded several thousand tons of TNT.[8]

A VBIED attack on the U.S. Embassy in Kenya in 1998 killed 213 people, including 44 American embassy personnel. Up to 2,000 pounds of explosives were used. Although there was little structural damage to the five-story reinforced-concrete embassy, the explosion reduced much of the interior to rubble, destroying windows, window frames, internal office partitions, and other fixtures on the building. It was secondary fragmentation from flying glass, internal concrete-block walls, furniture, and fixtures that caused most of the embassy casualties. The majority of the casualties, however, resulted from the collapse of an adjacent building and from flying glass from other buildings located within a two- to three-block radius. Other casualties were pedestrians or motorists in the crowded streets next to the embassy.[9]

Attacks like these understandably capture the headlines, but they can give a misleading picture about the destructive severity of a VBIED or IED attack. The vast majority of attacks kill far fewer people than in these. A few minutes after the Beirut attack, a similar truck bomb entered the underground parking garage of the French infantry barracks, killing 58 French paratroopers, far fewer than the attack on the Americans. And an attack on the American embassy in Tanzania, simultaneous with the one in Kenya, resulted in the deaths of 11. A one-ton truck bomb detonated in London in April 2003 killed one person, and a 2008 truck bombing of the Islamabad Marriott Hotel resulted in the deaths of 54. In 1993, six people were killed when a van containing 1,200 pounds of explosives was driven into an underground car park at the World Trade Center in New York and then detonated, carving out a crater of nearly 100 feet that was several stories deep and several more high.[10]

As noted in chapter 3, of 219 terrorist incidents in the United Kingdom involving explosives, only 2 inflicted damage that exceeded $1 billion, while 202 caused damage of less than $1 million. Even in the permissive terrorist environment in Iraq, where construction quality is highly variable, the number of fatalities from a VBIED attack against buildings and infrastructure has exceeded 50 people in fewer that 1 of every 200 attacks.[11]

Resilience

These and other experiences attest to the fact that well-designed and well-constructed buildings have significant reserve capacities enabling them to withstand forces they were never designed to meet, even the damage or loss of a supporting beam, slab, or column. Thus, although the intent of the 1993 World Trade Center bombers was to bring down one of the towers, the building proved to be structurally sound and suffered no serious damage to its integrity. Eight years later, both towers of the World Trade Center survived the massive aircraft impact and fire for between 56 and 102 minutes before they collapsed. With up to 60 percent of the buildings' columns fractured at impact and with fuel-fired temperatures of up to 1,500°F, many would have expected the immediate collapse of the towers because they were not designed for anything like this kind of damage. Yet the delay in the collapse enabled the safe evacuation of more than 33,000 occupants below the impact zone, and 99 percent of the people located below that point survived in each building.[12]

The number of fatalities is highest if the entire building experiences progressive or disproportionate collapse when one or two key structural members (usually supporting columns) are damaged, causing all, or a large part, of a structure to collapse upon itself. Fortunately, progressive collapse is extremely rare. Indeed, with the exception of the World Trade Center in 2001, no modern or well-designed tall or large building has fully collapsed as a result of terrorism, and only one as a result of fire.[13] The 12,000-pound truck bomb on the Marine barracks in Beirut and the 5,000-pound truck bomb in Oklahoma City caused only partial progressive collapse, and damage to the Pentagon on 9/11 was contained by the structure's resilience to progressive collapse—its continuity, redundancy, and energy-absorbing capacity.[14]

This is an important observation because it follows that it is nearly impossible for a single bomb, even one as massive as the one in Beirut, to blow up—to totally destroy—a properly designed and engineered multistory building normally comprised of structural steel and reinforced concrete floors, beams, and columns. Nearly all properly engineered buildings show a remarkable ability to absorb extraordinary blasts and have significant reserve capacity. Therefore, they cannot be destroyed by, or are resilient to, terrorist attack.[15] This also explains why there is so much terrorist devastation in Iraq, Afghanistan, and Pakistan: many buildings are made of unreinforced masonry, which is most vulnerable to explosives, just as it is to earthquakes.

The Costs of Hardening

Measures to enhance security for existing multistory, large commercial and institutional buildings typically focus on strengthening columns, walls, and roofs; installing perimeter walls and blast-resistant glazing; adding vehicle security barriers; restricting vehicle access; and hiring security personnel.

The National Academy of Sciences reports that for newly constructed commercial office buildings in the United States, "reasonable blast resistance can be accomplished for about a 5 percent premium in construction cost,"[16] and another study concludes that "substantial protection may be afforded by an increase in overall costs of the order of 5 percent to 10 percent."[17] Strengthening existing buildings is considerably costlier and is, in addition, inconvenient to owners and occupants.[18] For example, retrofitting existing U.S. Army administrative and housing buildings to resist a small IED of only 50 pounds costs 8 percent to 24 percent of the original building construction cost,[19] and to retrofit large buildings in the United States to mitigate progressive collapse costs roughly 30 percent of the initial building costs.[20]

As the building stock overwhelmingly consists of existing buildings, not new ones, substantial risk mitigation will most likely run well in excess of 10 percent of the original building cost, although this expense could decline over time as more effective and efficient protective measures are developed. This includes only the costs of reducing a building's vulnerability to damage by structurally hardening it. Perimeter security fences 1,000 feet long cost $120,000, a single bollard up to $26,000, handheld explosive detectors $34,000, vehicle crash barriers $70,000, and vehicle and cargo inspection systems between $2.7 and $6.6 million.[21] Expenses mount further with the addition of security guards, closed-circuit televisions, and alarm and communication systems.

We start our cost-benefit analysis by considering a representative multistory building for which occupancy and loss data are available—a three-story academic building, 250 by 110 feet, with teaching and office space, located at the U.S. Naval Postgraduate School in Monterey, California. Its replacement value in 2010 dollars is $20.3 million.[22]

There are four cost elements to the security process.

1. If the physical hardening of a building costs 10 percent of its original (or its replacement) cost, the cost of structurally hardening a $20 million building is $2 million. Annualized over a remaining service life of 20 years, this comes to approximately $150,000 per year.[23]
2. Additional (post-9/11) costs of extra gate security personnel at the Naval Postgraduate School was $1 million per year.[24] Since there are about ten large buildings on the U.S. Naval Postgraduate School campus,[25] this equates to $100,000 per building per year.
3. In addition, there would be the costs and maintenance of security equipment. To provide tighter security with personnel manning metal detectors and X-ray scanners to monitor access to the building and with guards to control access to an underground car park, delivery entrance, or perimeter security, four to six personnel would be required during the day and perhaps two more at night. If the salary and benefits for each employee total approximately $100,000 per year, the annual personnel bill will be near $1 million per building per year.
4. Security measures after 2001 also included closing three access gates and restricting parking within 80 feet of buildings. The opportunity cost of these

security measures is considerable. They include the increased travel distance to the gate (12.5 person years) costing $1.1 million per year, gate delays (19.2 person years) for another $1.7 million, and extra walking time to the building (3.3 person years) for $297,000, for a total opportunity cost of $3.1 million per year or $300,000 per building per year.[26]

The total costs of protecting a reasonably typical three-story building accumulate, then, to $250,000 per year by summing elements 1 and 2 and are well over $1 million per year if all four elements are included. Whatever the mix of security measures, the total direct cost to attain significant risk reduction will not be below $250,000 per building per year. We will use this estimate, essentially leaving out elements 3 and 4, in our cost-benefit analysis.

The Costs Inflicted by a Terrorist Attack

For a comprehensive risk assessment, we would want to consider a spectrum of threats in order to assess the cost-effectiveness of security measures.[27] But for the sake of brevity, we will primarily consider a high-consequence scenario, the one most likely to show that security measures are cost-effective: the detonation of a large, Timothy McVeigh–type truck bomb in close proximity to the building, an event that would trigger partial progressive collapse and require the building's replacement.[28]

As noted, the replacement value of a building that can be taken to be reasonably typical of large office buildings is $20.3 million in 2010 dollars. The value of its contents is placed at $8.2 million.[29] Demolition of a severely damaged building can be costly, as can design and utilities reinstallation costs, and we assume these costs to be 25 percent of the replacement value of the building. Hence, the cost of physical damage totals approximately $33 million and would easily reach $50 million or more if relocation costs, staff and student interruption costs, and other such factors are considered.

Beyond this would be the costs of the lives lost by the terrorist attack. For an average-size large commercial building, the number of occupants averages roughly 600 people.[30] As table 6.1 suggests, the average probability that an occupant will be killed in a terrorist attack with an explosive device on a building ranges from 7 percent to 15 percent. A mid-range of these figures multiplied by 600 gives roughly 80 fatalities, or $520 million in losses, based on the value of a statistical life considerations discussed in chapter 3.[31] It also is quite a conservative (that is, high) estimate: only 0.05 percent of VBIED or IED attacks against buildings have killed this many people worldwide over the past 40 years.[32]

The costs of physical damage and loss of life in this extremely destructive scenario add up, then, to about $555 million. However, there will also be indirect losses, mostly in terms of social disruption, loss of business, and other economic considerations. As we saw in chapter 3, the indirect losses arising from a terrorist attack to a building are unlikely to exceed a few billion dollars at most.[33]

We will take $1.5 billion as an upper limit for indirect costs and then add the costs of physical damage ($33 million) and loss of life ($520 million). A high estimate for the total cost inflicted by a large VBIED attack on a large multistory building in the United States, then, comes to around $2 billion.

Risk Reduction

In many cases, security expenditures buy little risk reduction. There have been a number of successful VBIED attacks on embassies, hotels, military facilities, and other high-profile targets because perimeter personnel either were not able to prevent entry of the truck or because the size of the truck bomb was large enough that it did not have to breach security barriers. Unlike aviation security, where there is considerable "defense in depth," overcoming perimeter security is simply a matter of breaching a security check point and perhaps a vehicle antiram barrier. At best, then, only two layers of security are provided, and risk reduction accordingly will be

Table 6.1 PROBABILITY OF OCCUPANT FATALITY FOR RECENT U.S. TERRORIST ATTACKS ON BUILDINGS

	Fatalities	Building Occupants	Probability of Occupant Fatality[1]
World Trade Center (1993)	6	17,550[3]	0.03 percent
Federal Building, Oklahoma City (1995)	165	361–850[2]	19–45 percent
World Trade Center (2001)	2427	35,100[3]	6.9 percent
Pentagon (2001)	125	16,200[3]	0.8 percent

[1]Calculated as fatalities divided by building occupants.
[2]Estimates of the number of occupants at time of attack vary considerably.
[3]Estimated from average occupant density of 3.7 people per 1,000 square feet (four people per 100 square meters).

nowhere near 100 percent and probably less than 50 percent. This consideration makes structural hardening particularly attractive: it is a passive layer of defense that, if properly designed and constructed, can reduce structural damage substantially—probably up to 90–95 percent.[34]

We will assume a risk reduction of 95 percent. This is quite substantial and biased in favor of showing that security measures are cost-effective.

Cost-Benefit Assessment

Once again, the *benefit of a security measure* is a function of three elements:

$$\text{Benefit} = (\text{probability of a successful attack}) \times$$
$$(\text{losses sustained in the successful attack}) \times (\text{reduction in risk})$$

The *probability of a successful attack* is the likelihood a successful terrorist attack will take place if the security measure were not in place. The *losses sustained in the successful attack* include the fatalities and other damage—both direct and indirect—that will accrue as a result of a successful terrorist attack. The *reduction in risk* is the degree to which the security measures foil, deter, disrupt, or protect against a terrorist attack. This *benefit*, a multiplicative composite of three considerations, is then compared with the *costs* of providing the risk-reducing security required to attain the benefit. A break-even cost-benefit analysis finds the minimum probability of a successful attack required, absent the security measures, for the benefit of security measures to equal their cost.

Table 6.2 arrays the annual attack probabilities required at a minimum for security expenditures on protecting a building to be cost-effective, assuming the expenditures reduce risk by an impressive 95 percent.[35] If, following our break-even analysis, the cost of security measures is taken to be approximately $250,000 per building per year (very much a low estimate) with losses of $2 billion (very much a high estimate), the protective measures would be cost-effective only if the probability of a successful terrorist attack without them exceeds 0.013 percent, or 1 in 8,000 per building per year (boxed in bold in the table). A sensitivity analysis of these results reveals that the results are relatively insensitive to parameter uncertainty.[36]

However, the yearly attack probability to a building in the United States is unlikely to be anywhere near that high because the bombings of buildings there are as rare as the number of potential targets is immense. During the entire 20-year period from 1988 through 2007, only two significant

Table 6.2 THE PROBABILITY OF AN OTHERWISE SUCCESSFUL TERRORIST ATTACK, IN PERCENTAGE PER YEAR, REQUIRED FOR PROTECTIVE SECURITY EXPENDITURES TO BE COST-EFFECTIVE, ASSUMING THE EXPENDITURES REDUCE THE RISK OF AN ATTACK BY 95 PERCENT

Cost of security measures (per year)	Losses from a successful terrorist attack							
	$10 million	$100 million	$250 million	$1 billion	$2 billion	$10 billion	$100 billion	$1 trillion
$1,000	0.01	0.001	0.0004	0.0001	0.00005	0.00001	0.000001	0.0000001
$100,000	1.0	0.1	0.04	0.011	0.005	0.001	0.0001	0.00001
$250,000	2.6	0.3	0.11	0.026	0.013	0.003	0.0003	0.00003
$500,000	5.3	0.6	0.21	0.053	0.026	0.005	0.0005	0.00005
$1 million	10.5	1.1	0.42	0.105	0.053	0.011	0.0011	0.00011
$5 million	52.6	5.3	2.10	0.526	0.263	0.053	0.0053	0.00053
$10 million	105.3	10.5	4.20	1.050	0.526	0.105	0.0110	0.00110
$100 million	1052.6	105.3	42.10	10.526	5.263	1.053	0.1060	0.01053
$500 million	5263.2	526.3	210.50	52.650	26.316	5.263	0.5263	0.05263

Note: A probability greater than 100 percent denotes more than one attack per year.

VBIED or IED attacks on buildings took place: the bombing of the World Trade Center in 1993 and of a federal building in Oklahoma City in 1995. We can also perhaps add in nine other attacks on buildings, mostly abortion clinics: although these were hardly as destructive as those on the WTC and in Oklahoma City (few resulted in any fatalities at all), they could have resulted in severe damage and/or casualties.[37] Over a 20-year period, then, there were 11 attacks by explosives on buildings. Since the average number of office or office-type buildings in the United States over this period, including office, education, health service, public assembly, police, and emergency service buildings, is 4.7 million,[38] the annual likelihood one would be attacked is one in 8.5 million or 0.000012 percent per building per year.[39]

Therefore, *in analyses applying assumptions substantially biased toward the opposite conclusion—leaving out many of the costs of protection, positing that protective measures would be especially effective, and assuming the damage inflicted by a successful attack would be exceptionally high—we find that the likelihood of a successful terrorist attack on a typical office-type building for which there is no specific threat would have to be a thousand times higher than it is at present for protective security measures to be cost-effective.*

The item in the table boxed in bold dashes denotes a condition for a building with a threat of one in a million (0.0001 percent) per year. Under that condition, protective measures would begin to be cost-effective only if the measures cost less than $100,000 per year and if losses were expected to be over $100 billion—far more than the value of the Twin Towers of the World Trade Center. It is difficult to imagine many (or even any) buildings whose damage would be that costly or that could be comprehensively protected for less than $100,000 per year—the cost of a security guard or two. If the expected losses are $1 billion—a lower but still very considerable sum—the cost of protective measures would need to be less than $1,000 per year. While there are many thousands of buildings with the potential for billion-dollar damages, none could be protected for only $1,000 per year—the price of a few "no standing" signs or of a lone security guard standing around for a few days.

Another way to look at this: for a building with a high threat (0.01 percent per building per year), $1 of expenditure yields only $0.19 in benefits.[40] For a building subject to a typical threat of one in a million per building per year, that same dollar yields less than a quarter of a cent in benefits.

We have attempted to describe cost data for a representative building to illustrate the net benefit calculations and their interpretation, and table 6.2 can be used to assess the required attack probability for a wide variety of cost and loss data. It will be applied in an analysis of bridge protection later in this chapter.

Where the attack probability is negligible, an investment of hundreds of thousands or a few million dollars in protective measures will ultimately lead to an expected net loss of the same amount—that is to say, it will be a waste of money.[41] Such a net loss may seem bearable for one building and thus an acceptable cost if the asset owner is risk averse and has plenty of other income, and it may accordingly be considered a prudent investment in a time of threat uncertainty. However, if this level of risk aversion is repeated across a portfolio of buildings, the accumulated costs (and expected losses) will be significant, running into tens or hundreds of millions of dollars. Expenditures like that could be used far more productively elsewhere.

Moreover, as discussed in chapter 5, many terrorist attacks are opportunistic in nature, and their activities should be modeled essentially as a random process. Related is the issue of risk transfer, where the hardening of one target may encourage terrorists to attack a softer one, resulting in no change in overall threat probability or consequences to society. These are issues with no clear outcome, but they need to be considered when assessing threat probability and deciding how such uncertainty might affect the outcome of a cost-benefit assessment.

Applying Data from the Insurance Industry

The insurance industry routinely calculates risks and risk reductions following standard procedures, and an examination of its pricing of premiums for property and business interruption, discussed briefly in chapter 1, is instructive.

Studies of several thousand firms encompassing 15 industry groups[42] show that, after the 9/11 shock, terrorism premiums in 2004 ranged from $1 for a total insured value of $500,000 to $6.75 million for one of $208 billion. The median terrorist premium, then, was $13,000 or 0.0065 percent, for a total insured value of $200 million. If we interpret this insurance cover according to standard risk calculations and apply median cost data, the probability of attack in 2004 was determined (premium divided by insured loss) by the insurers to be 0.0065 percent per firm per year. This estimate of the likelihood of a terrorist attack declined by 2006 to 0.0046 percent, a year later to 0.0040 percent, and by 2009 to only 0.0031 percent[43] In a period of only five years, then, the estimated likelihood of a terrorist attack was lowered by more than 50 percent. Terrorism premiums make up only 2.7 percent to 8.3 percent of the total property premium, demonstrating that insurance companies are more concerned with covering themselves from payouts related to fires, floods, storms, and other such losses than from terrorism.

In addition, these statistics relate to attacks on a "firm" and not to an individual property. Most firms, particularly larger ones, are spread across many locations and may have tens if not hundreds of buildings or other assets covered by their insurance portfolio. If we make the highly conservative assumption that the median-size firm is insuring only one building, the attack probability of 0.003 percent per *firm* per year becomes less than one in 30,000 per *building* per year. Since insurers include a healthy profit margin when setting their premiums, they must consider actual probabilities to be even lower than what we have inferred.[44]

In our analysis in this chapter, we determined, applying highly conservative assumptions, that the annual probability of an attack on a building must be higher than 1 in 8,000 (0.013) for protective measures to be cost-effective. Data from the U.S. insurance industry revealing that it considers that probability to be lower, probably *much* lower, than 1 in 30,000 per building per year further support our conclusion that expenditures on protective measures for buildings typically fail to be cost-effective.

PROTECTING BRIDGES

There are 600,000 highway bridges in the United States, a vital part of a transportation system that supports 86 percent of all personal travel and 80 percent of the nation's freight. Moreover, bridges are—or seem to be—especially vulnerable. As Chairman Bennie Thompson of the House of Representatives' Committee on Homeland Security insists, "The U.S. highway system is particularly vulnerable to potential terrorist attacks because of its openness—vehicles and their operators can move freely and with almost no restrictions, and some bridge and tunnel elements are easily accessible and located in isolated areas making them more challenging to secure."[45]

The Consequences of an Attack

While buildings have often been attacked by terrorists, there are very few reported attacks on bridges, suggesting that any supposed threat to them may well be overblown, even though bridges (like a near-infinite number of other targets) may be vulnerable to attack in some sense. An analysis of terrorism incidents compiled by the Global Terrorism Database (GTD)[46] shows that in the ten-year period 1998 to 2007 there were only two attacks on bridges in the United Kingdom (both IRA sponsored, generating only minor damage and no fatalities) and none in continental Europe or North America. Moreover, worldwide only 5 percent of guerrilla and terrorist attacks on public surface transportation systems in the 80-year period from 1920 to 2000 were directed at bridges and tunnels and only 1 percent during the last 3.5 years of that period.[47]

As it happens, a bridge is very difficult to damage severely because its concrete and steel construction makes it something of a hardened structure from the outset. Buildings are far more vulnerable, and many casualties can be caused if their thin and brittle masonry and glass facades are shattered.[48] By contrast, the GTD data show that of the 14 bridges attacked by insurgents in the war zones of Iraq and Afghanistan between 1998 and 2007, the total number of fatalities was relatively few at 59, and no more that 10 perished in any single attack.

Most highway bridges are two to four lanes wide with spans of 60 to 150 feet crossing rivers, roads, and railroad lines. An American Society of Civil Engineers Task Committee considers an upper bound practical threat to be a 4,000-pound TNT VBIED carried to the target by a light, single-rear-axle delivery vehicle.[49] Other engineers suggest that smaller explosives, on the order of 500 pounds, could cause "catastrophic damage" to a typical U.S. highway bridge.[50] Yet even a more massive VBIED may fail to totally collapse a bridge, or even cause too much disruption. Photos of damage caused by a huge VBIED, reputedly up to 5 tons, detonated on a highway bridge near Ramadi, Iraq, on October 17, 2009, show collapse of only one lane of one span, and the bridge seems to have been quickly reopened.[51] In addition, there were no casualties.

An explosive blast will not blow up a bridge, but will more likely damage and weaken supporting elements, causing only partial collapse. Even if a bridge collapses, however, not all vehicle occupants on it will be killed. For example, the collapse of the 10-lane, 14-span, 1,900-foot I35W bridge in Minneapolis in 2007 killed 13 people, but 111 vehicles were on the bridge at the time of collapse.[52] A bridge collapse over the Arkansas River in 2002 killed 14 people when 11 vehicles, of the many that were on the bridge, plunged into the river.[53] The unexpectedly high survival rates arise not only because the bridge only partially collapses but also because a car is designed to crumple on impact and thus absorb energy.

Costs of Damage

Because highway bridges have a large variety of spans, widths, geometry, and other characteristics, it is difficult to generalize about damage costs. However, several case studies of recent U.S. bridge collapses may be instructive. The replacement and demolition costs for two damaged U.S. interstate highway bridges were $4 million and $11.75 million, for bridges in Los Angeles from $6.2 million to more than $60 million, and for the I35W bridge in Minneapolis $234 million. Applying this experience, we set replacement costs for a typical bridge at $20 million. Traffic diversion and associated user delay costs for a bridge under construction can total $430,000 per day, which, even in the case of a rapid bridge replacement in Oklahoma of only 46 days, amounted to nearly $20 million.[54]

In addition to the economic cost of traffic diversion, there are other social and economic costs to a community. These are harder to quantify but may be in the order of tens to hundreds of millions of dollars because, although the loss of one bridge will not isolate a community, it will generally cause considerable inconvenience and disruption. We will assume this causes a loss of $100 million, and we round up the expected number of fatalities to twenty, at a cost of $130 million based on value of statistical life considerations.[55] The total losses for a damaged bridge including both the loss of life and economic considerations thus come approximately to $250 million, a rather high estimate.

Costs of Retrofitting

Although there is much information available about retrofitting bridges to mitigate the effects of blast damage,[56] there is little information about their cost. However, a broad estimate may be obtained from examining retrofit costs for bridges damaged by earthquakes because the stresses on the bridge are not dissimilar to those caused by explosions. The retrofit cost for the historic Cesar Chavez highway bridge in Los Angeles was 15 percent of its replacement value, and a "full-blown" rehabilitation of a U.S. four-span steel girder bridge was 51.5 percent of its replacement value.[57] Clearly, retrofit costs can be substantial.

We will conservatively assume that substantial mitigation of blast effects can be achieved at a cost of 20 percent of a bridge's replacement value. If the bridge replacement value is $20 million, the cost of strengthening it is then $4 million. Annualized over a remaining service life of 20 years, this comes to $268,000 per year.[58] If the cost is annualized over five years with the same discount rate, this equates to a present value cost of $872,000 per year. We will assume a middle value for strengthening of $500,000 per year.

Risk Reduction

As with the discussion of buildings, we will generously assume that protective measures reduce the risk by 95 percent.

The Cost-Effectiveness of Protection

As suggested earlier, the likelihood of a terrorist attack on a highway or railway bridge in western nations is remote. Engineering and design issues suggest that bridges should not be an attractive target for terrorists, and incident data suggest they aren't.

Table 6.2 on p. 118 shows that the likelihood of a successful attack needs to exceed 0.21 percent (underlined in the table) or one in 480 per bridge per year for bridge strengthening to be cost-effective under the assumptions we have applied:

- $250 million in losses, including the loss of life and economic considerations
- $500,000 per year to strengthen an existing bridge
- 95 percent risk reduction as a result of the bridge protection measures

If we assume risk is reduced only by 50 percent, the minimum attack probability per year required for bridge protective measures to be considered cost-effective increases to 0.4 percent per bridge. A sensitivity analysis of parameters is always useful, but the trends would not be dissimilar to those presented for buildings described earlier.

If there were one attack on a highway bridge every year in the United States, the attack probability would be only 1 in 600,000 (0.00017 percent) per bridge per year because there are 600,000 bridges in the country. This probability is obviously nowhere near the 1 in 480 likelihood of a successful attack required for bridge protective measures to be cost-effective. If lives saved is the only criterion for risk acceptability, protective measures would save only 0.0019 lives per year when the attack probability is below 0.01 percent per bridge per year.[59] The cost per life saved (cost of protection divided by lives saved) exceeds $263 million and thus fails a cost-benefit assessment because this is far in excess of the value of statistical life of $6.5 million.

If there is a specific threat such that the likelihood of attack massively increases, or if a bridge is deemed an iconic structure such that its perceived value is massively inflated, bridge protective measures may begin to become cost-effective. Thus, San Francisco's Golden Gate Bridge or New York's Brooklyn Bridge might be a more tempting target for terrorists than a more typical highway bridge, as evidenced by the embryonic plot in 2002 to use blowtorches to sever the cables of the Brooklyn Bridge.[60]

This plot and concerns about bridge vulnerabilities led a blue ribbon panel on bridge and tunnel security to inform the Federal Highway Administration in 2003 that "preliminary studies indicate that there are approximately 1,000 [bridges] where substantial casualties, economic disruption, and other societal ramifications would result from isolated attacks," that the "loss of a critical bridge or tunnel at one of the numerous 'choke points' in the highway system could result in hundreds or thousands of casualties, billions of dollars worth of direct reconstruction costs, and even greater socioeconomic costs," that the "ordinary cost of construction to replace a major long-span bridge or tunnel on a busy interstate highway corridor in the United States may be $1.75 billion," and that, summing reconstruction costs and socioeconomic losses, the "loss of a critical bridge or tunnel could exceed $10 billion."[61]

This is certainly alarming stuff, and an accompanying cost analysis of protective measures for four large U.S. bridges concludes that the cost to protect these bridges ranges from $20.6 million to more than $157.4 million.[62] The protection costs include strengthening (retrofitting) piers, anchors, road deck, tension hangars, and approach highways. While the blue ribbon panel report does not name the specific bridges, these costs clearly suggest they were considering the Golden Gate Bridge, Brooklyn Bridge, George Washington Bridge, and one other long span suspension bridge.

These are enormous protective costs. If the average cost of $95.6 million is annualized over a 25-year period, it comes to $5.5 million per year.[63] Referring again to table 6.2 and applying the panel's dire expected losses of $10 billion with protective costs rounded down to $5 million per year, the attack probability would need to exceed 0.05 percent (broken underline in the table), or 1 in 2,000, per bridge per year. Taking the panel's estimate of 1,000 critical U.S. bridges, this would mean that terrorists would otherwise be able to successfully conduct a massive attack on one of these bridges at least once every two years for these protective costs to be cost-effective. The evidence to date rather strongly suggests that such a high attack probability is not being observed.

OTHER INFRASTRUCTURE ELEMENTS

Pipelines, railroads, roads, power lines, communication facilities, and other utilities or lifelines are all vulnerable to terrorist attack because they are located in every community, are difficult to protect, and are often in isolated or remote locations. Damage to these infrastructure elements can cause short- and long-term social and economic effects, and this, in principle, should make them highly attractive targets for terrorists. For example, more than 65 percent of oil and gas pipelines are aboveground, and lost production can cost many billions of dollars.[64]

Yet most damage can be repaired fairly quickly. In Iraq, where there have been many IED attacks on such elements, repair teams from the Iraqi Ministry of Oil, working in the most hostile security environment imaginable, can right the damage in several days or in some cases several weeks.[65] The vulnerability of pipelines also makes them resilient because if they are easily accessible to terrorists, they are equally easily accessible to repair teams.

Offshore oil and gas platforms are vulnerable to terrorism because of their remote locations, but they are often located in severe marine environments that would make any attack particularly dangerous, if not impossible, for would-be terrorists. Offshore platforms are more vulnerable to hurricanes, earthquakes, storms, and ship impact. And as we have seen with the 2010 Gulf of Mexico BP oil spill, they are equally vulnerable to equipment malfunction and operator error—in fact, there have been numerous instances of explosions, blowouts, and other accidents over the years.[66] Contingency plans are available for most of these events, which in most cases would be equally appropriate to mitigate the effects of a terrorist attack.

Most other infrastructure is similarly resilient and can be readily repaired, resulting in minimal damage or disruption to communities. This can be seen, for example, when power poles or transmission towers are damaged in a storm, when communication cables are accidentally severed by construction workers, or when pipelines catch fire or explode because of accidents or lack of maintenance. Moreover, alternate means of supply are also often available, and diversions around damaged infrastructure can allow lines of transport, supply, or communication to be maintained.

Thus, terrorist attacks on such infrastructure elements are unlikely to cause significant long-term losses to society because damage is often repairable at an entirely bearable cost and in a timely fashion.

NUCLEAR AND CHEMICAL PLANTS AND MATERIAL

There are not a large number of nuclear plants, and an adept terrorist attack on them could potentially have devastating consequences. Consequently, they seem to be prime candidates for protection. However, the big ones, nuclear reactors, seem already to be quite secure from a terrorist attack—and, for a number of reasons, were so even before terrorism became much of an issue.

Nuclear reactors are surrounded by containment structures that are three to five feet thick, made of concrete heavily reinforced with steel, and designed to contain all radiation from nuclear accidents, as was successfully demonstrated with the Three Mile Island nuclear reactor accident in 1979. It was the lack of a containment structure that contributed to the massive release of radiation from Chernobyl in 1986—although that release, discussed in chapter 9, seems thus far to have had only quite limited health consequences. Containment structures were designed to withstand attacks by aircraft and missiles well before 9/11, and a 2002 analysis by the Electric Power Research Institute found that a fully laden Boeing 767–400 would not break through any U.S. containment structure, nor would used spent fuel pools, dry fuel storage facilities, or fuel transportation containers be breached.[67]

Since 9/11, armed security has been beefed up, including a "requirement that each nuclear power plant conduct security exercises every three years to test its ability to defend against the design basis threat." In these "force-on-force" exercises, "an adversary force from outside the plant attempts to penetrate the plant's vital area and damage or destroy key safety components."[68] The size of the security forces for the 65 U.S. nuclear plant sites now numbers more than 5,000, an average of about 75 per site.[69] Given the substantial invulnerability of nuclear reactors to terrorist attack (if not necessarily to extreme natural hazards) and given the low likelihood of such an attack, it may be questionable whether extravagant additional protective measures to deal with a potential terrorist threat (and quite possibly many of those already in place) are worth the cost.

There are a very large number of chemical plants, although mostly, like nuclear plants, they are placed away from population centers, a fact that may considerably reduce the urgency of protecting them further. It is possible to conjure damaging scenarios, but, except under the most severe circumstances, such as the 1984 chemical release, apparently by sabotage, at Bhopal, India, any dispersion is likely to have rather limited physical consequences. Panic, however, could enhance the effect. The same holds for biological pathogens, although in this case, the chief fear is that terrorists will be able to make the pathogens themselves, not steal them.

Oil and gas refineries are, in fact, chemical plants, producing the economic lifeblood of most modern economies, therefore presumably making them a tempting target for terrorists. Since most are placed away from population centers, loss of life is not a major consideration, but economic damages are. Yet, as with other infrastructure elements, damage to oil and gas infrastructure can generally be repaired relatively quickly, minimizing the economic damage.

A simulation and gaming scenario developed by the Heritage Foundation argues otherwise. It posits an extravagant *simultaneous* scenario: (1) "catastrophic destruction" of the Ras Tanura port and oil terminal in Saudi Arabia, causing a loss of more than 4 million barrels of oil per day for at least several months; (2) an attack by an explosives-laden plane on the Saudi Aramco headquarters, destroying the Internet facilities there and killing portions of the company's leadership; (3) speedboat attacks by the Indonesia-based terrorist group, Jemaah Islamiyah (JI), on oil tankers crossing the Strait of Malacca and emplacement in the strait of EM-52 mines coated with polymer (to reduce the likelihood of detection) that cause all oil traffic there to be halted because insurers will not give coverage to hydrocarbon cargo; and (4) the agile emplacement by an al-Qaeda affiliate of mines in the Strait of Sunda to further disrupt petroleum transport.[70]

The notion that al-Qaeda or any other terrorist organization (certainly including the increasingly pathetic JI) could successfully execute and coordinate a set of intercontinental attacks like this is clearly preposterous. But even if they could, oil refineries and ports can be rebuilt and naval protection to shipping can be provided in quick order. Moreover, if governments worldwide implemented sensible energy and policy responses to such a crisis and did not panic, the Heritage study itself concludes that, even with its imagined global mayhem, the world would recover within a year with short-term job losses of 164,000 and GDP losses of only $50 billion.[71] That is, even under the coordinated and highly destructive attacks posited in their fanciful scenario, American and European economies have the capacity to recover and respond in fairly short order.

KEY INFRASTRUCTURE NODES

It would make sense to protect any specific infrastructure nodes whose destruction could cause widespread damage—for example, by putting a large area out of electricity for months.[72] It is not at all clear that many, if any, such nodes exist. However, if they do, it would probably be most efficient to expend effort to establish backup emergency redundancies rather than seeking to protect the nodes themselves.

At any rate, investment in this area may be worthwhile because if such nodes are susceptible to terrorist disruption, they probably are as well to more likely events like lightning, heavy winds, and other natural hazards or to human error or sabotage by a disgruntled employee. A similar conclusion might hold for some dams and for concentrations of chemicals and explosives.

MAJOR PORTS

There are 361 ports in the United States, a few dozen of them major, and, as with most developed countries, the economy depends heavily on them. Accordingly, protecting them against at least a major attack may be a useful effort.

However, redirection of shipping is fairly easy, if costly and inconvenient. Moreover, the large linear layout of ports also makes them more resilient than most infrastructure simply because of their size. The Port of Los Angeles covers 3,200 acres and has 10 piers and berths for 80 ships. Other ports may be smaller, but even these include several piers and at least a dozen berths separated over thousands of feet. Any attack short of a nuclear one (for which protection measures beyond dispersion are substantially futile) is not likely to destroy an entire port. Some berths may be lost, but most ports would still be able to continue to operate, although perhaps at reduced capacity.

Therefore, the chief problem here seems to arise, as Stephen Flynn points out for the American case, from overreaction. He worries that policy makers could probably not restrain themselves from closing down all the ports if one were hit, thus inflicting massive losses on the economy.[73] The sensible solution in this case, obviously, is to have people in charge who are levelheaded and not overburdened by such considerations, an issue to be considered more extensively in chapter 8 and 9.

SYMBOLIC TARGETS

Protection measures may be justified for a small group of symbolic, even iconic, targets like the Capitol, the White House, the Statue of Liberty, the British Parliament buildings, the Sydney Opera House, the Eiffel Tower, the Washington Monument, and the Brooklyn and Golden Gate Bridges. In these cases, however, the main cost would be in embarrassment or in a painful loss of prestige because all (like the Pentagon after 9/11) could readily be repaired after an attack by a conventional explosive and because any loss of life might in many instances be smaller than for terrorist explosions in places of congregation. Moreover, in all cases, any protective benefits should be balanced with a reasonable cost consideration: the prevention of embarrassment is not an infinite good.

Given the low probability that even prime symbolic targets will be hit, limited protective measures might be all that are called for. Thus, huge amounts of money have been spent in an elaborate effort to make the Washington Monument secure, when one might tentatively speculate that the considerable bulk (though not all) of that benefit might have been achieved simply by hiring a few additional security guards.

There may be a small number of potential targets that are likely to appear so lucrative to terrorists that they would have difficulty restraining themselves if the targets were inadequately protected. One might be the person of the president of the United States, though, given assassination attempts in the past, protecting that person is unfortunately wise and necessary for quite a few reasons beyond the kind of terrorism that is of present concern. Given the proclivities of some terrorists, Israel's El Al airline would seem to be an attractive, high-visibility, rather trophylike target, and so Israel's extraordinary efforts to screen passengers and baggage may make sense. On the other hand, a very large number of potential Jewish targets—thousands of synagogues, for example—are highly visible and vulnerable (albeit not, perhaps, quite to the same degree as El Al), yet they seem to go substantially unmolested.

ASSESSING "CRITICAL" INFRASTRUCTURE

There is no doubt that a terrorist attack on many infrastructure elements could cause considerable damage and significant loss of life. However, while such targets as buildings, bridges, highways, pipelines, mass transit, water supplies, and communications may be essential to the economy and well-being of society, damage to one or even several of these, with few exceptions, will not be "critical" to the economy, to the state, or to just about anyone's way of life.

In part, this is because infrastructure designers and operators place much effort on systems modeling to ensure that a failure of one node will not keep the network from operating, even if at reduced efficiency. This is done routinely: for example, it is necessary to close many bridges from time to time for maintenance or repair, and therefore traffic is redirected so that the network is not interrupted. Other failures routinely planned for include traffic accidents, severe weather, earthquakes, and equipment malfunctions. In other words, as a matter of course, infrastructure is designed with built-in redundancies and backup systems to ensure resilience in the event of anticipated or unexpected hazards.

We have not assessed every possible element of homeland security protection, of course. However, applying the considerations laid out in chapter 5 and relying on standard evaluative measures accepted for decades by analysts, governments, regulators, and risk managers, efforts to protect people and structures from the effects of a terrorist attack are unlikely in general to be cost-effective because of the multiplicity of targets, the ability of terrorists to shift targets as needed, the capacity in many cases to quickly rebuild, the exceedingly low likelihood of an attack on a specific target, the limited capability of most terrorist groups (no Muslim terrorist in the United States has been able to set off even a tiny bomb over the last 10 years), and the difficulty of predicting which targets are most appealing to them.[74] If the terrorists' goal is to kill people, lucrative targets are essentially everywhere. If their goal is to destroy property, protection measures may be able to deter, inconvenience, or complicate, but only to the point where the terrorists seek something comparable among a vast—or even effectively infinite—array of potential unprotected targets.

Our cost-benefit assessment suggests, then, that many individual items of infrastructure, including bridges and buildings, require no protective measures unless, perhaps, there is a very specific threat to them.

CHAPTER 7

Protecting the Airlines

The protection of commercial airliners and their passengers may be feasible, or at least may seem to be so, because, although there are many airports, their number is at least somewhat limited. For example, there are only some 27 major ones (along with a few thousand smaller ones) in the United States, numbers that are vastly lower than, for example, the number of highway overpasses, fast-food restaurants, or places of congregation like stadiums, theaters, churches, and assembly halls. Although there are a very large number of commercial flights—nearly 30,000 daily in the United States alone[1]—the protection of airliners may be a comparatively manageable problem using the relatively small number of airports as key bases for protection.

In this chapter, we consider this problem from several angles and bring up a number of issues we feel should be given more systematic attention. In addition, we specifically assess the cost-effectiveness of measures designed to prevent a direct replication of a 9/11-type hijacking and of the full-body scanners that are designed to deal with the problem of smuggled plastic explosives.

THE SPECIAL IMPACT OF AIRLINER DESTRUCTION

The protection of airliners may be particularly important because, unlike the destruction of other modes of transportation, the downing of an airliner (or, especially, of two or three in succession) does seem to carry with it the special dangers of a widespread and at least somewhat lingering impact on the airline industry, as well as on related ones such as tourism. Three years after 9/11, domestic airline flights in the United States were still 7 percent below their pre-9/11 levels, and by the end of 2004, tourism even in distant Las Vegas had still not fully recovered.[2] One estimate suggests that the American economy lost 1.6 million jobs in 2001 alone, mostly in the tourism industry.[3] These numbers do not necessarily represent dead losses to the economy because, as discussed in chapter 3, much of that money may simply have been productively saved or spent elsewhere. However, they do suggest a very substantial disruption that unfairly affects a small number of industries, a disruption that was costly to all because it was felt necessary partly to mitigate the consequences by the infusion of tax money to the airline industry.

By contrast, if a bus or train is blown up, people still need to board them and will do so after a short period of wariness—as was found after the bombings in London and Madrid. To a considerable degree, people have a choice about whether to use commercial airliners, and many can turn to other types of transport—or, often, simply not take the trip. Riders of subways, buses, and probably even ferries often do not have the same luxury. Indeed, after 9/11 a man attempted to hijack a Greyhound bus in Utah, an exercise that had little consequence for the bus industry (or for just about anybody else).[4] As noted earlier, the effect on tourism of the 2005 bombings of the underground and of a bus in London proved to be comparatively transitory: international arrivals to the country increased after 2005, and the 10 percent drop in business in London hotels in the immediate aftermath of the attacks was matched by a 10 percent increase in other regions of the country.[5] Some of this may relate to the traditional British stiff upper lip and to previous experience with terrorism from the Irish Republican Army that inspired a resilience in the belief that "living life as normal represents a gesture of defiance against terrorists and may contribute to their ultimate defeat."[6] There is probably a lesson in this.

Similarly, if a building is attacked, people still enter them: after 9/11, people avoided airliners but soon returned to office buildings, even skyscrapers. Indeed, if the 9/11 attacks had been accomplished by explosives (as with the 1993 attempt on the World Trade Center or the 1995 bombing in Oklahoma City), there would have been a vastly lower social and economic impact because few would have systematically avoided buildings, or even urban office buildings. Put another way, if Timothy McVeigh had used an airplane to destroy the Murrah Building in Oklahoma City rather than explosives, the economic consequences would likely have been far greater, at least until the perpetrator was apprehended.

As noted in chapter 3, the events of September 11, 2001, suggest there can be another special cost in the case of airline terrorism. In fear of flying, many people canceled airline trips and consequently traveled more by automobile, and some studies have concluded that more than 2,300 people died in automobile accidents between September 11 and October 2003 because of such evasive behavior.[7]

It may matter as well that the airplanes on 9/11 were commercial passenger airliners. If they had been private or cargo planes, the effect on the airline industry (and on highway fatalities) would probably have been considerably less.

Interestingly, however, *failed* terrorist attempts on airliners do not seem to have had much in the way of a wider impact at all. The aborted effort by shoe bomber Richard Reid to blow up an airliner over the Atlantic occurred less than four months after 9/11. Yet in 2002, domestic and international passenger numbers continued to grow from the low point of September 2001.[8] Almost exactly eight years later, the foiled underwear bomber attempt on a Northwest Airlines flight resulted in no noticeable drop in airline patronage: International Air Transport Association data for the month following the attack (January 2010) reports that "demand shows further improvement" with a 2.1 percent increase in international passenger numbers in North America and 6.4 percent internationally.[9] Passenger numbers continued to increase after January 2010.

IS THE FLIGHT-AVOIDANCE RESPONSE TO 9/11, LIKE THE EVENT ITSELF, AN OUTLIER?

Much of the concern about airliner terrorism extrapolates from the 9/11 experience, which had, as noted, a crushing, if temporary, effect on airline passenger traffic. Particularly in the few years after 2001, it was commonly said that if terrorists were able to down two or three more airliners, they would destroy the airline industry.

But as the degree of destruction on 9/11 was extreme in the history of terrorism, so, possibly, is the extent of the reaction by airline passengers. From time to time, terrorists have been able to down airliners—the Lockerbie tragedy of 1988 high among them—but the response by the flying public has not been nearly so extreme. And after two Russian airliners were blown up by suicidal Chechen female terrorists in 2004, that country's airline industry seems to have continued with little interruption: airline passenger numbers after the attack did decline, but this has been attributed mainly to the 60 percent increase in fuel prices, and by the following year, passenger traffic had increased by 3.9 percent.[10]

It ought to be considered, then, that the downing by terrorists of additional airliners, however tragic, may not prove to be as consequential as sometimes envisioned—perhaps in part because 9/11 established such a vivid, and high, benchmark.

ARE AIRPLANES A PARTICULARLY ATTRACTIVE TERRORIST TARGET?

Moreover, contrary to many claims, airplanes may not actually be terribly attractive targets for terrorists. There have been remarkably few terrorist attempts on airplanes since 9/11 anywhere in the world, despite wide differences in security measures. There were the two attacks in 2004 on Russian airliners, plots to down planes with on-flight explosives were broken up in 1995 and 2006, and specific efforts to do so were thwarted in 2001 and 2009. That's not a high rate of frequency. Also relevant is the fact that, of the tens of billions of pieces of checked luggage transported on American carriers in the period after a bomb planted in checked luggage caused a PanAm jet to crash into Lockerbie, Scotland, in 1988, not a single one exploded to down an aircraft. This, even though mandatory screening of checked luggage was begun only after the September 11, 2001, attacks— though systems were put into place earlier to match passengers with luggage, thereby requiring that a terrorist trying to duplicate the deed would have to be suicidal.

A comparison may be helpful. In the 12-year period from 1999 through 2010, 9,605 passengers were killed worldwide in airline accidents.[11] During the same period, 363 passengers were killed by terrorism, 265 of them from the four aircraft downed on 9/11, and another 98 from the 2004 attacks in Russia.[12] Therefore, airline passengers were 26 times more likely to die from an accident than from terrorism during that period. Put another way, there was one chance in 22 million that an airplane flight would be hijacked or attacked by terrorists: there were 11 such events in the period 1999 through 9/11, and 5 more after 9/11 through 2010, several of which resulted in no deaths whatever.[13] Small odds indeed, albeit ones rarely or never pointed out by officials or by the media.

Also relevant is the fact that it is not necessarily easy to blow up an airliner. Airplanes are designed to be resilient to shock, and attentive passengers and airline personnel complicate the terrorists' task further.

Apparently, the explosion over Lockerbie was successful only because the suitcase bomb just happened to have been put at the one place in the luggage compartment where it could do fatal damage. According to Christopher Ronay, former head of the FBI bomb unit, if the bomb had been placed where it was surrounded by other luggage to absorb the blast, the passengers and the plane would have survived.[14]

Logically, then, a terrorist will not leave such matters to luck, which may be why the shoe and underwear bombers both carried their bombs onto the planes and selected window seats that are, of course, right next to the fuselage.[15] Yet even if their bombs had exploded, the airliner might not have been downed. The underwear bomber was reported to be carrying 80 grams of the explosive PETN,[16] and when his effort was duplicated on a decommissioned plane in a test set up by the BBC, the blast did not breach the fuselage, leading air accident investigator Captain J. Joseph to conclude, "I am very confident that the flight crew could have taken this aeroplane without any incident at all and get it to the ground safely."[17]

Moreover, an aircraft may not be doomed even if the fuselage is ruptured. A three-foot hole in the fuselage opened up on a Southwest Airlines plane in 2011, and the plane still landed safely.[18] In 2008, an oxygen cylinder exploded on a Qantas flight from Hong Kong, blasting a six-foot hole in the fuselage. The plane suddenly depressurized, but the aircraft returned safely to Hong Kong.[19] A Qantas spokeswoman remarked, somewhat optimistically perhaps, "There was no safety risk at any time."[20] In 1989, a cargo door opened on a United Airlines flight heading across the Pacific, extensively damaging the fuselage and cabin structure adjacent to the door. Nine passengers and their seats were sucked out and lost at sea, but the plane was able to make an emergency landing in Honolulu.[21] Aircraft, like other types of infrastructure discussed in chapter 6, are more robust and resilient than we often give them credit for.

Although PETN has a long history of use in terrorist attacks, like most stable explosives, it's not easy to ignite. Presumably because airport screening makes smuggling a metal detonator a risky proposition, the underwear bomber used a syringe filled with a liquid explosive like nitroglycerin to detonate the PETN. However, this adds to the difficulty: notes Jimmie Oxley, director of the Centre of Excellence Explosives Detection, Mitigation, Response and Characterization at the University of Rhode Island, "It looked like he was trying to use a chemical initiation, and that takes a lot of pre-experimentation to find out what would work."[22]

Another, albeit rather unlikely, way for terrorists to down an airliner involves shoulder-fired surface-to-air missiles or MANPADS (man-portable air defense systems). Measures to defend against this weapon could cost up to $38.2 billion for U.S. airlines alone.[23] Yet there were only six reported shoulder-fired missile attacks on Western-built civilian turbojet aircraft in the 20-year period 1978–2007. The results were the catastrophic loss of aircraft in two instances (Angolan Airlines in 1983 and Congo Airlines in 1998), one miss by two missiles (Arkia Israeli Airlines in Kenya in 2002), and three instances in which the aircraft were damaged but still landed safely.[24] The survivability of civilian airliners to such attacks is clearly high, as is the terrorists' difficulty. Moreover, except for the Israeli case, there have been no attacks against U.S. or Western aircraft, and, as Bartholomew Elias, a specialist in aviation policy for the U.S. Congressional Research Service, notes, "No credible intelligence has been reported to the public that al Qaeda or other terrorist groups may be planning such attacks."[25]

Since two Russian airliners were blown up by terrorists in 2004, the terrorist's task is obviously not impossible. However, there were some peculiarities in these cases that may limit their representativeness: in part through "police bungling" and the payment of "a petty bribe," the terrorist women passed "uninspected through layers of airport security and checks, even after being identified as possible terrorists."[26]

The terrorists' task, then, is a difficult one, and they are likely to end up with more duds than successes. Moreover, although their explosion may cause real damage and loss of life, this result is by no means guaranteed: blowing up an airliner is more challenging than we imagine. In assessing airline security measures, then, it should be considered that, while the measures may reduce the chances of downing or commandeering an airplane, the probability of that happening is already so low that any gain in security may not be worth the additional cost of the security measures.

AVIATION SECURITY MEASURES

The annual budget of the Transportation Security Administration (TSA) is $8.2 billion, which is 14 percent of the total Department of Homeland Security (DHS) budget.[27] In expending these considerable sums, the TSA developed what it calls a "layered approach" to airline security. That characterization implies a certain coordination and coherence—the establishment of an orderly set of sequential barriers. But the 21 specific layers TSA has come up with seem more nearly to be a somewhat haphazard listing of elements or measures that have been put in place.

At any rate, 15 of the layers are aimed at the deterrence and apprehension of terrorists before they board the aircraft:

Intelligence
International partnerships
Customs and border protection
Joint terrorism task force
No-fly list and passenger prescreening
Crew vetting
Visible intermodal protection response (or VIPR) teams
Canines
Behavioral detection officers
Travel document checker
Checkpoint/transportation security officers
Checked baggage
Transportation security inspectors
Random employee screening
Bomb appraisal officers

And the remaining six are designed to provide "in-flight security":

Federal Air Marshal Service (FAMS)
Law enforcement officers
Hardened cockpit door
Federal flight deck officers
Trained flight crew
Passengers

While these 21 layers may be appropriate for foiling or deterring terrorists smuggling themselves or bombs onto aircraft, they do little to reduce risks like shoulder-fired missile threats.

COST-EFFECTIVENESS OF SECURITY MEASURES DESIGNED TO PREVENT A REPLICATION OF 9/11

Since it is a primary (and very expensive) concern, we seek first to evaluate the costs and benefits of security measures designed to prevent a direct replication of 9/11, in which commercial passenger airliners were commandeered by small bands of terrorists, kept under control for some time, and then crashed into specific targets.

We will incorporate a general consideration of all airline security measures into our analysis, but to deal with the potential for a replication of 9/11, we want to initially focus in particular on those from the in-flight security list: (1) air marshals and other law enforcement officers, (2) hardened cockpit doors, and (3) crew and passenger resistance, a collection of the last three measure on the list.

A significant chunk of TSA's budget is spent on the *Federal Air Marshal Service*. There are now some 2,500 to 4,000 air marshals, up from 33 before 9/11,[28] and the FY2011 budget for the service is $950 million.[29] In addition, airlines are expected to provide free seats to air marshals, and these are generally in first class to allow observation of the cockpit door. The Air Transport Association estimates that this costs airlines $220 million per year in lost revenue.[30] A best estimate of the annual cost to government and airlines for the Air Marshal Service, then, is $1.2 billion.

Air marshals ride on no more than 10 percent of flights in the United States,[31] and some estimates are even lower, concluding that air marshals fly on less than 5 percent.[32] However, Thomas Quinn, director of the Air Marshal Service, has dismissed such reports and, while declining to give specifics, insists his agents cover "more than 5 percent" of some 28,000 daily commercial flights in the United States.[33] These are often high-risk flights, based on intelligence reports.[34] Exactly how that risk has been determined is difficult to fathom, particularly since air marshals have had almost nothing to do over the years. Additional law enforcement officers may be on some flights for reasons other than countering terrorism, such as escorting prisoners or protecting VIPs. However, their numbers will not significantly boost the percentage of flights that have an armed officer on board.

The Federal Aviation Administration required operators of more than 6,000 planes to install *hardened cockpit doors* by April 2003 to protect cockpits from intrusion and small-arms fire or fragmentation devices.[35] The purchase and installation cost of each hardened cockpit door is typically $30,000 to $50,000—rather remarkably high for a door, one might imagine, but anything to do with aircraft is expensive, and these doors are very heavy with all sorts of ballistics protection requiring that airframe supports be strengthened. The total cost to harden 6,000 cockpit doors is estimated as $300 to $500 million over a ten-year period, including the cost of increased fuel consumption due to the heavier doors.[36] A best estimate annual cost of hardening cockpit doors is $40 million. This cost will decrease over time because door installation costs for new aircraft will be less than for existing aircraft.

An important form of defense is *crew and passenger resistance*. One reason for the extent of the losses of 9/11 was the reluctance of crew and passengers to confront and resist the hijackers. This is understandable, as most previous hijackings ended peacefully or with minimal loss of life, and the main response to a hijacking was to "get the plane on the ground so negotiations can begin."[37] Indeed, only a few months earlier, three terrorists had commandeered a Russian airliner, demanding that it be flown to Saudi Arabia, at which point they were overcome by local security forces with almost no loss of life.[38]

The 9/11 suicide attacks on the World Trade Center and Pentagon radically changed this perception. As demonstrated on the fourth plane, where passengers had news of what had happened on the first three, passengers and crew will now fight back, particularly if there is any indication that the terrorists' intent is to enter the cockpit (or explode the airliner). As pilot Patrick Smith puts it forcefully:

> Conventional wisdom says the terrorists exploited a weakness in airport security by smuggling aboard box-cutters. What they actually exploited was a weakness in our mindset—a set of presumptions based on the decades-long track record of hijackings. In years past, a takeover meant hostage negotiations and standoffs; crews were trained in the concept of "passive resistance." All of that changed forever the instant American Airlines Flight 11 collided with the north tower. What weapons the 19 men possessed mattered little; the success of their plan relied fundamentally on the element of surprise. And in this respect, their scheme was all but guaranteed not to fail. For several reasons—particularly the awareness of passengers and crew— just the opposite is true today. Any hijacker would face a planeload of angry and frightened people ready to fight back. Say what you want of terrorists, they cannot afford to waste time and resources on schemes with a high probability of failure. And thus the September 11th template is all but useless to potential hijackers.[39]

There is now clearly a new paradigm, and crew and passengers will no longer be passive. Thus, an attempted hijacking of an Australian domestic flight in 2003 was foiled as flight attendants and passengers restrained a man attempting to enter the cockpit "armed" with two wooden stakes, an aerosol can, and a lighter.[40] Beyond hijacking, passenger and crew reactions were also effective in subduing the shoe bomber of 2001 and the underwear bomber of 2009. Moreover, flight crews have shown interest in the federal flight deck officer program, which allows volunteer pilots and crew members to transport and carry firearms to defend the flight deck of aircraft against acts of criminal violence or air piracy. It is estimated that 8 percent of pilots in the United States are federal flight deck officers (FFDOs).[41]

The FY2011 budget for the FFDO and crew training program is $25.7 million. Passengers, of course, receive no training whatever. That is to say, the single security layer that, according to Patrick Smith, is most important for foiling another 9/11 costs almost nothing at all.

Yet the issue may not be quite so clear-cut. Most reported incidents of fighting back have occurred when the terrorist was acting alone, not the coordinated resistance needed to overwhelm a team of hijackers spread throughout an aircraft—and a team of hijackers is what would be required for a 9/11 type of attack to be repeated. The time it takes for hijackers to take over an aircraft could be a matter of seconds or minutes, which could conceivably be less than passengers need to assess the situation, realize the dire threat, communicate with other passengers, and process other information needed for them to summon the courage to assault armed and dangerous terrorists. However, the realization that death is inevitable if the terrorists succeed would, as on the fourth flight on 9/11, have a mind-concentrating effect.

Cost-Benefit Analysis

Once again, the *benefit of a security measure* is a function of three elements:

$$\text{Benefit} = (\text{probability of a successful attack}) \times$$
$$(\text{losses sustained in the successful attack}) \times (\text{reduction in risk})$$

The *probability of a successful attack* is the likelihood that a successful terrorist attack will take place if the security measure is not in place. The *losses sustained in the attack* include the fatalities and other damage—both direct and indirect—that will accrue as a result of a successful terrorist attack. The *reduction in risk* is the degree to which the security measure foils, deters, disrupts, or protects against a terrorist attack. This *benefit*, a multiplicative composite of three considerations, is then compared to the *costs* of providing the security measure required to attain the benefit.

Probability of a Successful Attack

As discussed in earlier chapters, the 9/11 terrorist event was massively off the charts both in direct financial costs and in the loss of life when it took place, and that continues to be true today: there has never been a terrorist attack of remotely that magnitude. As Todd Sandler and Walter Enders note, "The casualties on 9/11 represent a clear outlier with deaths on this single day approximately equal to all transnational terrorist-related deaths recorded during the entire 1988–2000 period."[42] With this in mind, one could, in estimating the likelihood of another attack, remove that outlier from consideration on the grounds that it may well remain a (horrific) aberration with little relevance to the future. As Russell Seitz puts it, "9/11 could join the Trojan Horse and Pearl Harbor among stratagems so uniquely surprising that their very success precludes their repetition," and accordingly, "al-Qaeda's best shot may have been exactly that."[43] However, while it may be reasonable to leave 9/11 out of the statistics because of its exceptional status, it would not be conservative. Accordingly, this event needs to be included in the analysis.

Accordingly, we will assume that, in the absence of enhanced security measures, there would be a 9/11 replication every ten years in the United States. That is, the annual probability of a successful attack if there were no protection measures beyond those in place before 9/11 would be around 10 percent.

Losses Sustained in a Successful Attack

We saw in chapter 3 that the losses from the 9/11 attacks, including the deaths of nearly 3,000 people, direct physical damage of $30 billion including rescue and clean-up costs, and indirect losses to the U.S. economy, add up to approximately $200 billion. However, this is the total cost for four aircraft hijackings, not one. Most of the losses arose from the devastating attacks on the World Trade Center by two separate aircraft, so for a single aircraft we divide this figure by two, generating a loss of $100 billion for a hijacked aircraft that is subsequently flown into a significant building or target.

This is a high, upper-bound estimate because it would obviously be difficult for terrorists to again inflict such a huge loss of life and treasure as was accomplished with the attacks on the World Trade Center. Somewhat more plausible, actually, would be an attack like that on the Pentagon on 9/11. In that case, the damage bill came to $700 million,[44] while compensating the families of the 184 victims up to $1.2 billion if we use $6.5 million as the value of life. With the additional costs of social and business disruptions, loss of tourism, and the like, the total cost in this case might total $10 billion.

Reduction in Risk

The extra and more vigilant intelligence, immigration and passport control, airport screening, and other preboarding security measures implemented after 9/11 by TSA should result in a substantial likelihood of detection and apprehension of terrorists. Added to this are the preventive policing and investigatory efforts of the sort that upset a plan to blow up airliners that was apparently being hatched in Britain in 2006. Combined, we suggest, these measures by themselves reduce the risk of a replication of 9/11 by at least 50 percent, and this is likely to be a lower bound value. There has been no successful hijacking anywhere in the world since 9/11— and, for that matter, very few attempts to even blow up airliners. In consequence, we suspect, the risk reduction arising from preboarding security as well as from policing through deterrence and disruption is likely to be much greater than 50 percent.

If there is an attempt to hijack an aircraft, we further assume that all three in-flight security measures have an equal share in reducing the remaining risk. Risk reduction is therefore 16.7 percent each for air marshals, hardened cockpit doors, and crew and passenger resistance. For those who, like Smith, think crew and passenger resistance after 9/11 makes a replication of that event impossible or nearly so, this represents, of course, a massive underestimate for that particular barrier.[45]

However, the probability an air marshal will actually be on a hijacked flight is something like 5 percent. On the other hand, air marshals are supposedly more likely to be on flights deemed by intelligence reports to be high risk. Relevant is the Australian air marshals program finding that "following increases in screening at airports and the installation of bullet-proof cockpit doors, there is little intelligence indicating which flights are at risk," with the result that air marshals now only "have random assignments or fly to protect VIPs."[46] Despite this finding, we will assume that there is some coherent guidance from intelligence, and, to account for this, we will set the probability an air marshal is actually on a plane subject to terrorist hijacking at 10 percent.

Although small, the chance that air marshals will be on a flight might act as a deterrent to some terrorists. However, so, too, would hardened cockpit doors, airport screening, passenger and crew resistance, and the rest of TSA's 21 layers of security. Taken as a whole, these would not increase or reduce the *relative* reductions in risk we assume here.

Summarizing, we assume that preboarding security and policing reduce risk by 50 percent, that crew and passenger resistance reduce it by another

16.7 percent, that hardened cockpit doors reduce it by a further 16.7 percent, and that air marshals do so by a final 1.7 percent, a number that emerges when 16.7 percent, their share of presumed risk reduction, is multiplied by 10 percent, the likelihood an air marshal will actually be on the hijacked airline.[47] These risk reductions are our best estimate and are substantially conservative, biased to conclude that the FAMS, in particular, is cost-effective.[48]

Evaluating the Cost-Effectiveness of the Federal Air Marshal Service

We have assumed, then, that (1) in the absence of all post-9/11 security measures, the probability of a successful terrorist hijacking attack is 10 percent per year; (2) the successful attack would inflict $100 billion in damage (as an upper bound); and (3) the Federal Air Marshal Service reduces the risk of a successful hijacking by 1.7 percent. Multiplying these three items together as indicated in the previous equation generates a benefit of $170 million. This number is then compared with the cost of the FAMS of $1.2 billion per year. As shown in the boxed cell in table 7.1, the net benefit under our posited conditions comes out negative, a loss of $1,030 million per year.[49]

This can be looked at in another way. For the Federal Air Marshal Service to be cost-effective and therefore justify its $1.2 billion per year price tag, a break-even cost analysis shows that there would need to be more than one $100 billion attack every two years in the absence of enhanced (post-9/11) security measures. The annual attack probability would have to be at least 71 percent, a number that results when, following the approach on p. 84, the benefit or cost of the measure ($1.2 billion) is divided by the product of the losses sustained in the attack ($100 billion) and the reduction in risk (0.017).

The table allows for the evaluation of other possible scenarios. For a Pentagon-like attack where damage totals $10 billion, the cost-benefit loss becomes even greater at $1,183 million per year, underlined in the table. If the probability of a successful hijacking attack is taken to an astronomical 50 percent per year, still at an upper bound loss of $100 billion, the net benefit remains negative, a loss of $350 million per year. Even if the risk reduction is doubled, the analysis still shows significant losses.[50]

Therefore, at just about all reasonable (and not so reasonable) combinations of security measure effectiveness and attack likelihood, the Federal Air Marshal Service fails a cost-benefit analysis, usually quite miserably.

Table 7.1 NET BENEFIT IN MILLIONS OF DOLLARS FOR THE FEDERAL AIR MARSHAL SERVICE, ASSUMING IT COSTS $1.2 BILLION PER YEAR AND REDUCES THE RISK OF A 9/11 REPLICATION BY 1.7 PERCENT

Annual probability of a successful attack in the absence of enhanced security measures	Losses sustained in a successful terrorist attack				
	$1 billion	$10 billion	$50 billion	$100 billion	$200 billion
0.1 percent	-1,200	-1,200	-1,199	-1,198	-1,196
1 percent	-1,200	-1,198	-1,192	-1,183	-1,166
5 percent	-1,199	-1,192	-1,157	-1,115	-1,1030
10 percent	-1,198	-1,183	-1,115	-1,030	-860
25 percent	-1,196	-1,157	-988	-775	-350
50 percent	-1,192	-1,115	-775	-350	500
100 percent	-1,183	-1,030	-350	500	2,200

Each entry represents the benefit-minus-cost result for each loss and for each attack probability. Entries that are positive would be considered to be cost-effective. A value of -1,200 denotes no benefit.

Break-Even Analysis

The number of otherwise successful attacks averted by enhanced security measures at several loss levels necessary for the Federal Air Marshal Service to be cost-effective—that is, for the security benefit of the Service to equal its costs[1]

71 every year	7 every year	1 every year	1 every 2 years	1 every 3 years

[1]Put another way, for each of these loss levels, the annual probability of a successful attack would have to reach 7,159 percent, 706 percent, 141 percent, 71 percent, and 35 percent for the benefits of the enhanced security measure to equal its costs.

Evaluating the Cost-Effectiveness of Hardened Cockpit Doors

While the effectiveness of hardening cockpit doors has been questioned,[51] there is little doubt that they could deter and delay a hijacker's attempt to enter the cockpit.

We assume in this case that (1) in the absence of all post-9/11 security measures, the probability of a successful terrorist hijacking attack is 10 percent per year; (2) the successful attack would inflict $100 billion in damage (as an upper bound); and (3) hardened cockpit doors reduce the risk of a successful hijacking by 16.7 percent. Multiplying these three items together as indicated in the equation generates a benefit of $1.67 billion. This number is then compared with the cost of hardening cockpit doors of $40 million per year. Because this cost is far less than the FAMS budget and

Table 7.2 NET BENEFIT IN MILLIONS OF DOLLARS FOR HARDENING COCKPIT DOORS, ASSUMING IT COSTS $40 MILLION PER YEAR AND REDUCES THE RISK OF A 9/11 REPLICATION BY 16.7 PERCENT

Annual probability of a successful attack in the absence of enhanced security measures	Losses sustained in a successful terrorist attack				
	$1 billion	$10 billion	$50 billion	$100 billion	$200 billion
0.1 percent	-40	-38	-32	-23	-7
1 percent	-38	-23	44	127	294
5 percent	-32	43	378	795	1,630
10 percent	-23	127	795	1,630	3,300
25 percent	2	378	2,048	4,135	8,310
50 percent	44	795	4,135	8,310	16,660
100 percent	127	1,630	8,310	16,660	33,360

Each entry represents the benefit-minus-cost result for each loss and for each attack probability. Entries that are positive would be considered to be cost-effective. A value of -40 denotes no benefit.

Break-Even Analysis

The number of otherwise successful attacks averted by enhanced security measures at several loss levels necessary for hardened cockpit doors to be cost-effective—that is, for their security benefit to equal its costs[1]

1 every 4 years	1 every 40 years	1 every 200 years	1 every 400 years	1 every 800 years

[1]Put another way, for each of these loss levels, the annual probability of a successful attack would have to reach 24 percent, 2.4 percent, 0.5 percent, 0.2 percent, and 0.1 percent for the benefits of the enhanced security

because the risk reduction is greater, the measure is generally cost-effective: the net benefits as arrayed in table 7.2 are positive for most combinations of attack probability and losses. The net benefit for our central, if somewhat extreme, case of a 10 percent annual attack probability that inflicts $100 billion in losses comes to $1,630 million as boxed in the table.[52] For a Pentagon-like attack where damage totals $10 billion, the cost-benefit gain is much lower, but still positive, at $127 million, underlined in the table.

For the hardening of cockpit doors to be cost effective for prospective losses from a hijacking inflicting an upper bound cost of $100 billion, the likelihood of a success, absent enhanced security measures, must be at least 0.24 percent per year or one attack in every 400 years. If the attack probability is 10 percent, the minimum risk reduction needed for the hardening of cockpit doors to be cost effective is only 0.4 percent.[53] Since many security experts believe that strengthening cockpit doors is one of the few effective post-9/11 security measures,[54] it is highly likely that the risk reduction achieved by the hardening of cockpit doors is well in excess of 0.4 percent.

Under our analysis, then, hardening cockpit doors is a cost-effective security measure, a finding that is not overly sensitive to attack probability and to the relative weightings of risk reduction between security measures.[55] This finding is very similar to those that emerge from an assessment of Australian aviation security measures following a similar approach: strengthening cockpit doors appears to be cost-effective, whereas Australia's Air Security Officer program does not.[56] It is important to note, however, that our analysis assumes that crew and passenger resistance reduces the risk of a successful hijacking by 16.7 percent. As noted, there are people who would put that number much higher.[57]

THE COST-EFFECTIVENESS OF FULL-BODY SCANNERS

The TSA has been deploying advanced imaging technologies (AIT), full-body scanners to inspect a passenger's body for concealed weapons, explosives, and other prohibited items. In 2010, as noted in the preface, the U.S. Government Accountability Office (GAO) remarked: "Cost-benefit analyses are important because they help decision makers determine which protective measures, for instance, investments in technologies or in other security programs, will provide the greatest mitigation of risk for the resources that are available." And it then *specifically* went on to point out that "conducting a cost-benefit analysis of TSA's AIT deployment is important" and that "an updated cost-benefit analysis would help inform TSA's judgment about the optimal deployment strategy for the AITs, as well as providing information to inform the best path forward, considering all elements of the screening system, for addressing the vulnerability identified by this attempted terrorist attack."[58] Yet, before deciding to install AITs at very considerable cost the TSA does not appear, at least as far as we have been able to discover, to have conducted a cost-benefit analysis of the security measure.

AITs are primarily dedicated to preventing the downing of a commercial airliner by plastic explosives borne on the body by a passenger. Although both the shoe and the underwear bombers boarded their plane overseas, the AITs operated by the TSA have been deployed mainly (or perhaps only) in American airports. Accordingly, our analysis considers the threat probability, risk reduction, and losses for a suicide bomber who attempts to board an aircraft in the U.S. Additional deployment abroad would not materially alter the results.

Cost of the Security Measure

The TSA began rolling out the scanners in 2009 and says it plans to procure and deploy 1,800 of them by 2014 to reach full operating capacity at all checkpoints in the United States.[59] The costs are considerable, with staffing costs exceeding capital costs.[60] Gale Rossides, acting administrator of the TSA, states that the annualized cost of purchasing, installing, staffing, operating, supporting, upgrading, and maintaining the first 1,000 units is about $650 million per year.[61] We can then infer that the full quota of 1,800 units will cost approximately $1.2 billion per year.

Since AITs provide scans that reveal genitals and other personal characteristics, passengers who opt out of an AIT are subject to pat-downs with "TSA agents using their open hands to search the clothed genital areas of passengers," a prospect that adds to the staffing costs and that has "drawn huge web traffic, further escalating the controversy."[62] This perceived invasion of privacy, inconvenience, or extra delays during screening may deter some from traveling by air; short-haul passengers may drive to their destination instead. Since driving is far riskier than air travel, the extra automobile traffic generated by existing aviation security measures, as noted earlier, has been estimated to result in 500 or more extra road fatalities per year.[63] On the other hand, it may be argued that "full body scanners are a type of 'security theatre' and have little tangible effect on deterring terrorism, the mere act of making travelers *feel* safer may in itself be beneficial."[64] We will ignore opportunity costs in our analysis, although, as indicated, these have the potential to be very substantial. We also ignore any possible security theater benefits, which are likely, however, to be small as there is little evidence that AITs by themselves will make travelers feel much safer, and could well have the opposite effect.

Losses Sustained in a Successful Attack

The loss of an aircraft and follow-on economic costs and social disruption might be considerable. If we assume that the downed airline kills 300 and that each life is valued at $6.5 million, the total is approximately $2 billion. If we add the cost of a large commercial airliner at $200 to $250 million and include the costs of forensic and air transport crash investigations, direct economic loss sums approximately to $2.5 billion. If there are fewer passengers, say 150, direct losses would sum to $1.5 billion. However, we will select $2 billion as a reasonable lower bound.

A RAND study concludes that $15 billion would be a plausible upper value of economic loss.[65] However, it may fail to consider full losses to the economy. As we saw before, losses sustained after the 9/11 attacks ranged form 0.3 to 1.0 percent of annual GDP. The economic consequences of a successful terrorist airliner bombing would probably be less than that of those shocking events, so we will assume that a reasonable upper bound of losses is 0.3 percent of GDP, or $42 billion. If we add the direct costs of $2.5 billion, the total comes to about $45 billion, which we will round up to $50 billion.[66] This loss is half the loss figure we applied earlier in this chapter in the 9/11 replication scenario because that one involves crashing the airliner into a significant building, not only downing the airliner.

Since there is uncertainty about the extent of losses,[67] we will assume that loss is normally distributed with 95 percent confidence interval between $2 billion and $50 billion, resulting in a mean loss of $26 billion. We will apply this mean figure in our analysis.

Risk Reduction

A key motivation for the rapid deployment of full-body scanners was the foiled 2009 Christmas Day plot in which a terrorist hid plastic explosives in his underwear to be used to blow up a Northwest Airlines Flight on its way to Detroit from Europe. There is little doubt that that full-body scanners improve the ability to detect weapons and explosives. However, there is doubt about their ability to detect *all* explosives that may be hidden on a person. As the GAO points out, "While TSA officials stated that the laboratory and operational testing of the AIT included placing explosive material in different locations on the body, it remains unclear whether the AIT would have been able to detect the weapon" used in the attack.[68] Asked whether the new security measures would have caught the underwear bomber, TSA chief John Pistole essentially declined to answer:

> I know the threats are real. And I believe that the techniques and the technology we're using today are the best possible that we have. And it gives us the best opportunity for detecting a Christmas Day-type bomber.[69]

We will assume, however, that the full-body scanners are capable of detecting body-borne explosives that would be sufficient to blow up an airplane.[70] If not, they are obviously a complete waste of money except for a potential deterrent (or security theater) effect.

Once at the airport with his bomb, the terrorist confronts four hurdles to succeed in downing an airliner.

First, the terrorist must board the aircraft undetected, and that requires overcoming 10 of the 15 preboarding layers of security that apply—we do not include all of TSA's layers, only those likely to stop a suicide bomber. These layers include intelligence, international partnerships, customs and border protection, joint terrorism task force, no-fly list and passenger prescreening, behavioral detection officer, travel document checker, checkpoint/transportation security officers (TSO), transportation security inspectors, and bomb appraisal officers. We will assume he has a 90 percent chance of avoiding detection by each of these ten layers.

Second, the terrorist must be able to assemble and then trigger the explosive, despite the wariness of trained flight crew and passengers. We will assume that the terrorist has a high 50 percent chance of avoiding attention.[71]

Third, the bomb, once triggered, must actually explode. Although the competence of terrorist bombers, at least in the West, has not been impressive, we will assume there is a 75 percent chance the bomb is not a dud.

And fourth, the explosive must be of a sufficient size and be placed at a location in the airplane that can bring it down. We will assume there is a 75 percent chance the bomb will do so.

Figure 7.1 shows a reliability block diagram used to represent the system of foiling, deterring, or disrupting an IED terrorist attack on a commercial airplane.

For a series system where each event probability is statistically independent, the probability of airliner loss under our assumptions, which generally bias things in favor of terrorist success, is 9.8 percent.[72] The probability that the plot is unsuccessful, then, is 100 − 9.8 = 90.2 percent under existing security measures.

Full-body scanners have the potential to further lower the risk. They do so in three ways.

1. They reduce the likelihood the bomber will be able to board the aircraft undetected by increasing the likelihood that his explosives will be detected. We will assume the probability of detection is five times higher than any existing layer of TSA's preboarding security: 50 percent.

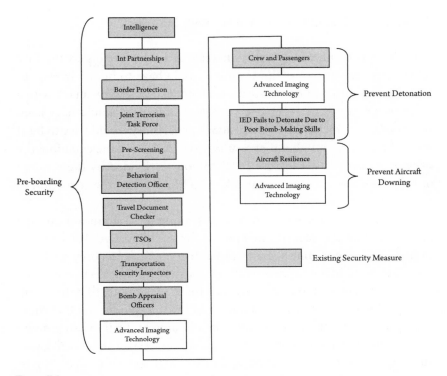

Figure 7.1
Reliability Block Diagram of Existing (shaded) and Enhanced Aviation Security Measures with Advanced Imaging Technology (AIT).

2. They deter the terrorist from using more reliable metal detonators, thus reducing the likelihood of successful detonation. As physicist Kurt Becker from the Polytechnic Institute of New York University notes, it is easier to detect a detonator than explosives "because most types of detonators have metal in them—a wire or a microchip, for example—that triggers a small spark or electrical signal."[73] We will assume the likelihood of this is 50 percent.

3. They deter the terrorist from using a larger, but more detectable, mass of explosives and hence reduce the likelihood that the explosion will be sufficiently large to down an aircraft. We will assume the likelihood the scanners will have this effect is 50 percent.

Again assuming a series system, the probability of airliner loss is now reduced to 1.2 percent,[74] and the additional risk reduction from this single security measure is 9.8 − 1.2 = 8.6 percent.[75]

Evaluating the Cost-Effectiveness of Full Body Scanners

For full-body scanners to be cost-effective and therefore justify the $1.2 billion per year price tag, the scanners would have to be solely responsible for disrupting or deterring more than one $26 billion attack with a body-borne explosive every two years that otherwise would have been successful. Specifically, the annual attack probability would have to be at least 54 percent, a number that results when, following the equation, the benefit or cost of the measure ($1.2 billion) is divided by the product of the losses sustained in the attack ($26 billion) and the reduction in risk (0.086).[76]

This result is derived from analyses applying assumptions biased toward finding the security measure to be cost-effective. We have assumed each preboarding security protective measure has only a 10 percent likelihood of being successful, that passengers and crew have only a 50 percent chance of foiling an attempt to set off a bomb, that the bomb is only 25 percent likely to be a dud or to fail to explode, and that there is only a 25 percent chance a rather small bomb will fail to bring down the aircraft. The analysis has also assumed a successful attack will cause an average $26 billion in damage, a rather high estimate according to some accountings, and it further ignores all opportunity costs inflicted by the body-scanning security measure, costs that could be quite substantial. Moreover, we are dealing here only with an attack in which the bomber boards an aircraft in the United States, even though the shoe and underwear bombers boarded their aircraft at international locations and not in the United States.[77]

Since it appears that exceedingly few suicide terrorists with body-borne explosives have planned, yet alone attempted, to board an aircraft anywhere, the likelihood of a successful attack, absent the body scanners, is unlikely to be anywhere near one every two years. By this criterion, the scanners fail a cost-benefit analysis quite comprehensively, and the $1.2 billion per year in taxpayer money might be used more productively elsewhere.

SOME ADDITIONAL CONSIDERATIONS

Stemming in part from these assessments, we offer a few further thoughts about airline security issues.

Evaluating Efforts to Prevent a Direct Replication of 9/11

Bruce Schneier concludes that the only two effective antiterrorism counter-measures implemented after 9/11 with regard to airliners were strengthened cockpit doors and passengers who learned they need to fight back. Similarly, Athol Yates, executive director of the Australian Homeland Security Research Centre says that air marshals are of "questionable" security value and that "hardening the cockpit doors and changing the protocols for hijacking has made it harder for terrorists to get weapons on board an aircraft and take control of it."[78] The assessment in this chapter generally supports these conclusions.

If the change of mind-set, together with the installation of hardened cockpit doors (an inexpensive measure that, as concluded in the analysis, is cost-effective), has made a direct replication of 9/11 essentially impossible, this means, as pilot Smith stresses, that we are "wasting billions of taxpayer dollars and untold hours of labor in a delusional attempt to thwart an attack that has already happened." Or in David Banks's words, "no pilot will relinquish control, and passengers will fight," yet "enormous resources are being invested to prevent this remote contingency."[79] It seems sensible to suggest, then, that all other measures designed entirely or almost entirely to prevent a direct replication of 9/11 are unnecessary and could be terminated. It should be stressed that in our analysis we have assumed that crew and passenger resistance reduces risk by only 16.7 percent. There are those, like Smith, who think it alone reduces the risk of a 9/11 replication pretty much by 100 percent. For those of that mind, no other security element (or layer) is necessary or, therefore, cost-effective.

However that may be, our analysis certainly suggests that the air marshal program would seem to be a prime target for cuts. There are thousands of these bored, seat-occupying entities with high attrition rates—some of this due, one suspects, to the boredom of the job, enhanced by the fact that the marshals presumably can't read, sleep, converse, watch movies, or listen to music as they keep their attention focused on the cockpit door. As noted earlier, the program not only costs the U.S. taxpayer $950 million dollars per year but also the marshals' free aisle seats cost airlines more than $220 million in lost revenue, a sum then passed on to the traveling public. Since 2001, air marshals have made 59 arrests, but none of these incidents has been related to terrorism.[80] Actually, they are best known so far for killing an apparently deranged and menacing, but innocent and unarmed, passenger during an altercation on the ground at a Florida airport in 2005.[81] In 2008, Australia announced a considerable cutback in the number of its sky marshals.[82] If this change is accepted in stride by the Australians, maybe the same result could be expected elsewhere.

Reducing Costs

Any consideration of the protection of commercial passenger airliners should include sensible cost-benefit analyses in an effort to provide the best benefit at the lowest cost. There clearly has been a demand for safety from the flying public, but not for specific measures such as vastly boosting the number of air marshals, forcing people to take off their shoes in security lines, or establishing a complicated no-fly list that generates enormous numbers of false positives.[83]

One might begin such a consideration by exploring areas in which protective measures might be relaxed with little or no likely effect either on the essential security of airline passengers or on their willingness to fly.

Actually, there have already been some modest relaxations, ones that seem to have been sensible, to have reduced costs, and to have been accepted by the flying public and these have not, it seems, led to a decline in airline passenger traffic.

- Passengers in the United States are no longer routinely required to undergo the unproductive, time-wasting process of answering questions about whether they packed their luggage themselves and have had their bags with them at all times. This exercise was instituted after the Lockerbie bombing of 1988, generating quite possibly the greatest amount of sustained mendacity in history, particularly among people who had checked their luggage at hotels for a period of time before going to the airport.
- Beginning in late 2005, passengers in the United States were allowed to take short scissors and knives with them on planes, as these were deemed too insignificant to pose much of a security risk, and Australia has followed suit.[84] The measure was justified on the grounds that it productively freed screening personnel to concentrate on weaponry potentially more lethal. Perhaps that has been its consequence, although a spokeswoman for the Association of Flight Attendants did alarmingly warn of another one at the time: "When weapons are allowed back on board an aircraft, the pilots will be able to land the plane safely but the aisles will be running with blood."[85]
- The inconvenient ritual of forcing passengers to remain in their seats during the last half hour of flights to Washington's Ronald Reagan National Airport has been eliminated.

- Considerations of permanently closing Washington's Ronald Reagan National Airport, potentially a very costly venture, were abandoned.
- Harassment of automobiles picking up and dropping off passengers appears to have been relaxed.
- Passengers are now usually required to show boarding passes only once to inspectors.
- Domestic passengers in the United States no longer need to show their identification at the gate.

Further advances have been variously suggested. Pilots have wondered forcefully why they need to be screened for weapons since, once in the cockpit, they scarcely need weapons to crash the airplane, should they take it into their mind to do so. The general requirement to screen crews at all has been questioned, particularly because ground crews and delivery personnel with equal or greater access to the plane are not screened.[86] There is some indication that this process has been, or will be, relaxed.

There ought also to be some discussion of why American airports were on orange alert from the time an airline bomb plot was rolled up in distant Britain in 2006 until 2011, when the color-coded scheme was officially abandoned, presumably ending the practice. Since the additional security cost for being on orange rather than yellow alert for the Los Angeles airport alone apparently could run to $100,000 per day, this issue would seem to deserve some reflection.[87]

Some consideration might also be given to assessing whether expensive procedures to assess checked baggage with elaborate machinery are cost-effective. As noted earlier, a bomb on a checked piece of luggage is likely to be able to bring down an airliner only if the luggage happens to be stowed at exactly the right (or wrong) place in the baggage compartment. Therefore, it is already a low-probability event, even if the timed or remote-controlled bomb does happen to explode. Expensive efforts to lower that likelihood further may be a sensible use of funds, given the costs and tragedy of an airliner loss, but it is an issue that should be investigated.

Reconsidering the Protection of Airports

Although there may be special reasons, as suggested earlier, to protect airplanes, it is not at all clear that there are any special reasons to protect airports. Compared with many other places of congregation, people are more dispersed in airports, and therefore, a terrorist attack is likely to kill far fewer than if, for example, a crowded stadium is targeted. The 2011 suicide bombing of the arrivals area of Moscow's Domodedovo airport, which killed 36 and injured 15 others, shows that airports are not unattractive targets, but in the previous year, suicide bombers targeted the Moscow metro, killing 25, and the year before that, derailed the Moscow to St. Petersburg high-speed train, killing 27.

In addition, airports sprawl and are only two or three stories high, and therefore damage to a portion is not likely to be nearly as significant as damage to a taller or more compact structure. Moreover, if a bomb does go off at an airport, the consequences would probably be comparatively easy to deal with: passengers could readily be routed around the damaged area, for example, and the impact on the essential function of the airport would be comparatively modest.

Assessing the Value, If Any, of Security Theater

It would be useful to fully explore the degree to which security theater may or may not be needed. If there is a measure that makes passengers feel substantially safer, it would have to be considered a benefit, even if the measure itself does not actually enhance security: to repeat Cass Sunstein's observation, "the reduction of even baseless fear is a social good."[88]

However, quite a few security measures presumably carry little theatrical value. For example, air marshals are not supposed to be identifiable by passengers (or terrorists, of course), and so the absence, or presence, of such people on a flight does nothing to affect feelings of security. Crew screening probably has a similar noneffect.

But there should be studies to determine if other measures are equally useless from this perspective. As noted, the relaxation of the ban on short, pointy objects does not seem to have enhanced fear or reduced passenger traffic. Would other such changes be acceptable? What would happen to fear levels and passenger traffic if security measures were severely reduced to, say, 2000 levels?

Many such issues could be studied in an experimental manner. For example, one might randomly assign passengers to security lines in which shoes must be taken off and to ones where that is not required and survey a sample of people in each line afterward to gauge their level of anxiety.[89]

Bringing Back Short-Haul Flying

Although the TSA sometimes claims that its measures stoke little resentment among passengers, there is good reason to believe otherwise. In 2007, when pilot Edward Smith put out a diatribe against airport security measures on his *New York Times* blog, it received hundreds of sympathetic comments from outraged passengers, mostly, it seems, from frequent-flying businesspeople.[90] Knowing that the expression of annoyance or frustration on a security line could trigger additional detention or inspection by TSA personnel, potentially causing them to miss their flight, they kept their views private there. However, they vengefully seized Smith's column as an opportunity to vent. The outrage over body-scanners and genital pat-downs that exploded at the end of 2010 gives further evidence of the problem.

This resentment, as suggested previously, can cause some people to avoid flying. Highly relevant is the important study by three Cornell University economists we mentioned earlier. They take note of the decline in short-haul flying since 2001, and attribute it primarily to delays caused by security measures.[91] They conclude that a result is that 500 Americans die each year because they accomplish their trips by the more dangerous automobile. As noted in chapter 2, this is considerably more death than has been visited by Muslim extremist terrorism worldwide since 9/11 outside of war zones.

There is an unspoken assumption by those in charge of airline security that, while their measures may sometimes be wasteful or inconvenient, they cause no harm. Clearly, this notion should be firmly reassessed by agencies charged with enhancing public safety.

Reconsidering General Aviation Restrictions

It seems likely that security restrictions on general aviation have been excessive—and therefore costly. Small planes are scarcely capable of doing the kind of damage that airliners can do. Richard L. Skinner, inspector general at DHS, concurs, observing that "general aviation presents only limited and mostly hypothetical threats to security."[92] Perhaps this is why the TSA plans to scale back a controversial plan to expand aviation security rules to thousands of private planes.[93]

A FULL EVALUATION OF AIRLINE SECURITY

Airline security consumes a major portion of the DHS budget, even as it exacts additional costs on the airlines and the public. It is also the area of activity that is most familiar to most people, and much of it is controversial.

In this chapter, we have sought to apply standard risk-analysis techniques to evaluate two aspects of TSA's layered approach to airline security: measures designed to prevent a direct replication of the 9/11 attacks and measures designed to prevent airliners from being blown up by body-borne explosives. As stressed in chapter 1, we decidedly do *not* argue that there will be no further terrorist attacks; rather, we focus on the net benefit of security measures and apply break-even cost-benefit analyses to assess how high the likelihood of a terrorist attack must be for security measures to be cost-effective. We also present our analysis in a fully transparent manner: readers who wish to challenge or vary our analysis and assumptions are provided with the information and data to do so.

Our analysis is not the end of the process, but a starting point. A complete risk analysis of airline security would, of course, need to be much more extensive, examining and evaluating in detail each of the security measures that have been initiated in an effort to make the skies safer from terrorist attack—canines, for example, or international cooperation, or those visible intermodal protection response teams. Some of these may well be worth the money (the cost-free passenger resistance layer is likely to pass with flying colors) while others may not be (the air marshals program seems unlikely to do well). That an agency with a budget approaching $10 billion a year appears to have failed to carry out this sort of elemental analysis is, well, rather depressing.

CHAPTER 8

Assessing Policing, Mitigation, Resilience

We have thus far applied widely accepted cost-benefit and risk analysis techniques to assess overall homeland security expenditures, that major portion of those expenditures designed to protect infrastructure (however "critical") and resources (however "key"), and those expenditures devoted to airline and aviation security. Given the limited capacity of the terrorists and the massive number of potential terrorist targets, we have found the quest to make the country less vulnerable to be a dubious enterprise, even quixotic. There may be a few specific protection measures among the many that have been massively enhanced since 2001 that make sense, but much of the effort, on reasonably close examination, seems to have been highly questionable.

However, although we find that the increase in overall spending on homeland security in the United States is not cost-effective, and although we find few protective measures that seem to pass a reasonable cost-effectiveness test, there may be some counterterrorism efforts that are cost-effective. These might include, or be found in, streams of homeland security spending only incidentally considered thus far: policing (or active defense), mitigation, and resilience (or absorption). The effectiveness of these measures is yet to be proven, but this book provides some of the tools to start the risk assessment process to identify which counterterrorism measures are effective and worthwhile and which are not, and in this chapter, we lay out some preliminary considerations for evaluating the effectiveness of policing, mitigation, and resilience.

POLICING

Some analysts, skeptical about protection measures—or passive defense—consider that, in contrast, there may be a cost-benefit payoff in active defense measures like policing and intelligence. Thus, Jeffrey Goldberg suggests that much of the money spent on airline security "would be better spent on the penetration of al-Qaeda social networks," and Bruce Schneier concludes that "the place where we can get the most leverage for our terrorism dollars" is "working with overseas police to roll up terrorist financing through effective intelligence."[1]

This seems plausible. Before an attack, standard policing methods of infiltration and surveillance may be able to uncover plots in preparatory stages. Since all, or nearly all, terrorist activities seem to require a conspiracy—that is, the participation of several people—the potential for leaks, detection of suspicious activity, and infiltration of informants is quite high. Policing can also be effective after an attack takes place. If it is not suicidal, one can seek to bring the attackers to justice, as in the case of the Madrid bombers. Even if it is suicidal, evidence from an attack or attempted attack can often aid police in tracing coconspirators, key suppliers, or instigators. Moreover, as with crime, repeated attacks or attempted attacks by a group are likely to establish patterns of operations that make them more predictable, and, unless they give up the game early, they are likely to make mistakes that lead to their apprehension.

Both Goldberg and Schneier stress the potential productivity of policing efforts *overseas*, where, as suggested in chapter 2, considerable successes have been achieved in rolling up, or rolling over, various terrorist cells and groups.[2] However, in this book, we are focusing on domestic homeland security expenditures and will consequently deal primarily with police and intelligence work within.

As noted in chapter 4, data from the Office of Management and Budget disclose that some 46 percent of the full total of "homeland security activities" in the United States focus on protecting people, infrastructure, and resources within the United States and its territories, while another 44 percent is devoted to "preventing and disrupting terrorist attacks" there. This latter activity includes "information sharing" among domestic governments, the private sector, and the public at large, but it does not include "most foreign intelligence collection," although it may make use of information gathered abroad.[3]

Although chasing after and gaining intelligence on terrorist networks certainly appears to be a useful undertaking, even this process should be evaluated systematically because of what seems to be the limited capacities of the terrorists. That is, given the low likelihood of a terrorist attack and the limited destruction it is likely to inflict, as discussed in chapters 2 and 3, are the massive enhancements in counterterrorism policing efforts cost-effective? Although there have been a considerable number of arrests, prosecutions, and apparent plot disruptions within the developed world over the post-9/11 decade, there also seems to have been a great deal of wasted effort in the massive accumulation of information and data. For example, the National Security Agency bombards the FBI with thousands of names, phone numbers, and e-mail addresses each month, and virtually all lead either to dead ends or to innocent Americans.[4] A recent *Washington Post* investigation points out that since 9/11 at least 263 military and intelligence agencies have been created or reorganized as a response to 9/11 and that the overload of reports is so great that it can actually be counterproductive, as "some policymakers and senior officials don't dare delve into the backup clogging their computers," relying instead on personal briefers.[5] As part of this process, the Department of Homeland Security has set up a vast array of "fusion centers," but it is unable to determine even for itself how much they cost.[6]

At any rate, a balanced assessment should be made of the issue, and we suggest that at least seven specific considerations should be embedded in it.

Civilian Surveillance

To begin with, after 9/11, the entire population, at no direct cost whatever, made itself into a surveillance force. Thus a specific tip from a Yemeni grocer eventually led to terrorism arrests in Miami, and a tip from a clerk in a video-duplicating establishment set an investigation going into a potential plot to raid Fort Dix in New Jersey. Sometimes people have even effectively made themselves into an active policing force: both the shoe bomber of 2001 and the underwear bomber of 2009 were forcibly and effectively interfered with by crew and passengers when they tried to set off their bombs on airliners.[7] One study conducted by a six-person research team surveyed 68 terrorist plots (both Islamist and non-Islamist) that were foiled in the United States between 1999 and 2009 and found that in 29 percent of them (19 or 20) the "initial clues" were supplied by the public.[8]

This surveillance force certainly (and especially) includes the Muslim community. Although the 9/11 conspirators wisely mostly avoided the Muslim community, homegrown terrorists or would-be terrorists have often foolishly failed to do so. Often, they have come out of it—and have been exposed in consequence. In fact, for 48 of the 120 instances in which Muslim Americans have been arrested for terrorism and in which the initial source of information has been disclosed, it came from the Muslim American community. Indeed, reports Charles Kurzman, "in some communities, Muslim-Americans have been so concerned about extremists in their midst that they have turned in people who turned out to be undercover informants."[9]

While it is true that civilian tipsters generally do their work free, processing the tips can still end up being rather costly. Specifically, any value that public awareness may have in the campaign against terrorism needs to be contrasted with the likely rather significant attendant costs of sorting through the haystack of tips, all of which need to be processed in one way or another: as the FBI's special counsel puts it, "Any terrorism lead has to be followed up.[10] A prominent example comes from the "If You See Something, Say Something" counterterrorism hotline run by the New York City police. It generates thousands of calls each year—8,999 in 2006 and more than 13,473 in 2007—but not one of these led to a terrorism arrest.[11] This could be taken to suggest that the tipster campaign has been something of a failure. Or perhaps it could be taken to suggest that there isn't all that much out there to be found. Undeterred by repeated failure, the number of calls then reportedly skyrocketed to 27,127 in 2008 before settling down some to 16,191 in 2009.[12] That would be 44 a day for the year, more than twice the number of success stories tallied over a decade, as trumpeted in the six-person survey. For its part, the FBI celebrated the receipt of its 2 millionth terrorism tip from the public in August 2008, though there seems to be no public information on whether these tips generally proved to be more useful than those supplied to the New York City police.[13]

It turns out that New York has received a trademark on its snappy slogan from the U.S. Patent and Trademark Office, and it has been willing to grant permission for its use by other organizations. However, it has refused permission sometimes because, according to a spokesman, "The intent of the slogan is to focus on terrorism activity, not crime, and we felt that use in other spheres would water down its effectiveness." Since it appears that the slogan has been *completely* ineffective at dealing with its supposed focus, terrorism, any watering down would appear, not to put too fine a point on it, impossible. In consequence, the irreverent may be led to wonder whether the $2 million to $3 million New York pays each year (much of it coming from grants from the federal government) to promote and publicize the hotline is perhaps not the wisest investment of taxpayer dollars.[14]

Those grants are likely to keep coming: in one of her early public announcements after becoming secretary of Homeland Security in 2009, Janet Napolitano indicated that she wanted to inspire even *more* participation by the public in the quest to ferret out terrorists.[15]

Limited Capacities

Many of those apprehended while planning to commit terrorism would probably have never actually been able to get either their act or their capacities together enough to carry out the deed. Hence, to have surveiled, arrested, tried, and jailed them has been, from a public policy perspective, a waste of resources; whatever the scope of their dire fantasies, they never would have done any (or much) damage anyway.

For example, James Dickey, in a book quite frankly impressed by the gritty prowess of New York's counterterrorism force, discusses a set of cases where homegrown people had been rolled up who were more or less plotting to blow up bombs or otherwise commit mayhem. In most, perhaps all, cases, concludes Dickey, the plotters were most notable for their boneheaded incompetence and disorganization and might never have pulled anything off.[16] No one can say for sure, of course, but for those cases where Dickey's suspicions would have proved sound, the policing effort and the costs of trial and incarceration can't be credited with having made us more secure. There is also the much-storied "Lackawanna Six," a group of guys, mostly disillusioned, who are accused of having gone to, and returned from, an al-Qaeda camp before 9/11, but not of even beginning to imagine committing violence in the United States.[17]

Inventing Terrorists

Others were significantly moved along the path to terrorism primarily by the efforts of informants—in many ways, the informants and their police patrons created terrorists. They close in on a hothead spouting violent jihadist bravado, create opportunities for him, set him up, and then arrest him when he pushes the (bogus) button they put before him. His intentions, or at least his thoughts, were foul, but his capacities suggest that, albeit dangerous in some sense, he might never have actually been able to do much of anything. Thus the hapless and impoverished would-be shopping mall bomber in Rockford, Illinois, pursued his quest because an FBI informant not only encouraged him but also promised to supply him, at a very favorable price (two used stereo speakers), with the weapons he needed to commit the deed.[18] Left to his own devices, it seems entirely possible he would never have done much of anything. As Karen J. Greenberg, executive director of the Center on Law and Security at the New York University of Law, observes of a case in New York: "They took people who might or might not commit hate crimes, and led them along the path to jihad."[19]

A problem here is policing terrorist intentions rather than their actions. The police do not scout out everyone who aspires to rob a bank, then provide him with the opportunity, and arrest him when he moves to carry out the actions they have choreographed. It would be an exceedingly expensive process and would result in very full jails since it seems likely that the number of people who aspire to rob a bank far exceeds the number who actually end up committing the crime. The same may hold for terrorism. But although the police do not spend time and effort creating bank robbers, they do essentially create terrorists in some cases.[20] And it may also be that as they get better and better at ferreting out and then subverting aspiring terrorists, the number of arrests will climb. It would be an increase more nearly attributable to policing that is more effective, or at any rate more aggressive, rather than to an increase in the actual number of terrorist plotters.[21]

Of course, there is no way to determine which of the people arrested for plotting terrorism would actually have done damage and which would have gone on to other things. However, there is little doubt that in many cases the informants' handiwork—supplying the would-be and gullible terrorist with a car or truck bomb or with antiaircraft missiles, for example—would be far beyond the capacity of the arrested.

In all this, the thoughtful words of analyst Brian Jenkins should be kept in mind. Many cases, he observes,

> may rest heavily on an interpretation of the ultimate intentions of the accused. That puts the American justice system perilously close to prosecuting people solely on the basis of what is in their hearts and on their minds. It is slippery terrain and not a domain where one ought to feel comfortable... informants can easily become *agents provocateurs*, subtly coaxing radicalized but hesitant individuals into action. Even without providing overt encouragement, the informant often plays the role of an enabler, offering people with extreme views but faint hearts the means to act, thereby potentially facilitating actions that otherwise might not occur.[22]

The Apprehension of Supporters of Terrorism Abroad

It should also be taken into consideration that many of the people arrested, tried, and incarcerated on terrorism charges were not planning to commit domestic terrorism at all but were focused on supporting or committing terrorism or other violence abroad. Thus, three of the five cases leading to arrests of "homegrown terrorists" in the last few months of 2009 involved foreign concerns: a recruiter of fighters to go to Somalia, a conspirator in an attack in India, and some Americans with plans to fight in Afghanistan who were arrested in Pakistan.[23] Another report, assessing the 50 "top plots" involving homegrown terrorists since 2001, finds that the plotter's targets were overseas in the third of the cases where a target could be identified.[24]

Rolling up these people may have been beneficial, but the process can scarcely be seen to have enhanced domestic security, although defenders of the policing efforts speculate that those going abroad might eventually return with enhanced skills and murderous intent.

Limited Capacity to Inflict Damage

Even if the aspiring domestic terrorists did try to pull off their plans (or fantasies), their track record suggests failure is far more likely than success. And even where successful, the consequences, while tragic, would probably have been far from monumental. Against the costs they might have been able to inflict must be balanced the costs of the efforts to find and apprehend them.

Preexisting Police Procedures and Capacities

Many of the policing techniques used to deal with terrorism after 9/11 were already funded and fully in place before that event and may not have needed much in the way of enhancement. Thus the investigative techniques—mostly, it seems, standard operating procedures—used by the New York police to capture the would-be Times Square bomber of 2010 were much the same as those used to find and arrest the people responsible for the failed attempt to topple one of the World Trade Center's towers in 1993.

Police do, of course, spend more time now worrying about terrorism and working on the problem, but there has long been a process of shifting focus without budgetary changes to threats that become current—against anarchists at one time, for example, or against the Weather Underground or the black power movement at another. And it is worth repeating the conclusion of Michael Sheehan, former New York City deputy commissioner for counterterrorism: "The most important work in protecting our country since 9/11 has been accomplished with the capacity that was in place when the event happened, not with any of the new capability bought since 9/11."[25]

Opportunity Cost

Finally, it seems imperative, as always, to take into consideration what else could have been done with the same money (an issue to be explored more broadly in the next chapter). Sheehan does take a refreshing no-nonsense approach to the subject of counterterrorism, and he has no trouble berating the tendency to spend "billions inside the Beltway on bloated bureaucracies and large-scale defensive measures that will most likely have little practical effect." But he goes on forcefully to fault other cities for failing to spend like New York on counterterrorism, complaining that they "are still under pressure to reduce street crime and are thus reluctant to put their best officers on terrorist investigations that may well come to naught." It is time, he continues, "to get beyond" such concerns.[26]

It is possible, of course, that funds spent on the vaporous, if dramatic, threat presented by terrorism will prove to be more cost-effective than funds spent on dealing with such distinctly nonvaporous concerns as street crime—some of which still exists even in Sheehan's beloved New York. But a systematic analysis of the issue is called for, not noisy posturing.

MITIGATION, RESILIENCE, ABSORPTION

Schneier supports spending on "emergency response and disaster relief," and Stephen Flynn puts this issue somewhat more broadly, arguing that it is important for society to become "resilient," arguing that "the more resilient we become as a society, the less consequential acts of terrorism become."[27] That is, particularly given the limited damage terrorism is likely to perpetrate, society should prepare itself to be able to absorb the effects, deal with them, keep things in perspective, and then, in an orderly manner, get on with its normal task without unnecessarily inflicting further damage on itself by excessive reaction or, as Flynn puts it, by "spooking" itself. To do otherwise is to play into the hands of the terrorists.

The quest here is laudable, but a reasonable discussion of how much money to spend on the process should accompany it.

Only about 9 percent of domestic homeland security expenditures are devoted to mitigation and resilience, and it is difficult to parse out which portions of these expenditures are devoted to which hazards because, obviously, enhancing the ability to respond quickly to emergencies and to have a better capacity for mitigating their consequences by rebounding from them is generally desirable for all hazards, not simply for the one presented by terrorism. Because terrorism is so rare and generally inflicts rather limited damage, it is not clear that all that much in the way of additional response preparedness is necessary to deal with the phenomenon. Emergencies, including ones caused by explosions or rampages by gunmen, are fairly common, of course, and police and other responders are generally poised to be diverted temporarily from other duties when an emergency occurs and to resume their normal work when it is over.

Conceivably, terrorism is of special concern in a few areas, particularly those focused on the deliberate use of nuclear or biological weapons. But terrorists are far more likely to use guns and explosives, and these scarcely present difficulties different from those presented by other hazards—including, of course, crime.

Moreover, as Frank Furedi points out, it often seems to be assumed that, contrary to experience, "resilience is not a normal state but the outcome of policies and programmes dedicated to its realization."[28] The British and Spanish rebounded quickly from the mass transit bombings of 2004 and 2005, and this has been widely attributed, in part, to their decades of experience battling homegrown terrorist movements. In terror-inflicted Israel, it is common procedure to clear up damage from terrorist attacks and to resume life as quickly as possible. The events of 9/11 came as a profound shock to the United States, but the public took foiled terrorist plots, including the 2009 underwear bomber and the 2010 Times Square bomber, pretty much in stride: as noted in chapter 7, there is little evidence of trip cancellation or other risk-averse behavior. It might be that the American public is becoming increasingly resilient and more in step with the behavior of their European counterparts. If so, it hasn't cost a dime.

To the degree that resilience is a normal state, its presence has important implications in counterterrorism strategies and expenditures. Instead of focusing on how to defeat terrorism, a resilient society can, as one commentator has put it, "endure terrorism much in the same way we endure road accidents. We face daily tragedies on our roads, yet these do not change the essential nature of our society."[29] Moreover, counterterrorism policies would not need to inspire resilience so much as be prepared to facilitate it when and if required, a process that can be quite inexpensive. Thus one analysis of bioterrorism points out that, although a biological attack could overwhelm hospital facilities, ordinary people, if properly instructed and supported, could use spare rooms in their homes to mitigate the results of an attack.[30]

Counterterrorism considerations have actually sometimes reduced the ability of specialist agencies to improve resilience while increasing the nation's vulnerability to natural hazards and perhaps to terrorist attack as well. The Federal Emergency Management Agency (FEMA) and many other government agencies were established with key responsibilities for disaster and emergency preparation and response, and these agencies were well in place before 9/11 and the homeland security obsessions it inspired. It was particularly renowned for its professional and community leadership in times of natural disasters. However, FEMA's incorporation into the Department of Homeland Security (DHS) in 2003 seriously impaired its effectiveness. According to a *Washington Post* report, two full years before the 2005 Katrina hurricane disaster, FEMA Director Michael Brown warned that plans forced on the organization by DHS would "break long-standing, effective and tested relationships with states and first responder stakeholders" and would result in "an ineffective and uncoordinated response to a terrorist attack or natural disaster." The infighting within DHS was so fierce that DHS Secretary Tom Ridge "stripped FEMA's power over billions of dollars worth of preparedness grants as well as the creation of a national disaster response plan. Most of the agency's top staff quit." And after taking over at DHS in February 2005, Michael Chertoff "decided to take away the rest of FEMA's preparedness duties."[31] No wonder, then, that FEMA failed so spectacularly to properly manage the response to Hurricane Katrina a few months later.

Evaluating Radiation Standards

We consider a terrorist atomic bomb attack to be highly unlikely. However, since many disagree, one might expect that there would be more public information disseminated about what to do if and when it happens— particularly about what to do if radiation levels significantly increase as a result of the explosion or, for that matter, as a result of a dirty bomb attack. But thus far, not much public information has been propagated on this.[32]

Radiological weapons or dirty bombs, in which radioactive materials are sprayed over an area by a conventional explosion, are often called "the poor man's nuclear weapon." However, unlike the rich man's version, they are incapable of inflicting much immediate damage at all, as noted in chapter 3. To repeat: it would be almost impossible to disperse radioactive material from a dirty bomb explosion so that victims would absorb a lethal dose before being able to leave the area, and it is likely that few, if any, in the target area would be killed directly, become ill, or even have a measurably increased risk of cancer.[33]

Accordingly, most analysts consider radiological devices to be more nearly weapons of mass disruption than of mass destruction. Dirty bombs simply raise radiation levels somewhat above normal background levels in a small area, something that would kill few, if any, people outright (perhaps some who happened to be nearby would be killed by the explosion itself). Accordingly, a common recommendation from nuclear scientists and engineers is that those exposed should calmly walk away. This bit of advice was not been advanced prominently (or even, perhaps, at all) by those in charge.

Effectively, therefore, they encourage panic, and the danger is, as one nuclear engineer puts it, "if you keep telling them you expect them to panic, they will oblige you. And that's what we're doing." Risk analyst Baruch Fischhoff, noting how rare real panic actually is, puts the issue most bluntly: "planning for panic" is at best "wasting resources on a future that is unlikely to happen," and at worst it "may be doing our enemies' work for them—while people are amazing under pressure, it cannot help to have predictions of panic drummed into them by supposed experts." Other specialists urge that the public should be "psychologically immunized" against a radiological attack through an extensive public education campaign stressing that such attacks rarely pose immediate threats to life.[34] It is surprising that the key facts about radiological weapons are so little known. Instead, the media and those in charge of our safety are content to let disinformation about the weapons' effect stand whether by implication or by default.

As part of this, there ought as well to be discussions assessing the standards now in place for determining when an area has become radiologically "contaminated." Agencies have evaluated radiation doses known to be lethal and have assumed that lesser doses are also harmful in proportionate degree: a dose one-tenth the size of a lethal one will be one-tenth as harmful. Questions have been raised about whether this procedure is justified.[35] In fact, the General Accountability Office in 2000 concluded that standards administered to protect the public from low-level radiation exposure "do not have a conclusive scientific basis, despite decades of research."[36] To return a contaminated area to acceptable radiation levels might in principle require expensive evacuation and decontamination procedures.

Estimates for the average background radiation routinely endured by people in the United States range from 3.00 to 3.60 millisieverts (mSv) per year, and the comparable figure for the United Kingdom is 2.70 mSv per year. Yet in both countries, agencies have declared a rise of more than 1 mSv per year above background levels to be unacceptable to individual members of the public.[37] A 1 mSv per year dose, according to standard models, increases the risk of cancer by a miniscule 0.004 percent[38] and is comparable to moving from the seacoast to a mountain in Colorado.[39] On the other hand, the dose limits for nuclear power plant workers is 50 times higher than that of the public, on the assumption that the risk is voluntary and that regular monitoring will reveal early signs of ill health. The U.S. Nuclear Regulatory Commission's mandated occupational dose limit of 50 mSv per year would increase an individual worker's chance of eventually contracting cancer by only 0.2 percent.[40] In the event of a radiological terrorist attack, the dose limit definition of *contaminated* might well be that adopted for worker safety, at least in the short term, after which regular monitoring of the public might warrant a review of dose limits, medical treatment, or evacuation.

This is a difficult issue to work with and certainly highly controversial, both among the public and among specialists. However, there are indications that DHS has from time to time toyed with the notion of reevaluating cleanup standards—which currently require that radiation leaks to be reduced to 15 percent of the amount of radiation that is routinely emitted by building materials in the U.S. Capitol and therefore is equally routinely absorbed by people working there. Overly strict rules, says one of the guideline examiners, only aids and abets the terrorists.[41]

Avoiding Overreaction

As has been suggested at various points in this book, avoiding overreaction, which requires no expenditure whatever, is by far the most cost-effective counterterrorism measure imaginable.

Terrorism can inspire self-destructive overreaction like no other hazard, and this can be massively costly—the two wars impelled or facilitated by 9/11 are only the most vivid examples. Indeed, the costs of overreaction can be far higher than those inflicted by the terrorists themselves—as they were even for 9/11, by far the most destructive terrorist act in history.[42] Osama bin Laden gloated over this phenomenon and claimed his goal was to bleed America into bankruptcy, something only the United States could do to itself.[43]

There would be no problem at all, of course, if decision makers are able to contain their temptation to overreact and engage in enterprises that do not reduce the terrorism risk nearly as much as they cost. As Sheehan puts it, "We mustn't overreact," pointing out that "it's in the national best interest to simply get over it."[44]

The notion that this may be the case seems only slowly to be dawning on people considering terrorism, but the trend may be positive. In 2004, Flynn began an article by dramatically proclaiming that the United States is "living on borrowed time—and squandering it" and ended the article with a warning about the "long, deadly struggle against terrorism." He also admitted that he often labored under a sense of despair and dread and suggested that officials must assume that terrorists will "soon" launch attacks far deadlier and more disruptive than those of 9/11.[45] Late in the same year, he contributed to an op-ed article vividly titled "'Our Hair Is on Fire,'" declaring that al-Qaeda had both the ability and the intent to detonate a weapon of mass destruction in the United States and envisioning graves by the hundreds of thousands, the collapse of the economy, and "perhaps a fatal blow to our way of life."[46] However, by 2010, he was arguing that the greatest threat from terrorism "comes from what we would do to ourselves when we are spooked" and that is it this "that makes it an appealing tool for our adversaries."[47]

In early 2005, Richard Clarke, counterterrorism coordinator from the Clinton administration, issued a scenario that appeared as a cover story in the *Atlantic* in which he darkly envisioned shootings at casinos, campgrounds, theme parks, and malls in 2005, bombings in subways and railroads in 2006, missile attacks on airliners in 2007, and devastating cyberattacks in 2008.[48] By 2010, however, he was advocating that "we should not adopt procedures that inconvenience the public more than they do the terrorists and amount to little more than security theater," that "those who seek political gain from the murder of Americans" should be "regarded as despicable," and that, should terrorists successfully attack again, we should "refine our tactics and procedures" but "not overreact." To do this, however, notes Clarke, would require "a good dose" of that oxymoronic commodity "political courage."[49]

But we are into the realm of politics now, a key consideration of the final chapter.

CHAPTER 9

Conclusions and Political Realities

We have sought in this book to evaluate the cost-effectiveness of the enhanced expenditures on overall homeland security measures that have taken place since 9/11 (chapters 2–4) and then more specifically on measures designed to protect (chapters 5–7). Finally, we have put forward some comments about evaluating policing and intelligence matters, as well as ones concerning mitigation, resilience, and overreaction (chapter 8). In doing so, we have applied standard risk and cost-benefit evaluation techniques that have been accepted and used throughout the world for decades by regulators, academics, businesses, and governments, and we have presented our analysis in a fully transparent manner.

Our key conclusion is that, given the quite limited hazard terrorism presents, enhanced expenditures designed to lower it have been excessive, sometimes massively so. We are in agreement, then, with security expert Bruce Schneier when he concludes, "In general, the costs of counterterrorism are simply too great for the security we're getting in return, and the risks don't warrant the extreme trade-offs we've been asked to make."[1] Or as Michael Sheehan puts it, although "gargantuan budgets" will enhance our capability over time, "the cost-benefit ratio does not compute favorably."[2]

We have not examined every aspect of enhanced homeland security in equal depth, but it is difficult to find many expenditures that, on balance, have clearly been a net benefit. Most enhanced homeland security expenditures since 9/11 fail a cost-benefit assessment, it seems, some spectacularly so, and it certainly appears that many billions of dollars have been misspent.

Increases in homeland security expenditures since 9/11 have, of course, been predominantly inspired by much heightened fears of terrorism, not by growing concerns about other hazards; as Veronique de Rugy has noted, by 2008 federal spending on counterterrorism had increased enormously, while protection for such comparable risks as fraud and violent crime had not, to the point where homeland security expenditures had outpaced spending on all crime by $15 billion.[3] It is possible that a systematic cost-benefit analysis of pre-9/11 expenditures on terrorism would uncover some additional areas in which there was excessive spending, but we have not done that analysis here. For now, our conclusion is that judiciously scaling back counterterrorism spending makes a great deal of sense. And increases in those expenditures seem ill-advised, unless perhaps they promise a notable improvement of security at very low cost.

We are not arguing that much of homeland security spending is wasteful because we believe there will be no more terrorist attacks in the United States or other Western countries. Like crime and vandalism, terrorism will always be a feature of life, and a condition of zero vulnerability is impossible to achieve. However, future attacks might not be as devastating as 9/11, as evidenced by the attacks on Western targets in the ten years since 9/11. Although tragic, each has claimed victims numbering in the tens to a few hundred—and none, certainly, has posed an existential threat. The frequency and severity of terrorist attacks are low, very low in fact, which makes the benefits of enhanced counterterrorism expenditures of a trillion dollars since 9/11 challenging, to say the least, to justify by any rational and accepted standard of cost-benefit analysis.

The 2004 article noted in chapter 8 in which Stephen Flynn proclaimed the United States to be "living on borrowed time—and squandering it" and warned about the "long, deadly struggle against terrorism" also includes something of a midcourse correction. In seeking to supply a standard for "how much security is enough," he suggested that that happy moment would come about when "the American people can conclude that a future attack on U.S. soil will be an exceptional event that does not require wholesale changes in how they go about their lives."[4] It seems reasonable to suggest that they can so conclude right now—and, for that matter, could have done so in 2004.

The Department of Homeland Security has come under close and critical scrutiny in this book, and it perhaps epitomizes many of the failings of the process. But it has a lot of company. Many other state and federal agencies apply similar sounding rhetoric, spend lavishly on security, and often pay little attention to the assessment of risk in order to allow objective measures of their performance. For example, Benjamin Friedman, after examining an important U.S. Defense Department policy document, notes that it "does not estimate the threats' likelihoods and recommend focusing on one or another on that basis." Rather, "it contends simply that 'managing risk' compels the United States to prepare for all of them. . . . It then recommends that we retain the weapons and forces we have, with a few tweaks."[5]

In this final chapter, we add a few additional considerations to the discussion. In particular, we take on the issue of the political context and constraints in which homeland security decisions must, of necessity, be made. We also seek to broaden the discussion by placing counterterrorism expenditures in the context of other expenditures designed to advance human welfare, many of them likely to be far more cost-effective. Finally, we consider the possibility that, given the way the terrorist threat has been internalized, and comparing the phenomenon with the quest for domestic Communists during the Cold War, it may essentially be impossible to alter public policy on this issue coherently. Accordingly, vast sums of money will continue to be misspent.

POLITICAL REALITIES

Politicians and bureaucrats do, of course, face considerable political pressure on the terrorism issue. In particular, they are fully wary of the fact that Jeffrey Rosen is onto something when he suggests that "we have come to believe that life is risk-free and that, if something bad happens, there must be a government official to blame."[6]

The dilemma is nicely parsed by James Fallows. He points out that "the political incentives here work only one way." A politician who supports more extravagant counterterrorism measures "can never be proven wrong" because an absence of attacks shows that the "measures have 'worked,'" and a new attack shows that we "must go farther still." Conversely, a politician seeking to limit expenditure "can never be proven 'right,'" and "any future attack will always and forever be that politician's 'fault.'" Or in the words of Michael Sheehan, "No terrorism expert or government leader wants to appear soft on terrorism. It's always safer to predict the worst; if nothing happens, the exaggerators are rarely held accountable for their nightmare scenarios."[7]

Thus politicians and bureaucrats have an incentive to pass along vague and unconfirmed threats to protect themselves from later criticism, should another attack take place. Bureaucrats have an additional incentive in that, if people come to devalue terrorism as a threat, there is a logical corollary suggesting that perhaps the agency's budget should be cut. In a speech at a Washington think tank in 2006, Homeland Security Secretary Michael Chertoff remarked, "I've never heard anyone say the Department is over-funded. Well, actually some people *do* say that—but no one *in* the Depart-ment has ever said that."[8] He got a laugh from his savvy audience, of course.

In Friedman's view, the problem is quite general not only in government and political agencies but also in associated think tanks: "The path of least resistance is to write about how to control a danger instead of evaluating its magnitude." And although such analysts "rarely take orders," at the same time "few offer analysis that harms their benefactors." It is a rare bureaucrat or expert, he contends, who "will voice opinions harmful to his organiza-tion or prospects for appointment, but even fewer will offer those opinions without being asked, and few policy-makers will ask."[9]

The political dilemma could be seen in full flower in two episodes during the 2004 presidential campaign in the United States. In September, George W. Bush, as columnist Gwynne Dyer sardonically noted, had "a brush with the truth" by opining that the war on terror could not be won but that conditions could be changed to make terrorism less acceptable in some parts of the world. "This heroic attempt to grapple with reality," notes Dyer, "was a welcome departure from Bush's usual style," but his Democratic opponents quickly pounced, declaring irrelevantly, "What if President Reagan had said that it may be difficult to win the war against Communism?" Bush promptly fled to safer ground, intoning in a later speech, "We meet today in a time of war for our country, a war we did not start, yet one that we will win."[10] Then in October, it was his opponent's turn. In an interview, John Kerry suggested, presumably by accident, that Americans would be able "to feel safe again" when we "get back to the place we were, where terrorists are not the focus of our lives, but they're a nuisance," reducing it "to a level where it isn't on the rise," where "it isn't threatening people's lives every day," and where "it's not threatening the fabric of your life." Bush and Vice President Dick Cheney jumped on that one, declaring it to be proof that Kerry was "unfit to lead." Kerry, sobered, was soon back to his more usual macho mantra: "I do not fault George Bush for doing too much in the War on Terror, I believe he's done too little." He has "no comprehensive strategy for victory in the War on Terror—only an ad hoc strategy to keep our enemies at bay," whereas, "if I am Commander-in-Chief, I would wage that war by putting in place a strategy to win it."[11]

However, nothing in all this relieves politicians and bureaucrats of the fundamental responsibility of informing the public honestly and accurately of the risk that terrorism presents. In 2002, when it was still in the process of being formed, the Department of Homeland Security officially intoned on the first page of its defining manifesto: "Today's terrorists can strike at any place, at any time, and with virtually any weapon."[12] This warning may be true in some sense (depending on how "virtually" is defined), but it should logically be followed by a sentence pointing out that, at present rates, anyone living outside a war zone stands 1 chance in 85,000 of being killed by terrorism over an 80-year period. But that second sentence never appears. Daniel Gardner notes that the failure of Bush administration "to put the risk in perspective was total."[13] That continues to be the case with the new one.

Instead, the emphasis has been on exacerbating fears. As Friedman aptly notes, "For questionable gains in preparedness, we spread paranoia" and facilitate the bureaucratically and politically appealing notion that "if the threat is everywhere, you must spend everywhere," while developing and perpetrating the myth, or at least the impression, that the terrorists are omnipotent and omnipresent.[14]

Thus it was in 2003 that Homeland Security Secretary Tom Ridge divined that "extremists abroad are anticipating near-term attacks that they believe will either rival, or exceed" those of 2001. And in 2004, Attorney General John Ashcroft, with FBI Director Robert Mueller at his side, announced that "credible intelligence from multiple sources indicates that al Qaeda plans to attempt an attack on the United States in the next few months," that its "specific intention" was to hit us "hard," and that the "arrangements" for that attack were already 90 percent complete.[15] (Oddly enough, Ashcroft fails to mention this memorable headline-grabbing episode in *Never Again*, his 2006 memoir of the period.)

In 2003, as noted in the introduction, Director Mueller reported that, although his agency had yet actually to identify an al-Qaeda cell in the United States, such unidentified (or imagined) entities nonetheless presented "the greatest threat," had "developed a support infrastructure" in the country, and had achieved both the "ability" and the "intent" to inflict "significant casualties in the US with little warning." At the time, not only were officials insisting that the number of trained al-Qaeda operatives in the United States was between 2,000 and 5,000 but also that cells were "embedded in most U.S. cities with sizable Islamic communities," usually in the "run-down sections," that they were "up and active," and that electronic intercepts had found some to be "talking to each other."[16] In 2005, at a time when the FBI admitted it *still* had been unable to unearth a single true al-Qaeda cell, Mueller continued his dire I-think-therefore-they-are projections: "I remain very concerned about what we are not seeing," he ominously ruminated. Needless to say, the media remained fully in step. Thus, on the fifth anniversary of 9/11, ABC's Charles Gibson dutifully intoned, "Putting your child on a school bus or driving across a bridge or just going to the mall—each of these things is a small act of courage—and peril is a part of everyday life."[17]

It should be stressed that terrorism-induced fears can be debilitating. For one thing, they can cause people to routinely adopt skittish, overly risk-averse behavior, at least for a while, and this can much magnify the impact of the terrorist attack, particularly economically. That is, the problem is not that people are trampling each other in a rush to vacate New York or Washington, but rather that they may widely adopt other forms of defensive behavior, the cumulative costs of which can be considerable. As Cass Sunstein notes, "In the context of terrorism, fear is likely to make people reluctant to engage in certain activities, such as flying on airplanes and appearing in public places," and "the resulting costs can be extremely high."[18]

Fear and anxiety can also have negative health consequences: Virtually any list of tips on how to live longer includes the admonition to "avoid stress." Physician Marc Siegel discusses a study that found Israeli women fearful of terrorism "had twice as high a level of an enzyme that correlates with heart disease, compared with their less fearful compatriots." A notable, if extreme, example of how severe such health effects can be comes from extensive studies conducted of the Chernobyl nuclear disaster that occurred in the Soviet Union in 1986. The largest health consequences came not from the accident itself (fewer than 50 people died directly from radiation exposure), but from the negative and often life-expectancy-reducing impact on the mental health of people traumatized by relocation and by lingering, and greatly exaggerated, fears that they would soon die of cancer. In the end, lifestyle afflictions like alcoholism, drug abuse, chronic anxiety, and fatalism have posed a much greater threat to health and essentially have killed far more people than exposure to Chernobyl's radiation. The mental health impact of 9/11 is, of course, unlikely to prove as extensive, but one study found that 17 percent of the American population outside New York City was still reporting symptoms of September 11–related posttraumatic stress two months after the attacks. And a later study found that those fearful of terrorism after 9/11 were three to five times more likely than others to be diagnosed with new cardiovascular ailments over the next several years.[19]

After conducting a national survey on the subject, risk analyst Baruch Fischhoff concluded that "Americans want honest and accurate information about terror-related situations, even if that information worries them."[20] Yet, despite the importance to responsible policy of seeking to communicate risk and despite the costs of irresponsible fearmongering, just about the *only* official who has *ever* openly put the threat presented by terrorism in some sort of context is, as noted in chapter 1, New York's Mayor Michael Bloomberg, who in 2007 pointed out that people should "get a life" and that they have a greater chance of being hit by lightning than of being struck by terrorism—an observation that, as table 2.4 suggests, may be a bit off the mark but is roughly sound.[21]

Things are not much better in the media. There seemed to be a brief glimmer on the December 28, 2009, PBS *NewsHour* when Gwen Ifill, in introducing a segment on the then-recent underwear bomber attempt to down an airliner, actually happened to note that the number of terrorist incidents on American airliners over the previous decade was 1 for every 16.5 million flights.[22] This interesting bit of information, however, was never brought up again either by Ifill or by the three terrorism experts she was interviewing. Nor, of course, did anyone think of suggesting that, at that rate, maybe the airlines are already safe enough.

In 2007, CIA Director Tenet revealed on CBS's *60 Minutes* that his "operational intuition" was telling him that al-Qaeda had "infiltrated a second wave or a third wave into the United States at the time of 9/11," though he added, "Can I prove it to you? No." (One might think that aging members of that wave would have since had a great incentive to actually *do* something since the longer they linger, the greater the likelihood they will be exposed and caught.) And DHS Secretary Michael Chertoff informed us a few months later that his gut was telling him there'd be an attack that summer. It would seem that when officials responsible for public safety issue fear-inducing proclamations based *by their own admission* on nothing, they should be held to account. As Ian Lustick puts it, the government "can never make enough progress toward 'protecting America' to reassure Americans against the fears it is helping to stoke." The result, as Bart Kosko points out, is a situation in which "government plays safe by overestimating the terrorist threat, while the terrorists oblige by overestimating their power."[23]

Spending on Counterterrorism

Political realities do present an understandable excuse for expending money, but not a valid one. In particular, they do not relieve officials of the responsibility of seeking to expend public funds wisely. Notes David Banks, "If terrorists force us to redirect resources away from sensible programs and future growth in order to pursue unachievable but politically popular levels of domestic security, then they have won an important victory that mortgages our future."[24]

Although political pressures may force actions and expenditures that are unwise, however, they usually do not precisely dictate the level of expenditure. Thus, despite public demands to "do something" about terrorism, nothing in that demand specifically requires removing shoes in airport security lines, requiring passports to enter Canada, spreading bollards like dandelions, or making a huge number of buildings into forbidding fortresses.

As noted in chapter 4, the United Kingdom, which seems to face an internal threat from terrorism that is considerably greater than that for the United States, appears nonetheless to spend proportionately much less than half as much on homeland security, and the same holds for Canada and Australia. Yet politicians and bureaucrats there do not seem to suffer threats to their positions or other political problems because of it.

As this may suggest, it is possible politicians and bureaucrats are overly fearful about the political consequences.

British, Canadian, and Australian officials have often used urgent American-style rhetoric about the threat of terrorism: it was very much a defining issue for Australian Prime Minister John Howard, for example. But while government expenditures on homeland security increased modestly and tougher counterterrorism legislation passed in parliament, the funding never matched his rhetoric about "safeguarding Australia." In contrast, the United States has matched rhetoric with phenomenal rises in homeland security spending with no apparent resulting marked increase in risk reduction and with no more apparent electoral gain to show for it than their Australian counterparts who talked equally big while doing much less.

Is Overreaction Required?

Although it is often argued that there is a political imperative for public officials to do something (which usually means overreact) when a dramatic terrorist event takes place—"You can't just not do anything"—history

clearly demonstrates that overreaction is not necessarily required. Sometimes, in fact, leaders have been able to restrain their instinct to overreact. Even more important, restrained reaction—or even capitulation
to terrorist acts—has often proved to be entirely acceptable politically.
That is, leaders have often done little or nothing after a terrorist attack
(or at least refrained from overreacting) and have not suffered politically
or otherwise.

Consider, for example, the two instances of terrorism that killed the
most Americans before September 2001. Ronald Reagan's response to
the first of these, the 1983 suicide bombing in Lebanon that resulted in
the deaths of 241 American Marines, was to make a few speeches and
eventually to pull the troops out. The venture seems to have had no negative impact on his reelection a few months later. The other was the
December 1988 bombing of a Pan Am airliner over Lockerbie, Scotland,
in which 187 Americans perished. Perhaps in part because this dramatic
and tragic event took place after the elections that year, the official
response, beyond seeking compensation for the victims, was simply to
apply meticulous police work in an effort to tag the culprits, a process
that bore fruit only three years later and then only because of an unlikely
bit of luck.[25] But that cautious, even laid-back, response proved to be entirely acceptable politically.

Similarly, after an unacceptable loss of American lives in Somalia in 1993,
Bill Clinton responded by withdrawing the troops without noticeable
negative impact on his 1996 reelection bid. Although Clinton reacted with
(apparently counterproductive) military retaliations after the two U.S. embassies were bombed in Africa in 1998 as discussed in chapter 2, his administration did not have a notable response to terrorist attacks on American
targets in Saudi Arabia (Khobar Towers) in 1996 or to the bombing of the
USS *Cole* in 2000, and these nonresponses never caused it political pain.
George W. Bush's response to the anthrax attacks of 2001 did include a
costly and wasteful stocking up of anthrax vaccine and enormous extra
spending by the U.S. Post Office. However, beyond that, it was the same as
Clinton's had been to the terrorist attacks against the World Trade Center in
1993 and in Oklahoma City in 1995 and the same as the one applied in
Spain when terrorists bombed trains there in 2004 or in Britain after attacks
in 2005: the dedicated application of police work to try to apprehend the
perpetrators. This approach proved to be entirely acceptable politically.
Similarly, the Indian government was able to neglect popular demands for
retaliatory attacks on Pakistan for the damage inflicted on Mumbai in 2008
by terrorists based there.[26]

Thus, despite short-term demands that some sort of action must be taken, experience suggests politicians can often successfully ride out this demand after the obligatory and essentially cost-free expressions of outrage are prominently issued.

It is true that few voters spend a great amount of time following the ins and outs of policy issues and even fewer are certifiable policy wonks. But they *are* grown-ups, and it is just possible they would respond reasonably to an adult conversation about terrorism. That has certainly been our experience in lectures and talks over the years. As noted in chapter 2, analyst Gregory Treverton says he found that his observation "Anyone's probability of being killed by a terrorist today was essentially zero and would be tomorrow, barring a major discontinuity" proved to be "hardly satisfying" to his audiences. That has not been our experience at all.

Thus both Bush and Kerry *assumed* in 2004 that there was danger in asserting that the battle against terrorism could never be decisively "won" or that policy should seek to reduce terrorism to where it would be at most a "nuisance." But while they quickly backed away from their unconventional comments, it is not at all clear they would have lost votes by continuing to issue such patently true statements. After all, Mayor Bloomberg's "get a life" outburst in 2007 did not have negative consequences for him. He is still in office, and, although he had some difficulties in his reelection two years later, his blunt comments about terrorism were not the cause.[27]

It may well be, as suggested in chapter 7, that there is also a tendency to assume that the outsize reaction to 9/11 will necessarily be repeated if there is another attack in the United States. However, London experienced a double hit in 2005: attacks on the underground two weeks apart (of which only the first was successful). But the politicians in charge survived. Also potentially relevant here is the fact that terrorist attacks on resort areas in Bali in 2002 had a far larger negative impact on tourism than did subsequent ones in 2005. Anecdotal sources state that there was "a mass exodus to the airport" in 2002 but not in 2005. After the later attacks, Robert Kelsali, chairman of the Bali Hotel Association, said: "We do expect some cancellations but nothing like on the scale of 2002."[28] And an analysis of foreign visitor arrivals in Bali confirms this: foreign visitor numbers dropped by nearly 300,000 in the year following the 2002 attack but only by 125,000 following the 2005 attack. By 2008, foreign arrivals were 46 percent higher than in 2001.[29]

Interesting in this regard is the remarkably muted reaction of the American public (and media) to the 2009 shootings by a Muslim psychiatrist at Fort Hood, Texas, that killed 13 and injured 30 more. Although this could be considered an act of a deranged man, it is generally taken to be a case of Islamic terrorism, and it is by far the worst since 9/11 in the United States. Although obviously far less costly than the earlier terrorist event, it could have been taken to be the next step in a terrorist onslaught—something that Americans have long been ominously waiting for. However, it failed to generate much outrage or demand for an outsize response. Indeed, a year later, it was scarcely remembered, as when the prominent journalist James Fallows mused about raising "the *certainty* that some day another terrorist attack will succeed" without noting that one had already taken place.[30]

Then in 2010, President Barack Obama candidly observed to *Washington Post* reporter Bob Woodward, "We can absorb a terrorist attack. We'll do everything we can to prevent it, but even a 9/11, even the biggest attack ever . . . we absorbed it and we are stronger."[31] This may have been the first time any official acknowledged the issue in public, and Obama even used the unpleasant word *absorb* rather than the more politically correct *resilient*. Obama's highly unconventional statement drew great attention in the press, but it hardly seems to have hurt the president's effectiveness or approval ratings.

THE TRADE-OFFS, OPPORTUNITY COSTS

Risk reduction measures that produce little or no net benefit to society or produce it at a very high cost cannot be justified on rational life-safety and economic grounds—they are not only irresponsible but also, essentially, immoral. When we spend resources on regulations that save lives at a high cost, we forgo the opportunity to spend those same resources on regulations and processes that can save more lives at the same cost or even at a lower one.[32] Homeland security expenditures invested in a wide range of more cost-effective risk reduction programs like flood protection, vaccination and screening, vehicle and road safety, health care, and occupational health and safety would probably result in far more significant benefits to society.

For example, diverting a few percent of the nearly $10 billion per year spent on airline security could save many lives at a fraction of the cost. Specifically, the money would be more effective—save far more lives—if it were instead spent on:

- Seat belts at a cost of $40,000 per life saved[33]
- Bicycle helmets for children at a cost of $120,000 per life saved[34]

- Tandem mass spectrometry screening program at a cost of $800,000 per life saved[35]
- Adult bike helmets for adults at a cost of $1 million per life saved[36]
- Front air bags at a cost of $2 million per life saved[37]
- Smoke alarms at a cost of $2 million per life saved[38]
- Tornado shelters at a cost of $6 million per life saved[39]

There are countless examples where governments can invest wisely in programs that provide a net lifesaving benefit to society. One more: a $27 billion flood protection system for New Orleans would reap benefits of more than $35 billion, including saving more than 1,000 lives.[40]

If diversions of funds like that would easily save many hundreds, if not thousands, of lives over time, a government obliged to allocate funds in a manner that best benefits society must explain why it is spending billions of dollars on security measures with very little proven benefit and why that policy is something other than a reckless waste of resources. This disregard of basic cost-benefit considerations not only wastes money but also costs lives, potentially in the thousands every year.

It may be useful in this light to put counterterrorism expenditures in the broadest comparative context. Bjorn Lomborg assembled a group of international experts to answer one question: "if we had an extra $75 billion to put to good use, which problems would we solve first?"[41] As our Trillion Dollar Table (1.2 on p. 4) indicates, this is less than what the United States spends on homeland security in a single year. More than 40 experts, tasked to do "what is rational instead of what is fashionable," applied cost-benefit thinking to a wide range of issues. The top ten overall solutions are given in table 9.1. The costs are modest, with most requiring expenditures of not just less than $75 billion but less than $1 billion. Yet the benefit is ten times greater than the cost in nearly every instance, and, most important, the number of lives saved is spectacular. According to these analysts, an investment of merely $2 billion could save more than 1.5 million lives: 1 million child deaths could be averted by expanded immunization coverage, and community-based nutrition programs could save another half a million.

In assessing expenditures for dealing with transnational terrorism, by contrast, costs were found by the experts to be 3 to 25 times higher than any benefits, except possibly for efforts to generate greater international cooperation on intelligence gathering and policing, where benefits were found to exceed costs—but only when the estimates behind the calculations were based on "heroic assumptions."[42]

In table 9.1, we have extended this consideration by providing comparable information about the lives saved and the benefit-to-cost ratio for

Table 9.1 COMPARISON OF RISK-REDUCING MEASURES

Rank	Risk-Reducing Measure	Numbers Affected (million)	Cost ($ million)	Lives Saved per Year	Benefits ($ million)	Benefit to Cost Ratio
1	Micronutrient supplements for children (vitamin A and zinc)	69.8	$60.4	12,000	$1,040	17.3
2	The Doha development agenda[1]	World	$154,000–$456,000		$173–$424 trillion	932–1121
3	Micronutrient fortification (from iron and salt iodization)	2,603	$286		$2,706	9.5
4	Expanded immunization coverage for children		$1,000	1,000,000	$20,000	20.0
5	Biofortification (plant breeding)[2]	36 countries	$60	50,000	$1,000	16.7
6	De-worming and other nutrition programs at schools	53	$26.5	–	$159	6.0
7	Lowering the price of schooling	Uganda	$140 per student per year		$3,675 per student per year	26.3
8	Increase and improve girls' schooling by 1 year	4.4	$9,269		$1,000	9.3
9	Community-based nutrition program	114	$798	500,000	$10,000	12.5
10	Provide support for women's reproductive role (routine maternity care)	2,060	$18,183	310,000	$213,577	11.7
Terrorism: US with a risk reduction of 45%						
	Mass transit attack: 50% yearly attack probability, $5 billion loss, 100 fatalities		$75,000	22.5	$1,125	0.015
	9/11 type attack: 10% yearly attack probability, $200 billion loss, 3,000 fatalities		$75,000	135	$9,000	0.12
	Nuclear attack: 10% yearly attack probability, $1 trillion losses, 100,000 fatalities		$75,000	4,500	$45,000	0.60

Source for the first ten: Lomborg 2009.
[1] World Trade Organization negotiations to lower trade barriers around the world, allowing countries to increase trade globally.
[2] A method of breeding crops to increase their nutritional value.

three terrorism attack scenarios in the United States. An expenditure of $75 billion per year would save at the very most 4,500 lives per year for a dire nuclear scenario. Spending on a more credible mass transit attack would save about 20 lives each year, the same as would be saved if everyone in the United States were to avoid driving in automobiles for six hours.[43] If a miserly $2 billion were redirected from the homeland security budget, the likelihood and consequences of such attacks would hardly change, but anywhere from 300 to 60,000 times more lives—albeit not necessarily American or Western ones—would be saved by instead spending the funds on the risk-reducing measures in the upper part of the list.

THE SELF-LICKING ICE CREAM CONE

In all this, however, it may be too late for careful cost-benefit analyses or for the judicious comparison of trade-offs and opportunity costs. Although it is possible the killing of Osama bin Laden in 2011 will begin to alter perspectives, homeland security has become, in venerable Washington parlance, a self-licking ice cream cone. It has become conventional, unexceptionable, and self-perpetuating.

Accordingly, homeland security and its attendant expenses may be with us for a very long time, even if there are no more terrorist acts to impel it along. The war on terror, at least in its domestic, homeland security aspects, has been fully launched and shows clear signs of having developed into a popularly supported governmental perpetual motion (or perpetual emotion) machine that has comfortably settled in for the long term.

What has happened is that terrorism and the attendant "war" thereon have become internalized—fully embedded in the public consciousness—with the effect that politicians and bureaucrats seem to have come to fear being accused of being soft on terrorism. Such fears may be unjustified, as we have argued here, but their existence—and continued existence—is likely to persist.

The Communist Comparison

The parallel is with comparable fears of being labeled soft on Communism during the Cold War. Impelled by several spectacular espionage cases and by an apparently risky international environment, fears about the dangers presented by the enemy within became fully internalized in the years after World War II. In a famous public opinion study conducted at the height of the McCarthy period in the mid-1950s, sociologist Samuel Stouffer found that 43 percent professed to believe that domestic Communists presented a great or very great danger to the United States (see figure 9.1). At the same time, however, when Stouffer asked more broadly about their primary worries, people mainly voiced concerns about personal matters. Unprompted, apprehensions about domestic Communism (or about restrictions on civil liberties) scarcely came up in the survey. There was, Stouffer concluded, no "national anxiety neurosis" over the issue.[44]

Problems arise, however, not from a national anxiety neurosis, but more from other results of the concern. One, already discussed, is that when a consensus about a threat becomes really internalized, it becomes—or seems to become—politically unwise to oppose it or even seem to oppose it. Another is that the internalized consensus creates a political atmosphere in which government and assorted pork barrelers and entrepreneurial opportunists can expend, or fritter away, considerable public funds and efforts on questionable enterprises as long as they appear somehow to be focused on dealing with the internalized threat.

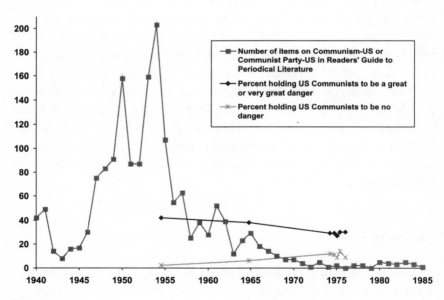

Figure 9.1
Domestic Communism: The Press and the Public, 1940–1985.
Source: John Mueller, "Trends in Political Tolerance," *Public Opinion Quarterly*, 52(1) 1988: 1–25.

In that atmosphere, politicians scurried to support billions upon billions to protect the country against potential Communist sabotage (a form of terrorism) and to surveil, screen, and spy on an ever expanding array of individuals who had come to seem suspicious for one reason or another. Organizations were infiltrated, phones were tapped (each tap can require the full-time services of a dozen agents and support personnel), letters were intercepted, people were followed, loyalty oaths were required, endless leads (almost all to nowhere) were pursued, defense plants were hardened, concentration camps for prospective emergency use were established, and garbage was meticulously sifted in hopes of unearthing scraps of incriminating information.

One of the few people to comment on the essential absurdity of the situation is Alexander Stephan in his book *"Communazis."* In this work, he systematically describes and evaluates the Federal Bureau of Investigation surveillance of a group of German émigré writers living in the United States and Mexico during and after the Second World War. None of the writers was ever found to pose much of a subversive threat, and the surveillance never led to real persecution of the writers—indeed, writes Stephan, few of them even noticed that they were being watched:

> Few exiles suspected that their telephone conversations were being recorded and their mail not only opened and read but translated, summarized, catalogued, photographed, and passed to other government bureaus. Hardly any guessed that the men parked in cars outside their homes were FBI special agents recording everyone who went in and out. In the diaries, autobiographies, correspondence, *romans à clef*, and interviews of the exiles we find virtually no references to the FBI burglaries of private homes and offices or the luggage searches.

Instead, what impresses Stephan is the "high efficiency and gross overkill" as hundreds of agents were paid to intercept and catalogue communications, to endlessly record goings and comings, and to sift enterprisingly through trash bins seeking scraps of incriminating information among the debris. For example, as he notes, there is something profoundly ludicrous about the fact that dozens of government employees spent their time in the middle of a world war monitoring pillow talk between Bertolt Brecht and his Danish coworker, Ruth Berlau, at taxpayers' expense.[45]

At the time, critics of this process focused almost entirely on the potential for civil liberties violations. This is a worthy concern, but it is not the only one. It appears that at no point during the Cold War did anyone say in public that "many domestic Communists adhere to a foreign ideology that ultimately has as its goal the destruction of capitalism and democracy and by violence if necessary; however, they do not present much of a danger, are actually quite a pathetic bunch, and couldn't subvert their way out of a wet paper bag. Why are we expending so much time, effort, and treasure over this issue?" It is astounding that this plausible, if arguable, point of view seems never to have been publicly expressed by anyone—politician, pundit, professor, editorialist—during the Cold War, although some people may have believed it privately. As can be seen in figure 9.1, only a lonely and obviously politically insignificant share of the population—2 percent—professed to believe that domestic Communists presented no danger at all in 1954.

The experience also suggests that once a threat becomes really internalized, the concern can linger for decades, even if there is no evidence to support such a continued preoccupation. It becomes self-perpetuating. In the two decades following the Stouffer survey, news about domestic Communism declined until it essentially vanished altogether: in the mid-1950s, *Readers' Guide to Periodical Literature* listed hundreds of articles under the categories "Communism-US" and "Communist Party-US," whereas in the mid-1970s there were scarcely any (figure 9.1). This, of course, reflected the fact that domestic Communism really wasn't doing very much of anything to garner attention. The Cold War continued elsewhere, but there were no dramatic court cases like the one concerning the State Department's felonious document transmitter, Alger Hiss, and his accuser, Whittaker Chambers, or atomic spy cases like the ones involving Klaus Fuchs and Julius and Ethel Rosenberg, cases that had so mesmerized the public in the late 1940s and early 1950s.[46]

However, even though the domestic Communist menace had pretty much settled into well-deserved oblivion by the mid-1970s, surveys repeating the Stouffer questions at the time found that fully 30 percent of the public *still* considered internal Communists to present a great or very great danger to the country, while those who found them to be of no danger had inched up only to around 10 percent (see figure 9.1).

That is, fear of domestic Communism persisted long after the press had become thoroughly bored with the issue, a development suggesting that, while the media may exacerbate fears about perceived threats, they do not particularly create them: fears often have an independent source and then take on a life of their own. Thus in 1972, by which time the public and press were paying almost no attention to the issue, the FBI in full perpetual motion mode opened 65,000 new files as part of its costly quest to ferret out Communists in the United States.[47]

Domestic Terrorism

Something comparable has now happened for the terrorist threat, and key to the dynamic is that the American public apparently continues to remain unimpressed by several of the inconvenient facts noted at several points in this book:

1. There have been no al-Qaeda attacks whatever in the United States since 2001.
2. No true al-Qaeda cell (nor scarcely anybody who might even be deemed to have a connection to the diabolical group) has been unearthed in the country.
3. The homegrown plotters who have been apprehended, while perhaps potentially somewhat dangerous at least in a few cases, have mostly been flaky or almost absurdly incompetent.
4. The total number of people killed worldwide by al-Qaeda types, maybes, and wannabes outside war zones since 9/11 stands at some 300 or so a year (smaller than the yearly number of bathtub drownings in the United States alone).
5. Unless the terrorists are somehow able to massively increase their capacities, the likelihood a person living outside a war zone will perish at the hands of an international terrorist over an 80-year period is about one in 85,000.

Despite all this, polls do not demonstrate much change since 2001 in the percentage of the public expressing fear that they themselves might become a victim of terrorists, even though the likelihood of that occurring is spectacularly low (see figure 9.2). The public has chosen, it appears, to wallow in what Leif Wenar has labeled a false sense of insecurity, and it apparently plans to continue to do so. Accordingly, it will presumably continue to demand that its leaders pay due deference to its insecurities and will uncritically approve shelling out huge sums of money in a quixotic and often mostly symbolic effort to assuage those insecurities.

This does not mean that people spend a great deal of time obsessing over terrorism, being spooked by it, or even paying all that much attention to it. There was a lot of evasive behavior after the 9/11 attacks, but behavior eventually settled down, and people pretty much seem now to carry out their lives without spending a lot of time thinking about the dangers of terrorism. There has been no great exodus from Washington or New York; few people seem to have gone to the trouble of stocking up on emergency supplies, despite the urgings of the Department of Homeland Security. And terrorism has for years now scored rather poorly on polls asking about the country's most important problem. As with domestic Communism, there is no "national anxiety neurosis" on this issue.

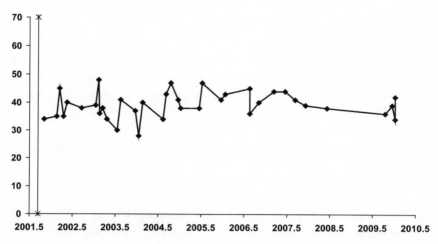

Figure 9.2
Percent Very Worried or Somewhat Worried About Becoming a Victim of Terrorism Since 9/11.
How worried are you that you or someone in your family will become a victim of terrorism? Very worried, somewhat worried, not too worried, or not worried at all?
Source: CNN/USA Today/Gallup/ORC.

However, people don't constantly think about motherhood either. Nonetheless, there are understandable fears that the public will not look kindly upon a politician or bureaucrat who is insufficiently sentimental about that venerable institution.

Thus, agencies like the FBI, redirecting much of their effort from such unglamorous enterprises as dealing with organized crime and white-collar embezzlement, have kept their primary focus on the terrorist threat. Like their predecessors during the quest to quash domestic Communism, they have dutifully and laboriously assembled masses of intelligence data and pursued an endless array of leads. Almost all of this activity has led nowhere, but it will continue because, of course, no one wants to be the one whose neglect somehow led to "another 9/11"—or, as the assistant chief for the FBI's National Threat Center puts it, it's the lead "you don't take seriously that becomes the 9/11."[48]

H. L. Mencken once declared "the whole aim of practical politics" to be "to keep the populace alarmed (and hence clamorous to be led to safety) by menacing it with an endless series of hobgoblins, all of them imaginary."[49] There is nothing imaginary about al-Qaeda, of course, though some of the proclaimed sightings of the group in the United States by officials do have an Elvis-like quality to them. However, the public seems to have been able to retain much of its sense of alarm about internal attacks even when the al-Qaeda hobgoblin doesn't actually carry any out.

Therefore, even without such declarations and even without further terrorist attacks (and, for that matter, even without Osama bin Laden), the war on terror seems likely, like the wars on drugs and on domestic Communism, to continue to grind on for a long time.

However, the situation after 9/11 may be different from the one that prevailed during the Cold War in one important respect. The Communist dragon, like Grendel (and his mother), could terminally and convincingly expire as a perceived threat. Like crime, however, terrorism can be carried out by an individual or small group and can therefore never vanish from the human experience. Other colorful monsters may arise from time to time to charm the attention and to strut and fret their hour upon the stage. But the monster of terrorism and the internalized fears it has inspired show distinct signs of being eternal. As a result, the additional trillion dollars expended to deal with terrorism in the United States in the first decade after 9/11 might well prove to be simply a down payment.

The Risk Assessment Process

A number of steps are basic to a quantitative risk assessment, and they are independent of the system or issue being considered. As applied in the engineering, insurance, pharmaceutical, and many other industries for many decades, the basic definition of risk has been standardized by international agreement.[1] The process is shown in figure A.1 and can be summarized as:

1. **Define context.** A risk assessment should take place within a well-defined context. This means that the system being examined and the internal and external influences must be known and defined.

2. **Analyze hazard scenarios.** Identification of what might go wrong—and when and where—are crucial to the analysis. Once the potential threats and scenarios have been identified, it is necessary to identify how and why these threats or scenarios can be realized. It requires the threat scenarios to be examined (and understood) in considerable detail. Information from databases and other past experience will play an important part in hazard scenario analysis.

3. **Analyze risk.**

$$\text{Risk} = (\text{probability of threat}) \times (\text{consequences})$$

This is concerned with determining the threat probabilities and the consequences (fatalities, damages) that would occur if the threat were realized. Typically, the probabilities are estimated from a combination of relevant data and subjective judgments.

4. **Evaluate risks.** Analyzed risk must be compared with criteria of risk acceptability, usually applying past experience as a guide. If the risk of

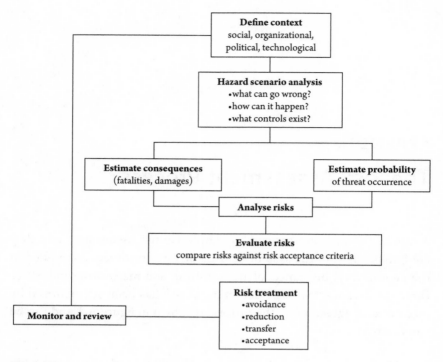

Figure A.1
The Risk Assessment Process.

death is less than one in a million per year, risks are conventionally considered acceptable if the benefit exceeds the cost.

5. **Treat the risk.** If the estimated risk exceeds the risk acceptance criteria, risk treatment is required. This may involve risk avoidance, risk reduction, or risk transfer. In some cases, the risk may be accepted but perhaps only for a limited time until measures can be taken to reduce it. In all cases, the proposed course of action requires careful evaluation. Consideration must be given to possible options and to the likely effect of their implementation, such as opportunity costs. This might involve one or more new risk analyses to gauge the effect of changes.

6. **Monitor and review.** Usually a risk analysis presents only a snapshot of the risks—for example, the effectiveness of control procedures may slacken with time. There is a need, then, to monitor the system and to repeat the risk analysis at regular intervals.

NOTES

INTRODUCTION

1. Howard Kunreuther, "Risk Analysis and Risk Management in an Uncertain World," *Risk Analysis*, 22(4) 2002: 662–663. See also John Mueller, "Some Reflections on What, If Anything, 'Are We Safer?' Might Mean," cato-unbound. org? September 11, 2006.

2. Operatives: Gertz 2002; Sale 2002. Giuliani: CNN, July 22, 2005.

3. As he put it mockingly in a videotaped message in 2004, it is "easy for us to provoke and bait. . . . All that we have to do is to send two mujahidin . . . to raise a piece of cloth on which is written al-Qaeda in order to make the generals race there to cause America to suffer human, economic, and political losses." His policy, he proclaimed, is one of "bleeding America to the point of bankruptcy," triumphally pointing to the fact that the 9/11 terrorist attacks cost al-Qaeda $500,000, while the attack and its aftermath inflicted, he claims, "a cost of more than $500 billion on the United States" (Full transcript of bin Laden's speech, aljazeera.net, October 30, 2004). However, this was not his original idea. Initially, he apparently expected that the United States would essentially *under* react to the 9/11 attacks. Impressed, in particular, with the American reaction to rather small losses in Lebanon in 1983 and in Somalia in 1993, he appears to have believed that the country would respond to an attack on itself by withdrawing from the Middle East (Wright 2006, 174, 200). Bin Ladin reformulated his theory after it was blown to shreds when the United States and its allies not only forced al-Qaeda out of its base in Afghanistan and captured or killed many of its main people but also toppled the accommodating Taliban regime there.

4. Government spending worldwide on homeland security reached a staggering $141.6 billion per year in 2009, about half of it by the United States (*Global Homeland Security 2009–2019—Our New Defence Report Explains How and Why This Market Will Grow Strongly*, Visiongain, June 2009). It is projected to reach $300 billion per year by 2016 (David Binning, "The Price of Homeland Security," Army-technology.com, June 5, 2009).

5. Kean 2004, 391, 396.

6. Mayer 2009, 62.

7. Troy Anderson, "Terror May Be at Bay at Port; Shipping Hubs Too Vulnerable," *Daily News of Los Angeles*, May 18, 2006.

8. James A. Thomson, "DHS AWOL? Tough Questions about Homeland Security Have Gone Missing," *RAND Review*, Spring 2007. The inbox management approach is perhaps suggested in an interview with Transportation Security Administration chief John Pistole: "Much of our approach is risk-based. To say: 'OK, what was the last threat from general aviation?'" James Fallows and Jeffrey Goldberg, "TSA Chief: 'We'll Never Eliminate Risk,'" theatlantic.com, January 8, 2010.
9. Shapiro 2007, 1–2, emphasis in the original.
10. Masse et al. 2007, 14.
11. Transportation Security Administration, Rail Transportation Security: Final Rule, RIN 1652-AA51, 2008.
12. National Research Council 2010, 108.
13. Transportation Security Administration, "DHS Announces Security Standards for Freight and Passenger Rail Systems," Press Release, November 13, 2008.
14. Lord 2010, 5. For our risk assessment of the scanners, see chapter 7 and Stewart and Mueller 2011.
15. United States Government Accountability Office, "Report to Congressional Requesters: Supply Chain Security: Feasibility and Cost-Benefit Analysis Would Assist DHS and Congress in Assessing and Implementing the Requirement to Scan 100 Percent of U.S.-Bound Containers," GAO-10-12, October 2009. See, however, Martonosi et al. 2007.
16. National Research Council 2010. For page references, see table P.3.
17. National Research Council 2010, 57.

NOTES TO THE TABLES IN THE INTRODUCTION

1. Somewhat high estimate. Hobijn and Sager (2007) give $20.1 billion. However, "The Budget of the United States Government Fiscal Year 2003" infers pre-9/11 homeland security expenditure to be $20 billion (p. 17), and "The National Strategy for Homeland Security" (Office of Homeland Security 2002, 64) states: "Including supplemental spending, the federal budget allocated $17 billion to homeland security in Fiscal Year 2001."
2. Estimate. Specific budget allocations to "homeland security" are available only after FY 2004 budget. FY 2002 estimate is based on "National Strategy for Homeland Security" (Office of Homeland Security 2002), reporting a $12 billion increase in funding over 2001 levels (p. 64). "Budget of the United States Government Fiscal Year 2003" states: "In the months since September 11th, the $10.6 billion of the $40 billion dedicated to homeland security" has been spent (p. 16), with more expenditure forecast. An increase of $12 billion over 2001 levels seems on the low side.
3. "Analytical Perspectives: Budget of the United States Government," Office of Management and Budget, Fiscal Years 2005 to 2011. Includes enacted and supplemental/emergency expenditures. Funding levels for 2010 and 2011 in this source are budget figures and do not represent actual expenditures.
4. 2011 budget request.
5. Approximately 70 percent of the DHS budget is allocated to border and transportation security: Customs and Border Protection, Transportation Security Administration, Coast Guard, Immigration and Customs Enforcement.

6. Nearly all is devoted to protecting "critical infrastructure" and "key resources" (CI/KR), including measures to counter chemical, biological, radiological, and nuclear (CBRN) threats. Includes programs focusing on physical security and improving the military's ability to prevent or mitigate the consequences of attacks against departmental personnel and facilities.
7. Mostly devoted to programs that help to plan, equip, train, and practice the capabilities of many different response units (including first responders such as police officers, firefighters, emergency medical providers, public works personnel, and emergency management officials) that are instrumental in the preparedness to mobilize without warning for an emergency. Includes developing new vaccines for biological weapons, maintaining vaccine stockpiles, and assisting local health providers to prepare for CBRN attacks.
8. Mostly domestic counterterrorism (FBI).
9. Nearly all devoted to protecting CI/KR, including measures to counter CBRN threats. Includes nuclear weapons facilities and nuclear power plants, as well as natural gas, oil, and other energy-related activities. Coordinates protection activities within the energy sector.
10. Nearly all is devoted to preventing and disrupting terrorist attacks. The State Border Security program includes visa, passport, American Citizen Services, and international adoption programs.
11. Includes the Departments of Agriculture, Treasury, and Transportation; the General Services Administration; the National Science Foundation; the National Aeronautics and Space Administration; and 19 other federal agencies.
12. Funding decline in 2004 because of one-time force protection investments by the Department of Defense in 2003.
13. Federal expenditures under the category of "homeland security" do not include national intelligence costs. However, Director of National Intelligence Dennis Blair disclosed at a conference call with reporters in 2009 that "the United States spent $75 billion over the past year to finance worldwide intelligence operations that employ 200,000 people" (Pincus 2009).

The intelligence community (IC) is divided into two programs: the National Intelligence Program (NIP) and the Military Intelligence Program (MIP).

The NIP "funds intelligence activities in several Federal departments and the Central Intelligence Agency (CIA)" and also includes foreign counterintelligence and intelligence activities of the FBI, the National Security Agency (NSA), the Department of State, the National Reconnaissance Office, and 11 other government agencies. Among its aims are "strengthening its component agencies' ability to collect intelligence; maintaining the security of Federal cyber networks; and protecting against the threat of international terrorism in the United States." This includes measures that enhance "Federal cybersecurity capabilities to protect a central part of our Nation's and economy's infrastructure" and the allocation of "resources in support of a U.S. Government-wide counterterrorism action plan" (Budget of the U.S. Government, Fiscal Year 2011, 61). The National Security Agency (NSA), which monitors, collects, deciphers, and analyzes signals intelligence, is funded mainly through NIP (Daggett 2004, 2). NIP clearly plays an important role in domestic counterterrorism and "homeland security." Further to this point, the director of national intelligence works to "closely effectively integrate foreign, military and domestic intelligence in defense of the homeland and in support of United States national security interests at home and abroad" and provides "fused domestic and foreign intelligence to quickly understand and disrupt homeland threats posed by alleged extremists." Moreover, the "IC rapidly produced and pushed relevant counterterrorism information to state, local, tribal, and private partners through the FBI and DHS" in an effort to forge "an integrated Intelligence Community that spans the historical divide between foreign and domestic intelligence efforts" (ODNI Fact Sheet, Office of the Director of National Intelligence, Washington, DC, February 17, 2010).

The National Intelligence Program finances intelligence activities for agencies both within and outside the Department of Defense (DOD). MIP finances only activities of the DOD, and expenditure goes toward funding tactical military programs and defensewide intelligence requirements (Daggett 2004, 2), which would have less relevance to homeland security than NIP funding.

Except for 1994, 1997, and 1998, budgets for NIP were classified until 2007, and since then, only a one-line budget for NIP, with no breakdown on expenditure by agency, has been provided. The "Joint Inquiry into Intelligence Community Activities before and after the Terrorist Attacks of September 11, 2001" (S. Rept. No. 107–351, House Permanent Select Committee on Intelligence and Senate Select Committee on Intelligence, December 2002) noted that the overall funding of intelligence agencies "fell or remained roughly even in constant dollars from the end of the Cold War until September 11, 2001" (p. 254). The last time budget figures were available for both NIP (formerly National Foreign Intelligence Program) and MIP was 1994, when the NIP budget was $16.3 billion and the MIP budget was $10.4 billion (Pincus 2009). Total intelligence expenditures were $26.6 and $26.7 billion in FY 1997 and FY 1998, respectively, and about two thirds of the intelligence budget at the time was for NIP (Daggett 2004, pp. 2–3). NIP budgets for 2007, 2008, and 2009 were $43.5, $47.5, and $49.8 billion, respectively ("DNI Releases Budget Figure for National Intelligence Program," News Release, Office of the Director of National Intelligence, Washington, DC, October 30, 2007, October 28, 2008, October 30, 2009). From this information, we can infer that over the period 1994 to 1998 the annual increase in the NIP budget was approximately $0.3 billion, and since overall funding of intelligence agencies remained constant until September 11, 2001, that the 2001 NIP budget was approximately $18.7 billion (or $23 billion in 2010 dollars). The NIP budget in the period 2007 to 2009 increased at an average of $3.15 billion per year. If we extrapolate these rises backward to 2002, we arrive at an estimated annual budget for NIP of $27.8 billion for that year (see figure I.1). As we would expect, figure I.1 shows a significant increase in NIP expenditure after 2001.

The MIP budget on intelligence is approximately $25.2 billion if the 2009 NIP budget of $49.8 billion ($50.6 billion in 2010 dollars) is deducted from the total of $75 billion estimated by Director Blair. This is about half of the NIP budget, which is a similar proportion to that observed before 2001 (Daggett

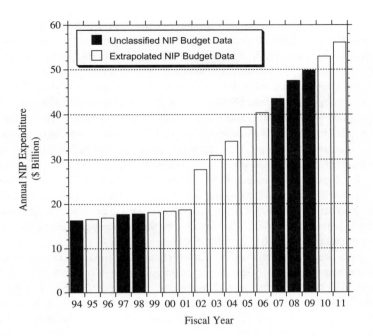

Figure I.1
Known (Unclassified) and Extrapolated NIP Annual Expenditures.

2004, 3). Approximately two thirds of the MIP is devoted to the TIARA program, which includes a "diverse array of reconnaissance and target acquisition programs which are a functional part of the basic military force structure and provide direct support to military operations" (Thomas J. Nicola, "9/11 Commission Recommendations: Intelligence Budget," CRS Report for Congress, September 27, 2004, 3). The remaining third of the MIP budget is to support the Joint Military Intelligence Program, which funds defensewide intelligence requirements (Daggett 2004, 3). Increases in the NIP budget since 2001, adjusted for inflation, resulted in enhanced expenditures of $27.6 billion in 2009 or $220 billion over the 2002 to 2011 period (in 2010 dollars). Enhanced MIP expenditures are 50 percent of NIP expenditures, resulting in $13.8 billion in 2009 and $110 billion over the period 2002 to 2010. Enhanced national intelligence expenditures in the decade since 9/11 thus sum to $330 billion.

Some of the federal homeland security budget described in table I.1 includes "intelligence and warning" activities by the DHS Office of Intelligence and Analysis and by the Department of Justice (mainly the FBI), as well as some domestic counterterrorism efforts to "identify, thwart, and prosecute terrorists in the United States," of which the largest contributors are the Department of Justice (largely for the FBI) and DHS (largely for Immigration and Customs Enforcement).

Because NIP includes intelligence activities of the FBI and DHS in its budget, we need to factor out these costs. The DHS Office of Intelligence and Analysis has an annual budget of $347 million (FY2011 Budget in Brief, DHS, 43), and the 2009 Department of Justice homeland security allocation for "preventing and disrupting terrorist attacks" is $3 billion ("Analytical Perspectives: Budget of the United States Government," Office of Management and Budget, Fiscal Year 2011, 380), while the intelligence activities of other agencies included in the federal government homeland security budget are minor by comparison: for example, Department of Energy's Office of Intelligence and Counter Intelligence spends some $50 million, Department of State's Bureau of Intelligence and Research $59.8 million, Department of Treasury's Office of National Security and Intelligence less than $75 million, and so on. We conservatively take the total enhanced expenditures of these government agencies on intelligence activities after 2001 levels to be $3.0 billion per year in 2010 dollars, cumulating to $30 billion over the decade.

Hence NIP expenditure not already included in enhanced federal government homeland security spending comes approximately to $24.6 billion in 2009 and $190 billion for the period 2002 to 2011. It is important to note that there is no Department of Defense allocation for federal government homeland security spending under the activities "intelligence-and-warning and domestic counterterrorism." A MIP expenditure of $110 billion is therefore a realistic estimate of all defense-related intelligence expenditure. Total enhanced intelligence expenditure is thus $300 billion for the decade after 2001.

The question is then how much of this expenditure relates to homeland security in the United States?

The distinction between domestic and foreign intelligence activities is increasingly becoming blurred because many, or most, serious threats to the U.S. homeland since 2001 have originated outside the United States. This is why national intelligence has *"fused* domestic and foreign intelligence to quickly understand and disrupt homeland threats posed by alleged extremists" (ODNI Fact Sheet, Office of the Director of National Intelligence, Washington, DC, February 17, 2010). Moreover, Director Blair testified after the 2009 Christmas bomb plot that "the Intelligence Community highlighted the growing threat to US and Western interests in the region posed by AQAP (Al Qa'ida in the Arabian Peninsula), whose precursor elements attacked our embassy in Sana'a in 2008. Our analysis focused on AQAP's plans to strike US targets in Yemen, but it also noted—increasingly in the fall of 2009—the possibility of targeting the United States." (Statement for the Record, Intelligence Reform: The Lessons and Implications of the Christmas Day Attack, Senate Homeland Security and Governmental Affairs Committee, January 20, 2010). "Intelligence community" refers to all civilian and defense intelligence agencies. While national intelligence clearly targets threats from foreign governments, such as identifying Iran's uranium enrichment facility in Qom, it also plays a pivotal role in identifying transnational threats to the United States homeland from al-Qaeda and related groups. The dramatic increase in national intelligence expenditure since 9/11 is a direct response to the need for improved counterterrorism capabilities and to military operations in Iraq and Afghanistan.

Since unclassified information about the intelligence community places significant emphasis on "defense of the homeland and in support of United States national security interests at home and abroad" (ODNI Fact Sheet), we will assume conservatively that, of increased NIP expenditures after 9/11 ($190 billion), half is devoted to homeland security. However, we omit two thirds of the increased MIP budget ($110 billion) because that is devoted to tactical reconnaissance and target acquisition programs that are not related to homeland security. Enhanced intelligence expenditure devoted to homeland security thus sums approximately to $15 billion for 2009 and to $110 billion for the ten-year period after 9/11.

14. Although the OMB does not collect detailed homeland security expenditure data from state, local, or private entities directly, it does note that "state and local governments and private-sector firms also have devoted resources of their own to the task of defending against terrorist threats" ("Analytical Perspectives: Budget of the United States Government," Office of Management and Budget, Fiscal Year 2009, 31). The "National Strategy for Homeland Security" (Office of Homeland Security 2002, 65) reports that "The National Governors Association estimates that additional homeland security–related costs, incurred since September 11 and through the end of 2002 will reach approximately $6 billion. Similarly, the U.S. Conference of Mayors has estimated the costs incurred by cities during this time period to be $2.6 billion. This totals $8.6 billion." Analytical Perspectives (FY 2005, p. 36) summarizes market reports from International Horizons Unlimited and Deloitte Consulting, which indicate that state and local expenditures varied from $6.5 to $29.2 billion in 2003 and from $7.5 to $15 billion in 2004. These estimates "removed spending that was funded by Federal grants to avoid double counting of spending that was reported by the Federal Government." A conservative estimate of annual state and local expenditure is $10 billion, which when adjusted for inflation is $110 billion over ten years.

15. Private-sector expenditures on security-related measures rose from approximately $36 billion to $45 billion per year between 2001 and 2005, equivalent to 0.36 percent of GDP (Hobijn and Sager 2007; there is a typographical error in this article incorrectly referring to 0.46 percent of GDP). This estimate includes only capital expenditure of electronic security systems and security guards, ignoring physical security, IT security, establishing and improving backup systems, and other measures to ensure that activities can be maintained in the event of a major disruption to normal operations. Based on 0.36 percent of GDP, enhanced private-sector costs would cumulate to $106 billion for the decade after 9/11, assuming 2 percent growth in GDP each year. By comparison, the Homeland Security Research Corporation report, "U.S. Homeland Security Government and Private Sectors Market Outlook 2007–2011," states that the private sector "will only trail the DHS in homeland security procurement volume," totaling $32.9 billion for the 2006 to 2011 period, and this sum applies to equipment only. A 2002 Brookings study estimates that the total annual homeland security costs for the private sector will be about $10 billion (Gunter et al. 2002, 84). Two private consulting firms have placed private-sector security spending between $4.8 and $46 billion for 2004 (Analytical Perspectives, FY 2005, p. 36). A conservative estimate of private-sector

expenditure, therefore, is $10 billion per year. Adjusted for inflation, that comes to $110 billion over ten years.

16. This total is conservative. The 2002 Office of Homeland Security report "National Strategy for Homeland Security" concludes: "The United States spends roughly $100 billion per year on homeland security" (p. xii). This figure includes federal, state, and local law enforcement and emergency services, but it excludes most funding for the armed forces. Another estimate is even higher. "The Homeland Security Market: The World's Most Challenging Emerging Business Environment," a 2002 Deloitte Consulting report, estimates that "$90 to $140 billion will be spent in 2003 towards antiterrorism or 'homeland security' preparedness across the U.S. including both government and industry spending" (as summarized in Bryan S. Ware, Anthony Beverina, Lester Gong, and Brian Colder, "A Risk-Based Decision Support System for Antiterrorism," August 14, 2002, 3; available at www.dsbox.com/Documents/MSS_A_Risk-Based_Decision_Support_System_for_Antiterrorism.pdf). These figures multiplied by ten years total more than one trillion dollars.

17. Annual terrorism risk insurance premiums total $3.6 billion, which in 2010 dollars is $40 billion over 10 years (Treverton et al. 2008, 76).

18. Enhanced TSA security measures increased average delays by 19.5 minutes in 2004. Based on 2004 passenger statistics of 785 million one-way domestic flights, resulting in 255 million hours waiting. Since surveys suggest that passengers value their time at about $37 per hour, total opportunity cost is $10 billion in 2010 dollars, and multiplied by ten years the cumulative cost is $100 billion. While average passenger delays may have been reduced since 2004, delays can still be considerable, especially at peak times. In general, many passengers continue to arrive early at the airport in anticipation of delays (Treverton et al. 2008, 75–76).

19. The inconvenience of extra passenger screening and added costs at airports after 9/11 caused many short-haul passengers to drive to their destination instead, and, since airline travel is far safer then car travel, this has led to an increase of 500 U.S. traffic fatalities per year. Using DHS-mandated value of statistical life of $6.5 million, this equates to a loss of $3.2 billion per year, or $32 billion over the period 2002 to 2011 (Blalock et al. 2007).

20. Many of the costs, delays, and inconveniences associated with enhanced security regulations will result in declines in the quantities of goods or services provided or an increase in their price. Consumers respond to price increases or lack of availability by purchasing less, resulting in an efficiency loss or "dead-weight loss." This can potentially cause losses in consumer welfare of between $5 billion (Ellig et al. 2006, 30) and $24 billion per year (Treverton et al. 2008, 76). When adjusted to 2010 dollars and multiplied by ten years, the cumulative losses are $52 billion to $250 billion. We will conservatively assume $10 billion per year or $100 billion over the decade after 9/11.

An additional deadweight loss arises from the marginal excess burden of taxes required to pay for homeland security expenditure because "under any tax system, every dollar collected in taxes results in distortions that reduce the efficiency of the economy and lower national income" (Office of Homeland

Security 2002, 65). For the United States, a reasonable estimate is $0.25 for every dollar of tax revenue (OMB, "Guidelines and Discount Rates for Benefit-Cost Analysis of Federal Programs (Revised)," Circular No. A-94, October 29, 1992, 13). When applied to enhanced federal, state, and local expenditures, the deadweight loss due to homeland security taxation over the 10 years since 9/11 is $580 billion. Multiplied by $0.25, this comes to $145 billion. When this is added to the deadweight loss associated with costs, delays, and inconveniences associated with enhanced security regulations ($100 billion) the total deadweight loss for the decade comes to approximately $245 billion.

21. "With enactment of the FY2009 Supplemental (H.R. 2346/P.L. 111–132) on June 24, 2009, Congress has approved a total of about $944 billion for military operations, base security, reconstruction, foreign aid, embassy costs, and veterans' health care for the three operations initiated since the 9/11 attacks: Operation Enduring Freedom (OEF) Afghanistan and other counter terror operations; Operation Noble Eagle (ONE), providing enhanced security at military bases; and Operation Iraqi Freedom (OIF)," and FY2009 war funding totals $150 billion (Amy Belasco, "The Cost of Iraq, Afghanistan, and Other Global War on Terror Operations since 9/11," CRS Report for Congress, Congressional Research Service, September 28, 2009, 1–2). If FY2011 war expenditure is similar to FY2010 levels, terror-related war expenditures in Iraq and Afghanistan exceed $1.2 trillion. For much higher estimates, including not only the direct costs during the wars' first several years, but longer term costs, see Stiglitz and Bilmes 2008. In domestic debate, the war in Iraq has commonly been justified as part of the war on terror, as in George W. Bush's "we fight them there so we don't have to fight them here." In his speech to the American people of September 8, 2003, requesting an additional $87 billion for the war in Iraq, Bush used the words *terror* or *terrorists* 26 times. Justifications for the Afghanistan war (and for related efforts in Pakistan) were similar at the beginning and continue to be so: according to Ambassador Richard Holbrooke, the "fundamental difference" between Afghanistan and Vietnam "is 9/11. The Vietcong and the North Vietnamese never posed a threat to the United States homeland. The people of 9/11 who were in that area still do and are still planning. That is why we're in the region with troops. That's the *only* justification for what we're doing" (Matthew Kaminski, "Holbrooke of South Asia: America's Regional Envoy Says Pakistan's Tribal Areas Are the Problem," *Wall Street Journal*, April 11, 2009, emphasis added).

22. In 2001, the postmaster general asked Congress for "a one-time appropriation of up to $2 billion to help offset the unanticipated decline in mail volume" that year, as well as "about $3 billion to help cover one-time direct costs, including the purchase of sanitization equipment; and the testing, cleaning and restoration of NY facilities lost or damaged in the September 11 attacks": www.usps.com/news/2001/press/mailsecurity/allfaq.htm.

23. Blalock et al. 2009. This equates to a loss of $15 billion.

24. The Air Transport Association estimates that this costs airlines $220 million per year in lost revenue. Ted Poe, Department of Homeland Security Appropriations

Act, 2006: Amendment No. 10, House of Representatives, May 17, 2005. Converted to 2010 dollars.

25. Deficit Reduction Act of 2005. Robert Pear, "Budget to Hurt Poor People on Medicaid, Report Says," *New York Times*, January 30, 2006.

CHAPTER 1: ASSESSING RISK

1. Gregory F. Treverton, *Intelligence for an Age of Terror* (New York: Cambridge University Press, 2009), 24–25, 188.
2. Chan 2007. On this issue, see also chapter 9.
3. Sunstein 2003, 122.
4. Michael Chertoff, "Security Efforts Well Worth Cost," *Philadelphia Inquirer*, January 4, 2008.
5. Warren S. Eller and Brian J. Gerber, "Contemplating the Role of Precision and Range in Homeland Security Policy Analysis," *Policy Studies Journal*, 38(1) February 2010: 38n2.
6. Bruce Schneier, "Worst-Case Thinking," www.schneier.com, May 13, 2010.
7. Sunstein 2007, 124.
8. George W. Bush, "The National Security Strategy of the United States of America," September 17, 2002, introduction and part V.
9. Sunstein 2007, 125.
10. Jessica Stern and Jonathan B. Weiner, "Precaution against Terrorism," *Journal of Risk Research*, 9(4) 2010: 393–447.
11. Sunstein 2007, 3.
12. Sunstein 2007, 8.
13. Masse et al. 2007, 6.
14. Such as the International Organization for Standardization standard, *Risk Management—Principles and Guidelines* ISO 31000–2009, AS4360–2004, Geneva, Switzerland, 2009.
15. Peter L. Bernstein, *Against the Gods: The Remarkable Story of Risk* (New York: John Wiley & Sons, 1996), 126.
16. Masse et al. 2007, 15.
17. National Research Council 2010, 137, emphasis in the original.
18. Mayer 2009, 64.
19. Office of Management and Budget, *Analytical Perspectives, Budget of the United States Government, Fiscal Year 2011*, Washington, DC, 381.
20. Department of Homeland Security 2009, 15n.
21. Department of Homeland Security 2009, 11.
22. Clark R. Chapman and Alan W. Harris, "Skeptical Look at September 11th: How We Can Defeat Terrorism by Reacting to It More Rationally, *Skeptical Inquirer*, September–October 2002: 32.
23. Myers: Jennifer C. Kerr, "Terror Threat Level Raised to Orange," Associated Press, December 21, 2003. Michael Scheuer [Anonymous], *Imperial Hubris: Why the West Is Losing the War on Terror* (Dulles, VA: Brassey's, 2004), 160, 177, 226, 241, 242, 250, 252, 263.
24. "All the Time He Needs," *New York Times*, April 16, 2008. For McCain, see, for example, "In Florida, Rivals Focus on Economy and Security," *New York Times*,

January 28, 2008; and "Obama Leads McCain in Four Key Battleground States," *Washington Post,* June 26, 2008. Chertoff: Shane Harris and Stuart Taylor Jr., "Homeland Security Chief Looks Back, and Forward," Government Executive. com, March 17, 2008.

25. Charles S. Faddis, *Willful Neglect: The Dangerous Illusion of Homeland Security* (Guilford, CT: Lyons, 2010); SC town discussed, p. 198.

26. Ervin 2006, 198, 225–226; Clark Kent Ervin, "Answering Al Qaeda," *New York Times,* May 8, 2007.

27. Randall Larsen, *Our Own Worst Enemy* (New York: Grand Central, 2007), 99.

28. Pam Fessler, "Auditors, DHS Disagree on Radiation Detectors," *Morning Edition,* National Public Radio, September 19, 2007.

29. Shapiro 2007, 4, 15–16; see also Veronique de Rugy, "Is Port Security Funding Making Us Safer? Audit of the Conventional Wisdom," Center for International Studies, MIT, November 2007.

30. Martonosi et al. 2005. Based on 3.2 million shipping containers (TEUs) per year for the Port of Long Beach with increased equipment and labor costs of approximately $100/TEU and $10/TEU, assuming existing and new technology scanners, respectively. Increases in yearly costs range from $32 to $320 million.

31. Martonosi et al. 2005, 228, 235.

32. Risk reduction would be 95 percent. Martonosi et al. 2005, 223.

33. Thomas H. Kean (Chair) and Lee H. Hamilton (Vice Chair), "Report on the Status of 9/11 Commission Recommendations, Part I: Homeland Security, Emergency Preparedness and Response," www.9-11pdp.org, September 14, 2005, 7.

34. Richard Forno, "Auditors Question TSA's Use of and Spending on Technology," *Washington Post,* December 21, 2010. Spencer Hsu, "Airports Won't Use 'Puffer' Machines," *Washington Post,* May 22, 2009.

35. Aaron Steelman, "Interview: W. Kip Viscusi," *Region Focus,* Spring 2007, 42. On later reflection, Viscusi was willing to estimate that the United States under current conditions was likely to lose an average of 50 lives per year to terrorism. See Bryan Caplan, "Viscusi Speaks," econlog.econlib.org, August 23, 2007. In the four years since then, a total of 14 lives have been lost to Muslim extremist terrorism.

36. Baird Webel, "Terrorism Risk Insurance: An Overview," CRS Report for Congress, Congressional Research Service, Washington, DC, April 11, 2005, 1.

37. "MarketWatch: Terrorism Insurance," Marsh Inc., 2005. Governments in the United Kingdom, continental Europe, Australia, South Africa, India, and elsewhere enacted similar terrorism reinsurance schemes. "Terrorism Insurance Update," Marsh Inc., Tower Place, London, June 2004.

38. Based on a survey of 1,382 firms in the United States. See "The Marsh Report: Terrorism Risk Insurance 2010," Marsh Inc., 16.

39. $9,541 divided by $303 million, or 0.003 percent.

40. For example, ISO 31000–2009, *Risk Management—Principles and Guidelines,* Geneva, Switzerland, 2009. See the appendix for a fuller description of the quantified risk assessment process. See also Henry H. Willis, Andrew R. Morral, Terrence K. Kelly, and Jamison Jo Medby, *Estimating Terrorism Risk* (Santa Monica, CA: RAND, 2005).

41. B. John Garrick, James E. Hall, Max Kilger, John C. McDonald, Tara O'Toole, Peter S. Probst, Elizabeth Rindskopf Parker, Robert Rosenthal, Alvin W. Trivelpiece, Lee A. Van Arsdale, and Edwin L. Zebrosk, "Confronting the Risks of Terrorism: Making the Right Decisions," *Reliability Engineering and System Safety*, 86(2) 2004: 129–176. Barry C. Ezell, Steven P. Bennett, Detlof von Winterfeldt, John Sokolowski, and Andrew J. Collins, "Probabilistic Risk Analysis and Terrorism Risk," *Risk Analysis*, 30(4) 2010: 575–589. Stewart 2010.

42. For studies that apply this approach to assess some of the effects of terrorism, see Henry H. Willis and Tom LaTourrette, "Using Probabilistic Terrorism Risk Modeling for Regulatory Benefit-Cost Analysis: Application to the Western Hemisphere Travel Initiative in the Land Environment," *Risk Analysis*, 28(4) 2008: 325–339; Detlof von Winterfeldt and Terrence M O'Sullivan, "Should We Protect Commercial Airplanes against Surface-to-Air Missile Attacks by Terrorists?" *Decision Analysis*, 3(2) 2006: 63–75; Juned Akhtar, Torkel Bjørns-kau, and Knut Veisten, "Assessing Security Measures Reducing Terrorist Risk: Inverse Ex-Post Cost-Benefit and Cost-Effectiveness Analyses of Norwegian Airports and Seaports," *Journal of Transportation Security*, 3 2010:179–195; and Scott Farrow and Stuart Shapiro, "The Benefit-Cost Analysis of Security Focused Regulations," *Journal of Homeland Security and Emergency Management*, 6(1) 2009: Article 25.

43. For many engineering systems, the hazard (or threat) rate is known or pre-dicted a priori, but for terrorism the threat is from an intelligent adversary who will adapt to changing circumstances to maximize the likelihood of success. Some statistical approaches exist for terrorist threat prediction. See M. Elisabeth Pate-Cornell and Seth Guikema, "Probabilistic Modeling of Terrorist Threats: A Systems Analysis Approach to Setting Priorities among Counter-Measures," *Military Operations Research*, 7(4) 2002: 5–23; Robin L. Dillon, Robert M. Liebe, and Thomas Bestafka, "Risk-Based Decision Making for Terrorism Applications," *Risk Analysis*, 29(3) 2009: 321–335; Louis A. Cox, "Improving Risk-Based Decision-Making for Terrorism Applications," *Risk Analysis*, 29(3) 2009: 336–341. However, these rely heavily on expert judg-ments from security experts, game theory, and the like, so the uncertainties of these predictions can still be high. Where possible, in our analyses the attack probability (the likelihood there would be an attack absent security measures) is the outcome of the cost-benefit analysis. It is the prerogative of the decision maker, based on expert advice about the likelihood of a successful terrorist attack, to decide whether security measures are worthwhile. Having said this, we find that such attack probabilities often have to be incredibly high for many security measures to be cost-effective.

44. Office of Management and Budget, "Guidelines and Discount Rates for Benefit-Cost Analysis of Federal Programs (Revised)," Circular No. A-94, October 29, 1992, Washington, DC. The OMB states that "the standard criterion for deciding whether a government program can be justified on economic principles is *net present value*—the discounted monetized value of expected net benefits (i.e., benefits minus costs)" and that "expected values (an

unbiased estimate) is the appropriate estimate for use." See also Michael Faber and Mark G. Stewart, "Risk Assessment for Civil Engineering Facilities: Critical Overview and Discussion," *Reliability Engineering and System Safety*, 80(2) 2003: 173–184; Bruce R. Ellingwood, "Mitigating Risk from Abnormal Loads and Progressive Collapse," *Journal of Performance of Constructed Facilities*, 20(4) 2006: 315–323; Cass R. Sunstein, *The Cost-Benefit State: The Future of Regulatory Protection* (Chicago: ABA Publishing, American Bar Association, 2002). As considered at various points in this book, terrorism is a frightening threat that influences our willingness to accept risk, a willingness that is influenced by psychological, social, cultural, and institutional processes. Moreover, events involving high consequences can cause losses to individuals that they cannot bear, such as bankruptcy or loss of life. On the other hand, governments, large corporations, and other self-insured institutions can absorb such losses more readily. Follow-on consequences from a terrorist attack, such as loss of consumer confidence leading to economic decline, reduced tourism, and reduced government tax revenue, should be included in the estimation of losses in a "risk neutral" risk analysis. Utility theory can be used if the decision maker wishes to explicitly factor risk aversion into the decision process.

45. For an analysis, see Mark G. Stewart, Bruce R. Ellingwood, and John Mueller, "Homeland Security: A Case Study in Risk Aversion for Public Decision-Making," *International Journal of Risk Assessment and Management*, forthcoming.

46. J. Brian Hardaker, Euan Fleming, and Gudbrand Lien, "How Should Governments Make Risky Policy Decisions?" *Australian Journal of Public Administration*, 68(3) 2009: 256–271.

47. Elisabeth Paté-Cornell, "Risk and Uncertainty Analysis in Government Safety Decisions," *Risk Analysis*, 22(3) 2002: 633–646.

48. Banks 2002, 10.

CHAPTER 2: TERRORISM AS A HAZARD TO HUMAN LIFE

1. Department of Homeland Security 2009, 11.

2. Gerges 2005, 1–3, 27–28, also 161–162. See also Michael Scheuer, *Through Our Enemies' Eyes: Osama bin Laden, Radical Islam, and the Future of America* (Washington, DC: Brassey's, 2002), 169–177.

3. Porter 2009, 300. committed suicide: Fawaz Gerges, *The Rise and Fall of Al-Qaeda* (New York: Oxford University Press, 2011). turned many: Peter Bergen and Paul Cruickshank, "The Unraveling: The Jihadist Revolt against bin Laden," *New Republic*, June 11, 2008; Wright 2008.

4. For "taxi drivers": Gerges 2008, 70–71. For rejection: Gerges 2005, 27, 228, 233, also 270; Gerges 2008, 71.

5. Gerges 2005, 232, and, for a tally of policing activity, 318–319; see also Pillar 2003, xxviii–xxix; Lynch 2006, 54–55; Sageman 2008, 149; Juan Cole, *Engaging the Muslim World* (New York: Palgrave Macmillan, 2009), 163.

6. Gerges 2005, 153; Sageman 2004, 47. For a discussion of a similar phenomenon during the war in Algeria during the 1990s, see Anneli Botha, "Terrorism in Algeria: The Role of the Community in Combating Terrorism," in Peter Katona, Michael D. Intriligator, and John P. Sullivan, eds., *Countering Terrorism and*

WMD: Creating a Global Counter-Terrorism Network (London: Routledge, 2006), 144–157. On the generally counterproductive effects for terrorists of targeting civilians, see Abrahms 2006, Mack 2008.

7. Indonesia: Sageman 2004, 53, 142, 173. Saudi Arabia: Gerges 2005, 249; Sageman 2004, 53, 144. Morocco: Sageman 2004, 53–54. Jordan polls: Pew Global Attitudes Project, "The Great Divide: How Westerners and Muslims View Each Other," June 22, 2006, pewglobal.org; see also Lynch 2006, 54–55. Religious grounds: Gerges 2008, 75. In sum, says Gerges, although al-Qaeda may retain local affiliates in Saudi Arabia, Yemen, Jordan, Pakistan, and elsewhere, "they are shrinking by the hour and bleeding profusely from the blows of the security services with substantial logistical support from the United States" (2005, 249). See also Pillar 2003, xxiv; Zakaria 2010.

8. Peter Bergen, "Where You Bin? The Return of Al Qaeda," *New Republic*, January 29, 2007, 19.

9. Porter 2009, 298.

10. Warrick 2008. See also Gerges 2005, ch. 5.

11. Gerges 2005, 252–253, 256–259. Bergen and Cruickshank 2007.

12. Zawahiri: Mack 2008, 15. Mindless brutalities: Bob Woodward, "Why Did Violence Plummet? It Wasn't Just the Surge," *Washington Post*, September 8, 2008. Iraq polls: Mack 2008, 15–17. Grenier: Warrick 2008. See also Bergen and Cruickshank 2007; Jenkins 2008, 191.

13. Uncomfortable hosts: Burke 2003, 150, 164–165; Wright 2006, 230–231, 287–288; Brown 2010. No foreign fighters: Brian Glyn Williams, "Return of the Arabs: Al-Qa'ida's Current Military Role in the Afghan Insurgency," *CTC Sentinel*, 1(3) 2008: 22–25. American commander: Craig Whitlock, "Facing Afghan Mistrust, al-Qaeda Fighters Take Limited Role in Insurgency," *Washington Post*, August 23, 2010. Panetta: Daniel W. Drezner, "Why I'm glad I'm not a counter-terrorism expert," foreignpolicy.com, June 28, 2010. Extensive study: Seth G. Jones, "The Rise of Afghanistan's Insurgency: State Failure and Jihad," *International Security*, 32(4) 2008: 7–40. Distanced: Brown 2010, 2. House arrest, Borchgrave: Scott Atran, "Turning the Taliban against Al Qaeda," *New York Times*, October 26, 2010.

14. Glenn L. Carle, "Overstating Our Fears," *Washington Post*, July 13, 2008; see also Sageman 2008, Gerges 2008.

15. Sheehan 2008, 14. Dickey 2009, 118–119.

16. This discussion stems from Sageman 2008, from conversations with Sageman, and from a talk on the book he gave in Washington as televised on C-SPAN in early 2008 (ably summarized in David Ignatius, "The Fading Jihadists," *Washington Post*, February 28, 2008).

17. Wright 2008. See also Zakaria 2010.

18. Sageman 2008, 128. Kenney 2010a, 185. On the case of Bryant Neal Vinas, an American who sought to join al-Qaeda and was then arrested and has become an informer, see "American Al-Qaeda," CNN, May 15, 2010. See also Mueller 2011.

19. Martin C. Libicki, Peter Chalk, and Melanie Sisson, *Exploring Terrorist Targeting Preferences* (Santa Monica, CA: RAND, 2007), 67, 70. The authors suggest an

attack in Taba, Egypt, in October 2004 may have been run by al-Qaeda, but, as they note (p. 46), Egyptian officials have ruled that out based on confessions and evidence at the scene. See also Friedman 2008, 37. On al-Qaeda's threats, see also Mueller 2010, 218–220.

20. Johnson 2009.

21. On this point, see also Hoffman 2006, 271–272.

22. 2002 reports: Gertz 2002. Testimony by Mueller can be found through www.fbi.gov/congress/congress.htm.

23. 2005 report: Brian Ross, "Secret FBI Report Questions Al Qaeda Capabilities: No 'True' Al Qaeda Sleeper Agents Have Been Found in U.S.," ABC News, March 9, 2005. Press conference: Michael Isikoff and Mark Hosenball, "The Flip Side of the NIE," Newsweek.com, August 15, 2007. Officer: Bill Gertz, "Al Qaeda Seen In Search of Nukes: Defense Official Warns U.S. Still Group's Target," *Washington Times*, July 26, 2007. In 2005, FBI Director Robert Mueller testified that his top concern was "the threat from covert operatives who may be inside the U.S." and considered finding them to be his top priority; however, they had been unable to find any (Dana Priest and Josh White, "War Helps Recruit Terrorists, Hill Told; Intelligence Officials Talk Of Growing Insurgency," *Washington Post*, February 17, 2005).

24. During 2008, for example, nonimmigrant admissions to the United States alone totaled 175 million (Randall Monger and Macreadie Barr, *Nonimmigrant Admissions to the United States: 2008* [Washington, DC: Department of Homeland Security, Office of Immigration Statistics, Annual Flow Report, April 2009]). Not all of these, of course, enter at international airports; the total includes people repeatedly going back and forth across the borders with Canada and Mexico.

25. Spencer S. Hsu, "Homeland Security Chief Warns of Threat from al-Qaeda Sympathizers in U.S.," *Washington Post*, December 3, 2009.

26. Peter Bergen and Bruce Hoffman, *Assessing the Terrorist Threat: A Report of the Bipartisan Policy Center's National Security Preparedness Group* (Washington, DC: Bipartisan Policy Center, September 10, 2010), 4 (mass-casualty), 32 (less sophisticated operations, worrisome trend), 3 (more complex), 31 (public safety officials). See also Philip Mudd, "Evaluating the Al-Qa'ida Threat to the Homeland," *CTC Sentinel*, August 2010, 1–4. For a debunking of the supposed trend, see Joshua L. Dratel, "Nothing New about Homegrown Terrorism," centerlineblog.org, July 27, 2010. For additional argument on the unlikelihood of a major attack on the United States, see "Biden: Major Terror Attack on U.S. Unlikely," cnn.com, February 11, 2010.

27. Richard A. Serrano, "U.S. Faces 'Heightened' Threat Level," *Los Angeles Times*, February 10, 2011.

28. Max Abrahms, "Fear of 'Lone Wolf' Misplaced," *Baltimore Sun*, January 5, 2011.

29. Jenkins 2010, 4 (tiny), 5 (Mao), 13 (one-off). See also Brooks 2011.

30. David Schanzer, Charles Kurzman, and Ebrahim Mooza, "Anti-Terror Lessons of Muslim-Americans," Triangle Center on Terrorism and Homeland Security, January 6, 2010.

31. Lawson 2008. Splintering analogy: Karl Mueller, personal communication. See also Kenney 2010b; Bruce Schneier, "Portrait of the Modern Terrorist as an Idiot," schneier.com, June 14, 2007; Daniel Byman and Christine Fair, "The Case for Calling Them Nitwits," *Atlantic*, July–August 2010; Brooks 2011.
32. *Times*: David Johnston and Scott Shane, "Terror Case Is Called One of the Most Serious in Years," *New York Times*, September 25, 2009. Most serious: Johnson 2009. Riedel: *Lehrer NewsHour*, PBS, October 16, 2009.
33. Mueller 2011.
34. Ivan Moreno and P. Solomon Banda, "Prosecutor: Terror Plot Focus was 9/11 Anniversary," Associated Press, September 26, 2009.
35. Johnson 2009.
36. Shikha Dalmia, "What Islamist Terrorist Threat?" reason.com, February 15, 2011.
37. Kenney 2010b. To demonstrate how we face "a thinking enemy that is constantly adapting to defeat our countermeasures," former Deputy Secretary of Homeland Security James Loy argues that when cockpit doors were hardened to prevent hijackings, the terrorists moved to shoe bombs to "penetrate our defenses" ("Al-Qaeda's Undimmed Threat," *Washington Post*, November 7, 2010). However, the hardened doors (which anyway were not much in place in late 2001, when the shoe bomber made his move) were in no sense a defense against bombings, only, as Loy admits, against hijacking. Similarly, Loy's (widely accepted) contention that terrorists "nearly succeeded in blowing up seven planes crossing the Atlantic" is simply preposterous. The terrorist group was under constant police surveillance and could be closed down at any time, and it was nowhere near having sufficient materials or personnel or effective bombs. Moreover, many of the conspirators did not possess passports that would have allowed them to board the planes. See Mueller 2011.
38. Mette Eilstrup-Sangiovanni and Calvert Jones, "Assessing the Dangers of Illicit Networks," *International Security*, Fall 2008. See also Brooks 2011.
39. Kenney 2010a. Stenersen 2009, 56. See also Stenersen 2008. By contrast, see Gabriel Weimann, *Terror on the Internet: The New Arena, the New Challenges* (Washington, DC: United States Institute of Peace, 2006).
40. Clare Dyer, "'There Is No War on Terror': Outspoken DPP Takes on Blair and Reid over Fear-Driven Legal Response to Threat," *Guardian*, January 24, 2007.
41. After 2003, the State Department changed its definitions so that much domestic terrorism—including much of what is happening in the war in Iraq—is now included in its terrorism count (see National Counterterrorism Center, "Report on Incidents of Terrorism 2005," April 11, 2006, ii–iii). Current numbers, therefore, are not comparable to earlier ones. However, when terrorism becomes really extensive in an area, we generally no longer call it terrorism, but rather war or insurgency. Thus, the Irish Republican Army was generally taken to be a terrorist enterprise, while fighters in Algeria or Sri Lanka in the 1990s were considered to be combatants who were employing guerrilla techniques in a civil war situation—even though some of them came from, or were substantially aided by, people from outside the country. Insurgents and guerrilla combatants usually rely on the hit-and-run tactics employed by the terrorist, and the difference between terrorism and such wars is not in the method, but in

the frequency with which it is employed. Without this distinction, much civil warfare (certainly including the decade-long conflict in Algeria in the 1990s in which perhaps 100,000 people perished) would have to be included in the terrorist category. And so would most "primitive warfare," which, like irregular warfare more generally, relies mostly on raids rather on set-piece battles (see Lawrence H. Keeley, *War before Civilization: The Myth of the Peaceful Savage* [New York: Oxford University Press, 1996]; and for more on the distinction between terrorism and civil war, Mueller 2004, 18–20). That is, with the revised definition, a huge number of violent endeavors that have normally been called wars would have to be recategorized. Indeed, the concept of civil war might have to be retired almost entirely. Most of the mayhem in the American Civil War did take place in set-piece battles between uniformed combatants, but that conflict was extremely unusual among civil wars in this respect—the rebels in most civil wars substantially rely on tactics that are indistinguishable from those employed by the terrorist. When people in the developed world worry about terrorism, however, they are not particularly concerned that sustained civil warfare or insurgency will break out in their country. They are mainly fearful of random or sporadic acts of terrorism carried out within their homeland. For this concern, the original State Department definition, not an expanded one stemming from the sustained violence in Iraq, seems to be the most appropriate for our purposes here.

42. Todd Sandler, Daniel G. Arce, and Walter Enders, "Transnational Terrorism," in Lomborg 2009, 524.

43. About 100 Americans die per year from accidents caused by deer: Andrew C. Revkin, "Coming to the Suburbs: A Hit Squad for Deer," *New York Times*, November 30, 1998. The same number holds for peanut allergies: http://blogcritics.org/archives/2004/09/19/161029.php. See also Schneier 2003, 11, 237, 241–242.

44. See also Schneier 2003, 237–242.

45. Anthony H. Cordesman, *The Challenge of Biological Weapons* (Washington, DC: Center for Strategic and International Studies, 2005), 29–31, tallies "major attacks by Islamists" outside of Iraq: 830 fatalities for the period April 2002 through July 2005; we have corrected the total for the 2005 London bombings, given as 100 in this source, to 52. Brian Michael Jenkins, *Unconquerable Nation: Knowing Our Enemy and Strengthening Ourselves* (Santa Monica, CA: RAND, 2006), 179–184, tallies "major terrorist attacks worldwide" by "jihadist extremists" outside Afghanistan, Iraq, Israel, Palestine, Algeria, Russia, and Kashmir: 1,129 fatalities for the period October 2001 through April 2006. "Jihadi Attack Kill Statistics," IntelCenter, August 17, 2007, 11 (www.intelcenter.com), tallies "most significant attacks executed by core al-Qaeda, regional arms and affiliate groups excluding operations in insurgency theaters": 1,632 fatalities for the period January 2002 through July 2007.

46. John Stossel, *Give Me a Break* (New York: HarperCollins, 2004), 77.

47. Blalock et al. 2007.

48. Fatality data are based on GTD terrorist incidents that satisfied the following criteria: the act must be aimed at attaining a political, economic, religious, or

social goal; there must be evidence of an intention to coerce, intimidate, or convey some other message to a larger audience (or audiences) than the immediate victims; the action must be outside the context of legitimate warfare activities; and there is essentially no doubt as to whether the incident is an act of terrorism. Terrorist incidents that did not satisfy these criteria were filtered out of the database.

49. New York City–Northern New Jersey–Long Island. The U.S. Census Bureau estimates the 2009 population as 19.1 million.

50. The August 2006 transatlantic plot to detonate liquid explosives on up to ten commercial aircraft is not included, as this plot was disrupted by British police and security services and was not a direct threat to the American homeland.

51. For example, there was absolutely nothing of substance behind the "plot" to blow up the Sears Tower in Chicago. It was a fantasy (or con) inspired by the movies, according to its creator, that he anticipated would generate confusion (possibly by generating a tsunami in Lake Michigan), during which Muslim prisoners from a jail could be liberated to form an army for an independent nation. Walter Pincus, "FBI Role in Terror Probe Questioned," *Washington Post*, September 2, 2006. Amanda Ripley, "Preemptive Terror Trials: Strike Two," *Time*, December 13, 2007. See also Mueller 2011.

52. This would also be the number the underwear bomber of 2009 would have been able to kill, had he been successful at blowing up his airliner.

53. Howard: *Sydney Morning Herald*, October 18, 2002. Clark: Associated Press, October 14, 2002.

54. As is common practice, we have in this book valued every life equally. Following the definitions laid out in chapter 1 then, risk, which is the product of consequences and likelihood, in the present discussion becomes entirely a function of likelihood. This is because the consequence (loss of life) is held essentially to be a constant, and we seek to assess the likelihood a particular hazard will cause loss of life (the annual fatality rate) and then compare it with other hazards on this dimension. However, it is clearly true that from society's standpoint young adults, who are yet to make their contribution (and pay their taxes), are essentially more valuable than older people, who have already made their contribution and have disproportionately become a cost to society. If one adds in such a consideration, automobiles, which very disproportionately lead to the deaths of young adults (particularly male ones), inflict peculiarly high costs. If one adds in as well the loss of future progeny, the costs to society of the automobile would become even higher.

55. This does not include the deaths of people who suffer fatal falls trying to board a subway train by jumping on the landing between cars.

56. Some argue that an important issue is that the automobile system is voluntary—no one is forced to drive around in a car. However, fully 12 percent of automobile accident victims in the United States in 2008 were pedestrians, and no one really has much of an effective choice about being one of those from time to time. Others argue that it is important to point out that the deaths caused by automobiles are unintentional—deaths, unlike war or terrorism, for example, are not its point but an unfortunate side effect.

However, in an important sense, the deaths are indeed intentional: unlike most deaths from cancer and heart disease, they happen because the United States has systematically chosen to encourage the automobile over means of transportation that are well known to be less dangerous. A reduction of the speed limit for private passenger automobiles to 13 miles per hour in the country would, if enforced, save over 3 million lives by the end of the century at present fatality rates. To oppose such a law is to pay this price willingly to get there faster by automobile.

57. "The Tolerability of Risk from Nuclear Power Stations," Health and Safety Executive, HMSO, London.

58. International Traffic Safety and Analysis Group, OECD, 2009.

59. Lawrence J. Blincoe, Angela G. Seay, Eduard Zaloshnja, Ted R. Miller, Eduardo O. Romano, Stephen Luchter, and Rebecca S. Spicer, *The Economic Impact of Motor Vehicle Crashes 2000*, Report No. DOT HS 809 446 (Washington, DC: National Highway Traffic Safety Administration, May 2002), 3.

60. Stewart and Melchers 1997, 208–216. Slovic et al. 1980.

61. *Industrial Union Department, AFL-CIO v. American Petroleum Institute*, 448 U.S. 607, 655 (1980).

62. Travis et al. 1987.

63. Specifically that the risk to an individual or to the population in the vicinity of a nuclear power plant of prompt fatalities that might result from reactor accidents should not exceed 0.1 percent of the sum of prompt fatality risks resulting from other accidents to which members of the U.S. population are generally exposed, and that the risk of cancer fatalities should not exceed 0.1 percent of the sum of cancer fatality risks resulting from all other sources. "Safety Goals for the Operation of Nuclear Power Plants; Policy Statement," U.S. Nuclear Regulatory Commission, *Federal Register*, 1986, 51, 30028.

64. "Safety Assessment Principles for Nuclear Facilities," Health and Safety Executive, Merseyside, UK, 2006, 100–103.

65. "Safety Goals," Nuclear Safety Commission of Japan, 2006, www.nsc.go.jp/NSCenglish/topics/safety_goals.htm.

66. "Risk Criteria for Land Use Safety Planning," Hazardous Industry Planning Advisory Paper No. 4, Department of Planning, Sydney, Australia.

67. Travis et al. 1987.

68. Richard A. Meserve, "The Evolution of Safety Goals and Their Connection to Safety Culture," *NRC News*, S-01-013, U.S. Nuclear Regulatory Commission, Office of Public Affairs, Washington, DC, June 18, 2001.

69. See also "The Tolerability of Risk from Nuclear Power Stations," Health and Safety Executive, London, 1992; Stewart and Melchers 1997, 227–241. An acceptable risk is not one that is negligible or *de minimus* meaning essentially zero risk: V. Martin Petersen, "What Is a de Minimis Risk," *Risk Management*, 4(2) 2002: 47–55. It is simply a risk that we can learn to live with. Our discussion is mainly focused on public risks that are generally involuntary; acceptable risk levels for workers are often an order of magnitude higher than those for the public. See Paté-Cornell 1994.

70. Slovic et al. 1980.

71. See also Kenneth T. Bogen and Edwin D. Jones, "Risks of Mortality and Morbidity from Worldwide Terrorism: 1968–2004," *Risk Analysis*, 26(1) 2006: 56; Gardner 2008, 250–251.
72. Paul Slovic, Baruch Fischhoff, and Sarah Lichtenstein, "Rating the Risks," in Paul Slovic, ed., *The Perception of Risk* (London: Earthscan, 2000), 115.
73. As noted earlier, this includes the New York–Northern New Jersey–Long Island area, populated in 2009 by 19.1 million. The calculation of the annual fatality rate is, of course, sensitive to the denominator: the population exposed to the risk. Further reductions in the size of the denominator in this case to embrace, say, only the population of Manhattan seem ill-advised. Among the complications: the 9/11 attacks on the World Trade Center claimed more than 300 foreign victims, and the populations of their countries are not, of course, included in the denominator.
74. Mack 2008.
75. For rare, perhaps unique, exceptions, see Mueller 2002; Seitz 2004.
76. Walter Laqueur, "Postmodern Terrorism: New Rules for an Old Game," *Foreign Affairs*, September–October 1996. For a lively and insightful discussion of expert prediction, see Dan Gardner, *Future Babble* (New York: Dutton, 2011).

CHAPTER 3: THE FULL COSTS OF TERRORISM

1. Paul Slovic, "Perception of Risk from Radiation," in Paul Slovic, ed., *The Perception of Risk* (London: Earthscan, 2000), 264–274. However, the relation between risk aversion and VSL is less clear: L. R. Eeckhoudt and J. K. Hammitt, "Does Risk Aversion Increase the Value of Mortality Risk?" *Journal of Environmental Economics and Management*, 47 2004: 13–29.
2. Paté-Cornell 1994.
3. Viscusi 2000. Inflation adjusted to 2010 dollars.
4. Robert W. Hahn, "The Cost of Antiterrorist Rhetoric," *Regulation*, 19(4) 1996.
5. Robinson et al. 2010. See also Lisa A. Robinson, "Valuing Mortality Risk Reductions in Homeland Security Regulatory Analyses, Final Report," U.S. Customs and Border Protection, Department of Homeland Security, June 2008.
6. 9/11 and insurance payouts: Lloyd Dixon and Rachel K. Stern, *Compensation for Losses from the 9/11 Attacks* (Santa Monica, CA: RAND Institute for Civil Justice, 2004), 31, 17. Oklahoma City: Jennifer Brown, "Oklahoma City Bombing Victims Feel Neglected Because of 9/11 Compensation Fund," *Argus Press*, August 27, 2002. Aviation: James S. Kakalik, Elizabeth M. King, Michael Traynor, Patricia A. Ebner, and Larry Picus, *Costs and Compensation Paid in Aviation Accident Litigation* (Santa Monica, CA: RAND Institute for Civil Justice, 1988), x; in 2010 dollars. Iraq: Stiglitz and Bilmes 2008, 17.
7. Viscusi 2000, 215.
8. J. Bram, J. Orr, and C. Rapaport, "Measuring the Effects of the September 11 Attack on New York City," *FRBNY Economic Policy Review*, November 2002: 5–20.
9. World Bank estimate of U.S. 2009 GDP of $14,256,300 million.

10. Hook 2008.
11. S. Brock Blomberg and Adam Z. Rose, "Editor's Introduction to the Economic Impacts of the September 11, 2001, Terrorist Attacks," *Peace Economics, Peace Science, and Public Policy* 15(2), 2009: 1–14.
12. Paul Krugman, "The Costs of Terrorism: What Do We Know?" Briefing Note, the Nexus of Terrorism & WMDs: Developing a Consensus, Princeton University, 12–14 December 2004. David Wyss, "Where Terror Hurts Less," *BusinessWeek*, July 11, 2005.
13. Todd Sandler and Walter Enders, "Economic Consequences of Terrorism in Developed and Developing Countries: An Overview," World Bank Working Paper, 2005.
14. Carl Bonham, Christopher Edmonds, and James Mak, "The Impact of 9/11 and Other Terrible Global Events on Tourism in the United States and Hawaii," *Journal of Travel Research*, 45(1) 2006: 99–110.
15. Blalock et al. 2009.
16. One study (Gordon et al. 2007) has concluded, however, that the impact on the airline industry of a single plane being blown up would alone be in this range. This finding is assessed in chapter 7.
17. "London Bombing Liability Limited," *Claims Magazine*, August 4, 2005.
18. "The Radical Islamic Group That Acts as 'Conveyor Belt' for Terror," *Independent*, August 7, 2005. Using an exchange rate of £1.0 = $1.5.
19. "Terror Strikes to Cost London £600m," *Scotsman*, August 1, 2005.
20. London Chamber of Commerce and Industry 2005, 5.
21. O'Connor et al. 2008.
22. Bill Keane and Phillip Esper, "Forensic Investigation of Blast Damage to British Buildings," *Proceedings of Institution of Civil Engineers (Civil Engineering)*, 162 2009: 4–11.
23. London Chamber of Commerce and Industry 2005, 8.
24. Paul Hamilos, "The Worst Islamic Attack in European History," *Guardian*, October 31, 2007.
25. Buesa et al. 2007. Direct costs included cost of rescue operations and of the loss of life, health costs, loss of wages for injured people, damage to rail infrastructure and adjacent houses, cost of services of psychological support, and opportunity cost that the citizens incurred in order to express their solidarity with the victims the day after the attacks. Compensation to victims was €220,000 for each fatality and €455,000 for each critical or seriously injured victim.
26. O'Connor et al. 2008.
27. Buesa et al. 2007, 5.
28. The estimate is based on $1.2 billion for loss of life plus $282 million in direct losses plus loss of tourism and business interruption.
29. Statistics Indonesia, Number of Foreign Visitor Arrivals to Indonesia by Port of Entry 1997–2008.
30. A 2003 report by the Australian Centre for International Economics tell us that the cost of the Bali bombings at an economic level is about A$3 billion ($2.5 billion).

31. Gunter et al. 2002, 7.
32. Zycher 2003. In this study, lives are valued at $4.9 million each. It defines the "moderate" case as one that uses the 1999 experience in Northern Ireland, scaled up to be proportional to the U.S. population. In 1999, there were 7 deaths and 878 injuries resulting from sectarian violence in Northern Ireland.
33. S. Ungerer, H. Ergas, S. Hook, and M. Stewart, *Risky Business: Measuring the Costs and Benefits of Counter-Terrorism Spending*, Special Report, Issue 18, Australian Strategic Policy Institute, Canberra, November 2008.
34. Only 8 of the 219 attacks resulted in the death of more than ten people, the worst being the 28 killed in the 1998 bombing in Omagh, Northern Ireland. In some instances, republican terrorists warned authorities of impending attack; they did so in Omagh, but the warnings were unclear, and the wrong areas were evacuated. The GTD defines a single terrorist attack as one occurring in the same geographic area and at the same point in time. Hence the 2005 London attacks are included in the count as four separate incidents.
35. Global Terrorism Database.
36. See also Gardner 2008.
37. Obama: see also Woodward 2010, 363. Lugar: Fox News Sunday, June 15, 2003. Charles Krauthammer, "Blixful Amnesia," *Washington Post*, July 9, 2004. G. Allison 2004, 191. Joshua S. Goldstein, *The Real Price of War: How You Pay for the War on Terror* (New York: New York University Press, 2004), 145, 179. Michael Ignatieff, *The Lesser Evil: Political Ethics in an Age of Terror* (Princeton, NJ: Princeton University Press, 2004), 147.
38. Oppenheimer: Kai Bird and Martin Sherwin, *American Prometheus: The Triumph and Tragedy of J. Robert Oppenheimer* (New York: Knopf, 2005), 349; for a similar comment by President Barack Obama, see Woodward 2010, 363. Predictions: for example, John McPhee, *The Curve of Binding Energy* (New York: Farrar, Straus and Giroux, 1974), 195–197; G. Allison 1995.
39. Karl P. Mueller, "The Paradox of Liberal Hegemony: Globalization and U.S. National Security," in Jonathan Kirshner, ed., *Globalization and National Security* (New York: Routledge, 2006), 156.
40. For example, John Negroponte at www.globalsecurity.org/security/library/report/2003/n0335167.pdf; G. Allison 2004, 15; Michael Scheuer on *60 Minutes* (CBS), November 14, 2004: "probably a near thing."
41. Jenkins 2008, 250–251.
42. Mueller 2010, xi.
43. Tenet and Harlow 2007, 279. For an array of similar assertions, see Mueller 2010, ch. 2.
44. See also Woodward 2010, 383.
45. Charles Meade and Roger C. Molander, *Considering the Effects of a Catastrophic Terrorist Attack* (Santa Monica, CA: RAND, 2006). On this study, see also Mueller 2010, 270, n. 30.
46. On this issue, see in particular W. Allison 2009.
47. Matthew Bunn, Anthony Weir, and J. P. Holdren, *Controlling Nuclear Warheads and Materials: A Report Card and Action Plan* (Washington, DC: Nuclear Threat Initiative and Cambridge, MA: Project on Managing the Atom, Harvard

University, 2003). Gunter et al. posit, probably more than bit fancifully, similar trillion dollar losses as a result of a "weapon of mass destruction" shipped via containers or the mail that would trigger an extended shutdown in deliveries, physical destruction, and lost production in the contaminated area; massive loss of life; and medical treatment for survivors (2002, 7).

48. For a much more extensive discussion of this issue, see Mueller 2010, chs. 11–12. See also Gardner 2008, 253–259; Jenkins 2008.

49. Wirz and Egger 2005.

50. Disassembled: Mitchell Reiss, *Bridled Ambition: Why Countries Constrain Their Nuclear Capabilities* (Washington, DC: Woodrow Wilson Center Press, 1995), 11, 13; Joby Warrick, "Pakistan Nuclear Security Questioned: Lack of Knowledge about Arsenal May Limit U.S. Options," *Washington Post*, November 11, 2007. Younger 2009, 153–154. See also Levi 2007, 125.

51. Levi 2007, 26; Lugar 2005, 17. See also Ferguson and Potter 2005, chs. 3–4.

52. Gilmore Commission 1999.

53. See also Levi 2007, 29, 32–33.

54. Wirz and Egger 2005.

55. Younger 2009, 146.

56. G. Allison 2004, 97.

57. It appears reasonable to suggest that terrorists seeking to create a bomb would have to overcome at least 20 hurdles that can be taken to be essentially independent of each other. Even under the generous assumption that they have a fighting chance of 50 percent of overcoming each of these obstacles, the probability that a concerted effort would be successful comes out to be less than one in a million. If one assumes, somewhat more realistically, that their chances at each barrier are one in three, the cumulative odds they will be able to pull off the deed drop to one in well over 3 billion. For details on the hurdles and on the calculations, see Mueller 2010, ch. 13.

58. On the history of WMD and for data on the use of the term, see W. Seth Carus, *Defining "Weapons of Mass Destruction"*, Center for the Study of Weapons of Mass Destruction Occasional Paper 42006 (Washington, DC: National Defense University Press, 2006). Actually, as Carus notes, the 1994 legal definition of the concept is so broad that hand grenades, bombs bursting in air, and Revolutionary War muskets would be considered to be WMD (see also John Mueller and Karl Mueller, "The Rockets' Red Glare: Just What Are 'Weapons of Mass Destruction,' Anyway?" foreignpolicy.com, July 7, 2009). See also Pillar 2003, 21–26; David C. Rapoport, "Terrorists and Weapons of the Apocalypse," *National Security Studies Quarterly*, 5(1) 1999: 49–67; Peter Bergen, "WMD Terrorism Fears are Overblown," cnn.com, December 5, 2008; Mueller 2010, 11–15.

59. World War: Mueller 2006, 18–19. Matthew Meselson, "The Myth of Chemical Superweapons," *Bulletin of the Atomic Scientists*, April 1991: 13. Gilmore Commission 1999, 28.

60. Jonathan B. Tucker and Amy Sands, "An Unlikely Threat," *Bulletin of the Atomic Scientists*, July–August 1999: 51. See also Gilmore Commission 1999, 25; Milton Leitenberg, *Assessing the Biological Weapons and Bioterrorism Threat*

(Carlisle, PA: Strategic Studies Institute, U.S. Army War College, 2005); David Ropeik and George Gray, *Risk: A Practical Guide for Deciding What's Really Safe and What's Really Dangerous in the World around You* (Boston: Houghton Mifflin, 2002), ch. 22.

61. Zimmerman and Loeb 2004, 11. Ferguson et al. 2003, 19. G. Allison 2004, 8. See also Rockwell 2003.

62. Michael A. Levi and Henry C. Kelly, "Weapons of Mass Disruption," *Scientific American*, November 2002.

63. Stenersen 2008, 39, 35–36. See also Mueller 2010, ch. 14.

64. Craig Whitlock, "Homemade, Cheap and Dangerous: Terror Cells Favor Simple Ingredients in Building Bombs," *Washington Post*, July 5, 2007.

65. Stenersen 2009, 59. The excitable jihadist is at least somewhat more accurate than bomb maker Oppenheimer, who maintained, as quoted here, that an atomic bomb could "blow up" *all* of New York.

66. On this issue more broadly, see Mueller 2006.

67. For the (controversial) argument that, absent the assassinations, World War I would not have taken place, see Richard Ned Lebow, *Forbidden Fruit: Counterfactuals and International Relations* (Princeton, NJ: Princeton University Press, 2010), ch. 3.

68. Pillar 2003, xv.

69. Burke 2003, 167–168; Wright 2006, 267–268, 287–289, 354.

70. Michael Ignatieff, "Lesser Evils: What It Will Cost Us to Succeed in the War on Terror," *New York Times Magazine*, May 2, 2004. This article also includes his confident prediction that there would terrorist events in connection with the 2004 U.S. elections.

71. See Gardner 2008, 259. On the notable spike in confidence in government engendered by the 9/11 attacks, see Pew Research Center, *The People and Their Government: Distrust, Discontent, Anger and Partisan Rancor* (Washington, DC: Pew Research Center, April 18, 2010).

72. However, top members of the Obama administration have strongly indicated to Pakistani leaders that, if the United States is hit by a terrorist attack "connected to a Pakistani group," there are some things Obama "would not be able to stop" because "there are political realities in the United States," and he would accordingly be "forced to do things that Pakistan would not like." Pakistani leaders have sensibly pointed out that this could well be foolish and self-destructive: "if we have a strategic partnership, why in the face of a crisis like you're describing would we not draw close together rather than have this divide us?" The Americans' tunnel-vision reply was that "President Obama's only choice would be to respond. There would be no alternative." Woodward 2010, 364.

73. Lugar 2005, 14–15.

74. G. Allison 2004, 15. Calculation based on a series system probability analysis where Allison claims a 50 percent chance in ten years, leading to the calculation $0.5 = 1 - (1 - 0.066)^{10}$. Allison had presumably relied on the same inspirational mechanism when he predicted in a 1995 article: "In the absence of a determined program of action, we have every reason to anticipate acts of nuclear terrorism against American targets before this decade is out."

75. Graham T. Allison, "How Likely Is a Nuclear Terrorist Attack on the United States?" New York Council on Foreign Relations, April 2007. None of these estimates assumes, however, that the explosion would necessarily be set off in the rare location where, as in the worst-case scenario, it could cause $5 trillion in damage. Nor do they assume that the terrorist device would be as large as ten kilotons: see G. Allison 2004, 15.

CHAPTER 4: EVALUATING INCREASES IN HOMELAND SECURITY SPENDING

1. As required, for example, by the U.S. Office of Management and Budget: "Executive Order 12866 requires agencies, to the extent permitted by law, to 'propose or adopt a regulation only upon a reasoned determination that the benefits of the intended regulation justify its costs'" (2009 Report to Congress on the Benefits and Costs of Federal Regulations and Unfunded Mandates on State, Local, and Tribal Entities, Office of Management and Budget Office of Information and Regulatory Affairs, 2009, 16). And by the Australian government, which says it "is committed to the use of cost-benefit analysis to assess regulatory proposals to encourage better decision making" (*Best Practice Regulation Handbook* [Canberra: Office of Best Practice Regulation, Australian Government, August 2007], 115). See also Stewart and Melchers 1997, 216–227.

2. System modeling and reliability techniques exist to calculate risk reductions for any system (see Stewart and Melchers 1997; Stewart 2010) While there are many advantages to probabilistic and reliability analyses for calculating risk reductions, they are not always appropriate, particularly for the "new hazard" of terrorism. Hence, as is the case with any risk analysis of a complex system, information about risk reductions may be inferred from expert opinions, scenario analysis, statistical analysis of prior performance data, and system modeling, as well as from probabilistic and reliability analysis. The discussion to follow draws on all these aspects to arrive at quantifiable risk reductions.

3. Kean 2004, 108. Thus, in a speech at the U.S. Naval Academy in May 1998, President Bill Clinton said, "First, we will use our new integrated approach to intensify the fight against all forms of terrorism, to capture terrorists no matter where they hide, to work with other nations to eliminate terrorist sanctuaries overseas, to respond rapidly and effectively to protect Americans from terrorism at home and abroad. Second, we will launch a comprehensive plan to detect, deter and defend against attacks on our critical infrastructures—our power systems, water supplies, police, fire and medical services, air traffic control, financial services, telephone systems and computer networks. . . . We can and we must make these critical systems more secure, so that we can be more secure. Third, we will undertake a concerted effort to prevent the spread and use of biological weapons. And to protect our people in the event these terrible weapons are ever unleashed by a rogue state or terrorist group or an international criminal organization" (Kean 2004, 101). On this issue, see also Benjamin H. Friedman, "Perception and Power in Counterterrorism: Assessing the American Response to Al Qaeda before September 11," in Trevor Thrall and Jane K. Cramer, eds., *American Foreign Policy and the Politics of Fear: Threat Inflation since 9/11* (London: Routledge 2009), 210–229.

4. Kean 2004, 108.
5. Frederick Mosteller and Cleo Youtz, "Quantifying Probabilistic Expressions," *Statistical Science*, 5(1) 1990: 2–12.
6. Sheehan 2008, 263.
7. Jenkins 2010, 8–9.
8. Terry McDermott, "The Mastermind: Khalid Sheikh Mohammed and the Making of 9/11," *New Yorker*, September 13, 2010.
9. Transportation Security Administration, "DHS Announces Security Standards for Freight and Passenger Rail Systems," Press Release, November 13, 2008. As noted in the introduction this is the only instance in published DHS literature we have been able to find where risk reduction methods are specifically and coherently used.
10. LaTourrette et al. 2006, 48.
11. While it might be expected that additional benefits not directly related to mitigating terrorist threats (e.g., reduction in criminal behavior due to enhanced building security, increased consumer confidence) may be gained, there are also opportunity costs of enhanced security measures, such as increased inconvenience and delays, that would most likely counterbalance any of these relatively minor gains in benefit.
12. Office of Management and Budget, *Analytical Perspectives, Budget of the United States Government, Fiscal Year 2011*, Washington, DC, 2010, 380.
13. Hobijn and Sager 2007.
14. OMB, *Analytical Perspectives 2010*, 379. FY2009 is the most recent year where actual expenditures, as opposed to budget requests, are known. The federal budget includes expenditures from aviation security fees and other fee-funded homeland security programs.
15. Defined by OMB as "activities of both intelligence-and-warning and domestic counterterrorism aim to disrupt the ability of terrorists to operate within our borders and prevent the emergence of violent radicalization."
16. For OMB, "critical infrastructure includes the assets, systems, and networks, whether physical or virtual, so vital to the United States that their incapacitation or destruction would have a debilitating effect on security, national economic security, public health or safety, or any combination thereof."
17. Defined by OMB as "the ability to respond to and recover from incidents requires efforts to bolster capabilities nationwide to prevent and protect against terrorist attacks, and also minimize the damage from attacks through effective response and recovery."
18. Actual expenditures for FY2010 and FY2011 are not known at this time.
19. Pincus 2009.
20. Budget of the U.S. Government, Fiscal Year 2011, 61.
21. $75 billion divided by risk reduction (45 percent) divided by $5 billion.
22. The ratio of benefit to cost is equal to (attack probability) x (losses) x (risk reduction)/(security cost)
23. Interesting in this respect is Vice President Dick Cheney's "one-percent doctrine." When a top CIA analyst told him in 2001 that al-Qaeda probably didn't have a nuclear weapon, but that he couldn't "assure you that they don't,"

Cheney replied, "If there's a one percent chance that they do, you have to pursue it as if it were true" (Tenet and Harlow 2007, 264). Table 4.1 suggests in the last column, however, that there would have to be at least a 3.3 percent yearly chance that al-Qaeda not only had a nuclear weapon but also possessed the capacity to set one off in a key place in a crowded American city. Under that circumstance, enhanced homeland security expenditures would be deemed cost-effective.

24. $75 billion divided by value of life ($6.5 million).
25. Lives saved equals the attack probability (1 percent) multiplied by risk reduction (100 percent) multiplied by losses (3,000 lives).
26. Attack probabilities reduce by the ratio 0.45/0.749 = 60 percent.
27. HM Treasury, *2007 Pre-Budget Report and Comprehensive Budget Review* (London: Stationary Office, October 2007).
28. Treverton et al. 2008, 72.
29. HM Treasury 2004, *2004 Spending Review*, 76.
30. HM Treasury 2007.
31. Jonathan Stevenson, "The Role of the Armed Forces of the United Kingdom in Securing the State against Terrorism," *Connections*, Fall 2005, 26.
32. Exchange rate used is an average of approximately US$1.7/GBP.
33. For example, the Scottish government increased counterterrorism expenditure on its eight police forces by a modest £3.8 million ($6 million) over two years after the June 30, 2007, attack at Glasgow Airport. "Fighting Terrorism," News Release, Scottish Government, June 22, 2008.
34. Richard Norton-Taylor, "Cost of War in Afghanistan Soars to £2.5 bn," *Guardian*, February 13, 2009.
35. Based on 2009 U.K. population of 62 million and World Bank estimate of U.K. 2009 GDP of $2.2 trillion. Source: http://siteresources.worldbank.org/DATASTATISTICS/Resources/GDP.pdf.
36. Based on 2009 U.S. population of 308 million and World Bank estimate of U.S. 2009 GDP of $14.2 trillion.
37. In their analysis of homeland security costs, Treverton and his colleagues conclude that "post-9/11 security spending by Britain appears to have been substantially smaller than that by the United States" (Treverton et al. 2008, 74).
38. A ratio of 15 is equal to $75 billion divided by $5 billion because threshold attack probability is directly proportional to homeland security expenditure.
39. We tried, without much success, to assess as well the homeland security budgets for Israel, France, Germany, and other Western countries. A 2006 Congressional Research Service report surmises that "France also has a budget system that largely lacks line items; instead, executive authority may move funding around to respond to needs, with minimal parliamentary oversight. For this reason, even general budget figures for the country's anti-terror effort cannot be described" (p. 9) and "There is no agency comparable to the U.S. Office of Management and Budget, able to make decisions about expenditure of funds. There is also no department or agency comparable to the U.S. Department of Homeland Security or to FEMA that directs disaster relief or counterterrorist action. And there is no Government Accountability Office (GAO) that investigates such matters as appropriate funding of government action" (p. 15).

The story for Germany is similar: "Funding for 'homeland security' functions is spread throughout the federal and state governments. Although the German Ministry of Finance provides detailed breakdowns of spending by ministry and agency, there is not a spending category combining activities that would fall under the rubric of 'homeland security'" (p. 22). Kristin Archick, Carl Ek, Paul Gallis, Francis T. Miko, and Steven Woehrel, *European Approaches to Homeland Security and Counterterrorism*, CRS Report for Congress (Washington, DC: Congressional Research Service, July 24, 2006). On Israel, see note 45.

40. Eric Lerhe, *"Connecting the Dots" and the Canadian Counter-Terrorism Effort— Steady Progress or Technical, Bureaucratic, Legal and Political Failure* (Calgary, AB: Canadian Defence and Foreign Affairs Institute, March 2009).

41. The Canadians have a somewhat peculiar homeland security (or as they prefer to put it, public safety) concern. They are essentially required to do anything, however absurd or irrational, that might prevent the elephant next door from closing off its northern border, a venture that would be highly costly to the American economy but devastating to the Canadian one.

42. Athol Yates, *2008–09 Federal Budget Briefing on Homeland Security Expenditure* (Canberra: Australian Homeland Security Research Centre, 2008). The increase in expenditure in the 2008–2009 budget was the smallest since 2002–2003, and, as Yates remarks somewhat wistfully, "This appears to reflect the declining priority given to counter-terrorism issues" illustrated by the absence of the word *terrorism* in the treasurer's speech for the first time since 2002–2003. The following year, though, the word *terrorism* was back in the budget, and so projected spending in the period increased to A$8.6 billion over the ten years from 2002–2003 to 2011–2012. Athol Yates, *Safeguarding Australia Newsletter*, May 31, 2009.

43. As with the United Kingdom, Australian and Canadian homeland security spending is dominated by national government expenditure because of their more centralized police and security structures in that country. Yates surmises that state expenditure is typically on emergency response, which is dual capability and not counterterrorism specific, and that spending at the state or local level specifically on counterterrorism is quite possibly only 5 percent of federal spending (personal communication, March 2, 2010).

44. World Bank estimate of Canadian and Australian 2009 GDP of $1.34 and $0.92 trillion, respectively.

45. Although U.S. expenditures are high in comparison with many other Western nations, they are not as high, unsurprisingly, as those of Israel, where the Ministry of Homeland Security budget exceeds 1.3 percent of GDP, or $1,235 per capita (State Budget Proposal for the Fiscal Years 2009–2010, Jerusalem, June 2009; based on a 2010 Israeli population of 7.69 million, a World Bank estimate of Israeli 2009 GDP of $195.4 billion, and an exchange rate of NIS1 = US$0.272). This would be somewhere between twice and fivefold the U.S. expenditure rate. In addition, this estimate excludes military budgets. The Israel Defense Force has primary responsibilities for antiterrorism activities in the West Bank and Palestinian administered areas, and, if the costs for those were included, Israeli "homeland security" expenditures would increase to well above

our rough estimate. On these issues, see also David Weisburd, Tal Jonathan, and Simon Perry, "The Israeli Model for Policing Terrorism: Goals, Strategies, and Open Questions," *Criminal Justice and Behavior*, 36(12) 2009: 1259–1278. Homeland security expenditures for Israel are opaque and not as detailed as their American counterparts, and, although the 2009–2010 Israeli budget specifically refers to a "Ministry of Homeland Security," other Israeli government Web pages refer to this ministry interchangeably as the Ministry of Public Safety or the Ministry of Internal Security. The Ministry of Homeland Security (or Public Safety or Internal Security) budget includes police and possibly fire brigade expenditures.

46. Series system calculation. Probability of occurrence over ten years equals $0.85 = 1.0 - (1.0 - 0.17)^{10}$.

CHAPTER 5: PROTECTING THE HOMELAND: SOME PARAMETERS

1. Office of Management and Budget, *Analytical Perspectives, Budget of the United States Government, Fiscal Year 2011* (Washington, DC: OMB, 2010), 380.
2. Alec MacGillis, "Paralyzed Roads Envisioned near Belvoir," *Washington Post*, August 1, 2006. Charles S. Clark, "Base Realignment Faces a Case of Road Rage," *National Journal*, September 11, 2010.
3. Department of Homeland Security 2009, 7.
4. Mueller 2006, ch. 7. Shapiro 2007, 16. Flynn 2007.
5. For a discussion of their low success rate at achieving their goals, see Abrahms 2006; Mack 2008.
6. U. S. Department of Energy, Energy Information Administration, "2003 Commercial Buildings Energy Consumption Survey."
7. Abrahms 2008 and, for further discussion of the group cohesion and camaraderie issue, see Horgan 2009 and Mueller 2011. In contrast, see Department of Homeland Security 2009, 33, 37. On the importance of this quality in the formation of military organization, see Mueller 2004,12–13.
8. Jeffrey B. Cozzens and William Rosenau, "Training for Terror: The 'Homegrown' Case of Jami`at al-Islam al-Sahih," *CTC Sentinel*, 2(8) 2009: 22, 23.
9. NEFA Foundation, "Target: America: A NEFA report on the Little Rock, Arkansas Recruiting Station Shooting," nefafoundation.org, June 2009, 3.
10. Mueller 2011.
11. Horgan 2009, 44.
12. Lou Michel and Dan Herbeck, *American Terrorist: Timothy McVeigh and the Oklahoma City Bombing* (New York: ReganBooks, 2001), 167–168.
13. Ellig et al. 2006, 7.
14. Stratfor, "U.S. Shopping Malls: Unlikely al Qaeda Targets," November 9, 2007.
15. James A. Lewis, "Assessing Counterterrorism, Homeland Security, and Risk," in Benjamin H. Friedman, Jim Harper, and Christopher A. Preble, eds., *Terrorizing Ourselves: Why U.S. Counterterrorism Policy Is Failing and How to Fix It* (Washington, DC: Cato Institute, 2010), 96.
16. On this issue, see also Robert Powell, "Defending against Terrorist Attacks with Limited Resources," *American Political Science Review*, 101(3) 2007: 527–541; Ervin 2006, 156–158.

17. Department of Homeland Security 2009, 11.
18. *Highway Infrastructure: Federal Efforts to Strengthen Security Should Be Better Coordinated and Targeted on the Nation's Most Critical Highway Infrastructure* (Washington, DC: U.S. Government Accountability Office, January 2009), 1.
19. Spencer S. Hsu, "New York Presses to Deploy More Bioweapons Sensors," *Washington Post,* January 9, 2008, and personal communication with Hsu. See also Dubay 2010.
20. Nick Childs, "Pentagon Staff Reclaim Destroyed Offices," *BBC News,* August 15, 2002.
21. Jason Tedjasukmana, "In Jakarta, after Bombings, the Ritz Reopens," *Time,* August 3, 2009.
22. For an application of this line of thought to the 1941 attack on Pearl Harbor, in which almost every damaged or "destroyed" ship and aircraft was repaired or replaced in a matter of a few weeks, see John Mueller, *Quiet Cataclysm* (New York: HarperCollins, 1995), ch. 7.
23. Personal communication.
24. Veronique de Rugy, "The Case for Doing Nothing," www.cato-unbound.org, September 28, 2006; Mueller 2006, 147. For an otherwise impressive study where this is not done, see LaTourrette et al. 2006.
25. Hook 2008. Zycher 2003, 22, 32.
26. Mueller 2006, 31.
27. LaTourrette et al. 2006. After undergoing considerable pressure about shopping mall security, the International Council of Shopping Centers announced shortly after Christmas 2006 that it was instituting a program to train guards to help in the fight against terrorism (Ylan Q. Mui, "From Monitoring Teens to Minding Terrorists: Mall Security Guards to Receive New Training, but Feasibility Is Questioned," *Washington Post,* January 3, 2007). If the council was more worried about terrorism than about deterring shoppers by bringing up the unpleasant subject of terrorism, it should logically have announced and carried out the program *before* the busy holiday season. One might be set to wondering, no doubt quite unfairly, why they announced it at a time of the year when there is some advantage in deterring customers, made up disproportionately by people returning and exchanging goods.
28. Ellig et al. 2006, 35; Blalock et al. 2007.
29. Furedi 2008, 651.
30. Grosskopf 2006.
31. Sunstein 2003, 132. See also Mueller 2006, 157–159.
32. Rosen 2008.
33. Schneier 2003.
34. Office of Inspector General 2006. For an extended discussion, see Mayer 2009.
35. Lustick 2006.
36. Veronique de Rugy, "What Does Homeland Security Spending Buy?" Working Paper #107, Washington, DC: American Enterprise Institute for Public Policy Research, 2005, 26. See also Mayer 2009.
37. Mueller 2011. See also Steve Emerson, *Jihad Incorporated: A Guide to Islam in the US* (Amherst, NY: Prometheus, 2006), 120.

38. Mimi Hall, "Terror Security List Way Behind," *USA Today*, December 9, 2004.
39. Mary Spicuzza, "Weeki Wachee Mermaids in Terrorists' Cross Hairs?" *St. Petersburg Times*, April 22, 2005.
40. Office of Inspector General 2006, 9, 11, 13, 24.
41. Ripley 2004. On this issue, see also Lustick 2006 and, in contrast, Tyler Prante and Alok K. Bohara, "What Determines Homeland Security Spending? An Econometric Analysis of the Homeland Security Grant Program," *Policy Studies Journal* 36(2) 2008: 243–256.
42. New York newspaper: Carol Eisenberg, "Waking Up to Terror: City Counterterror Chief Says Each Day He Expects Subway Attack Because Feds Fail to Protect Rails," *Newsday*, March 7, 2007. Other quotes: Ripley 2004. On this issue, see also Lustick 2006.
43. Department of Homeland Security 2009, 34.

CHAPTER 6: HOMELAND PROTECTION: INFRASTRUCTURE

1. A. G. Sulzberger, "When Bus Drivers Stopped Giving Change," nytimes.com, August 31, 2009. As this experience shows, crime deterrence due in considerable part to protective measures can reduce the value of crime to the point where it essentially doesn't pay economically, though there may be other reasons for criminals to engage in the practice. See John Mueller, "Crime Is Caused by the Young and Restless," *Wall Street Journal*, March 6, 1985.
2. *Protecting Infrastructure*, Civil Engineering Research Foundation Monograph Series (New York: American Society of Civil Engineers, 2001). *Engineering a Safer Australia: Securing Critical Infrastructure and the Built Environment* (Canberra, Australia: Institution of Engineers, 2003).
3. DHS's duct tape and plastic sheeting campaign of 2003 seems sensibly to have been abandoned—although the program's chief promoter was later promoted to become head of the Federal Emergency Management Administration. Melissa McNamara, "Bush Nominates New FEMA Director," cbsnews.com, April 6, 2006.
4. Lakamp and McCarthy 2003.
5. Little 2007.
6. "Report of the DoD Commission on Beirut International Airport Terrorist Act, October 23, 1983." United States Department of Defense, December 20, 1983, 33.
7. Jarrett Murphy, "Beirut Barracks Attack Remembered," *CBS News*, October 23, 2003.
8. Michael I. Greenberg, *Disaster! A Compendium of Terrorist, Natural and Man-Made Catastrophes* (Sudbury, MA: Jones and Bartlett, 2006).
9. "Report of the Accountability Review Boards on the Embassy Bombings in Nairobi and Dar es Salaam on August 7, 1998," U.S. Department of State, January 1999. As discussed later, the progressive collapse of a building in the developed world is virtually unknown.
10. "FBI 100 First Strike: Global Terror in America," Headline Archives, Federal Bureau of Investigation, February 26, 2008. "Terrorism in the United States: 1996," Counterterrorism Threat Assessment and Warning Unit National Security Division, 13.

11. Global Terrorism Database.

12. No serious damage: Ennala Ramabhushanam and Marjorie Lynch, "Structural Assessment of Bomb Damage for World Trade Center," *Journal of the Performance of Constructed Facilities*, 8(4) 1994: 229–242. Columns fractured: Yukihoro Omika, Eiji Fukuzawa, Norihide Koshika, Hiroshi Morikawa, and Ryusuke Fukuda, "Structural Response of World Trade Center under Aircraft Attacks," *Journal of Structural Engineering*, 131(1) 2005: 6–15; Glenn G. Thater, Gary F. Panariello, and Daniel A. Cuoco, "World Trade Center Disaster: Damage/Debris Assessment," *Proceedings of the Third Forensic Engineering Congress*, American Society of Civil Engineers, 2003, 383–392. Temperatures to 1,500, 99 percent survived: W. Gene Corley, "Lessons Learned on Improving Resistance of Buildings to Terrorist Attack," *Journal of the Performance of Constructed Facilities*, 18(2) 2004: 68–78. Evacuation: Kean 2004, 316; improved evacuation measures put in place after the 1993 bombing also proved helpful.

13. The term "tall building" indicates buildings that are taller than surrounding buildings, slender in their proportion, and nominally taller than 15 to 20 stories. The World Trade Center Building 7 suffered total progressive collapse due to uncontrolled fire, which according to the NIST report "was the first known instance of the total collapse of a tall building primarily due to fires" ("Final Report on the Collapse of World Trade Center Building 7," NIST NCSTAR 1A, National Institute of Standards and Technology, U.S. Department of Commerce, November 2008, xxxv). While terrorist blast attacks have caused extensive damage to buildings, these are nearly always of low height—houses or shops, for example—and have not been designed by engineers. The collapse of a 21-story concrete building adjacent to the U.S. embassy in the 1998 attack in Kenya is the only example of total progressive collapse of a tall building due to a VBIED. However, it is questionable whether the building was designed and constructed to the same standards as European or American tall buildings.

14. ASCE 2003. Progressive collapse provisions are now being incorporated into U.S. and international design codes. ASCE 7–2002, *Minimum Design Loads for Buildings and Other Structures* (New York: American Society of Civil Engineers, 2002).

15. Smith and Rose 2002. Progressive collapse is defined as collapse of all or a large part of a structure caused by damage to a relatively small part of the structure: the damage is normally disproportionate to the initiating or triggering event. Even a damaged column will provide partial support to a building; it is the destruction or disintegration of a key supporting column that can cause progressive collapse. In contrast, the quality of construction in the developing world is, in many cases, of poor quality. In Bangladesh, the quality of cement is poor. Enno Koehn and Mohsin Ahmmed, "Quality of Building Construction Materials (Cement) in Developing Countries," *Journal of Architectural Engineering*, 7(2) 2001: 44–50. And in Turkey, higher than expected earthquake damage is attributed to project errors, poor quality of construction, unlicensed modifications to buildings, and so on. Erdel Irtem, Kaan Turker and Umut Hasgul, "Causes of Collapse and Damage to Low-Rise RC Buildings in Recent Turkish Earthquakes," *Journal of Performance of Constructed Facilities*, 21(5) 2007: 351–360. A magnitude 7.0

earthquake in Haiti in 2010 killed more than 230,000 people, mainly because of poor building construction, whereas a larger earthquake in densely populated Kobe, Japan, in 1995 killed around 6,000, and a magnitude 6.9 earthquake in 1989 in the San Francisco Bay area killed some 63 people. Surveying the damage caused by an earthquake in China in 2008, in which many schools collapsed, killing hundreds of children, a field team of Australian and Hong Kong earthquake experts observed that "many buildings had inadequate construction quality including insufficient reinforcement, poor detailing and poor quality concrete" (Ari Wibowo, Bidur Kafle, Alireza Kermani, Nelson Lam, John Wilson, and Emad Gad, "Damage in the 2008 China Earthquake," *Proceedings of 2008 Australasian Earthquake Engineering Society Conference,* 2008, Ballarat, Victoria). In addition, building codes have been bypassed with the complicity of corrupted officials and construction site staff. As Penny Green notes for Turkey, "Violations were part of a well entrenched political process," and she quotes an adviser to the mayor in one of the worst hit earthquake areas of Turkey, who admits, "The project managers, they take bribes, we do it ourselves. There is no project inspection." Penny Green, "Disaster by Design," *British Journal of Criminology,* 45(4) 2005: 528–546.

16. *Protecting Buildings from Bomb Damage: Transfer of Blast-Effects Mitigation Technologies from Military to Civilian Applications* (Washington, DC: National Academy Press, 1995).

17. Peter D. Smith and John G. Hetherington, *Blast and Ballistic Loading of Structures* (Oxford: Butterworth-Heinemann, 1994), 279.

18. K. A. Marchand, "Retrofitting Existing Structures," in E. J. Conrath, ed., *Structural Design for Physical Security: State of the Practice* (New York: ASCE, 1999), 8.1–8.22.

19. B. L. Morris, J. W. Strybos, and K. A. Marchand, *Minimum Hardening Measure for Protection of People Intensive Army Facilities from Exterior Explosive Attack,* SwRI Project 06-2914-700 (Omaha, NE: U.S. Army Engineer District, 1991).

20. N. C. Gould, V. Winn, and D. Drevinsky, "Progressive Collapse Analysis, Retrofit Design, and Costs for Existing Structures," in B. Cross and J. Finke, eds., *Structures Congress 2006,* ASCE, 2006, CD-ROM. A single blast-resistant window for the Pentagon renovation project weighs 1,500 pounds and costs $10,000: Sherie Winston, "Pentagon's Construction Team Beats The Odds on One-Year Rebuild," *Engineering News Record,* September 2, 2002.

21. David D. Owen and RSMeans Engineering Staff, *Building Security: Strategies and Costs,* Reed Construction Data, 2003.

22. Lakamp and McCarthy 2003.

23. Assuming discount rate of 3 percent. The time before a building will be renovated, demolished, or rebuilt is variable. The annualized cost for 10 years is $234,500 per year and for 30 years $102,000 per year. A cost of $150,000 per year is a reasonable middle value.

24. Lakamp and McCarthy 2003.

25. Estimate from Google Maps.

26. Lakamp and McCarthy 2003. The opportunity cost of the increased travel distance to the gate is estimated this way: "An average driver will spend a total of

over a minute of extra driving time coming on the base. Because the parking spaces within eighty feet of buildings are now restricted, the person will then walk thirteen extra seconds to cover that ground (four miles per hour for eighty feet). Thus, for every time a person comes to and subsequently leaves the base, there is about two and a half minutes of extra time spent traveling. Multiplied by the daily number of people that come on base and the number of days they come to the base, the total additional time spent traveling is upwards of 25,000 man-hours or the equivalent of greater than a dozen full-time employees. This example does not even include the added delays at gates during peak hours; however, it illustrates the substantial loss of time that must now be translated in financial terms. Using a realistic average salary for the population that works and studies at NPS, the total cost of this time is over one million dollars per year."

27. See Stewart 2010 for an example of a risk assessment that considers a spectrum of threats.

28. Although a VBIED with lower explosive force or a large stand-off will likely cause few casualties, it may inflict enough physical damages to require demolishing and replacing the building.

29. Lakamp and McCarthy 2003.

30. A typical large building is 250,000 square feet. A survey of 100 U.S. buildings reveals an average occupant density of 3.7 people per 1,000 square feet (4.0 people per 100 square meters) and that occupied floor area is approximately 66 percent of gross floor area. See Andrew Persily and Josh Gorfain, *Analysis of Ventilation Data from the U.S. Environmental Protection Agency Building Assessment Survey and Evaluation (BASE) Study*, NISTIR 7145 (Washington, DC: National Institute of Standards and Technology, 2004).

31. Applying a value of $6.5 million per life (in 2010 dollars) as in Robinson et al. 2010. We do not include the risk and safety of people outside the building (such as pedestrians and other passersby) because these fatalities are mostly unavoidable whatever the security measures in place to protect the building.

32. Ten VBIED or IED attacks against buildings killed more than 80 people out of approximately 20,000 attacks in the period 1970 to 2007 in the Memorial Institute for the Prevention of Terrorism (MIPT) database. This statistic does not include the insurgencies in Iraq or Afghanistan, but even if it did, there are fewer than five instances of 80 or more fatalities from VBIED or IED attacks on buildings in these countries.

33. There is the case, for example, of the 1993 World Trade Center bombing, where, in addition to the $500 million to repair the damage, up to 400 plaintiffs, including families of the dead, people hurt in the attack, and businesses, have sought $1.8 billion for "lost wages, damage to businesses, and pain and suffering." Anemona Hartocollis, "Port Authority Found Negligent in 1993 Bombing," *New York Times*, October 27, 2005.

34. Mark G. Stewart, "Cost-Effectiveness of Risk Mitigation Strategies For Protection of Buildings Against Terrorist Attack," *Journal of Performance of Constructed Facilities*, 22(2) 2008: 115–120. Stewart 2010.

35. As in chapter 4, the minimum attack probability equals (security costs)/ [(reduction in risk) × (losses sustained in the attack)].

36. If risk reduction is increased to an overwhelming 99.9 percent, the attack probability required decreases only slightly to 0.012 percent. Doubling the cost of physical damage in our estimate from $33 million to $66 million has a negligible effect on the cost-effectiveness result because the expected losses are dominated by loss of life and damage to business, not by direct physical damage of the building. However, if the value of life (or the number of deaths) is doubled, total losses would increase by $500 million to $2.5 billion, reducing the required probability of a successful attack to 0.011 percent, or 1 in 9,000 per building per year. If protective measures cost $500,000 per year rather than $250,000, required probability of a successful attack is 0.026 percent or 1 in 4,000 per building per year. For protective measures to be cost-effective, the probability of a successful attack on a building must be between one and three one-hundredths of 1 percent, or between 1 in 4,000 and 1 in 9,000 per year.

37. This excludes those who used Molotov cocktails or other incendiary devices to firebomb a building, the preferred technique of the Animal Liberation Front and other such "terrorist" groups.

38. Mark G. Stewart, "Cost-Effectiveness of Risk Mitigation Strategies For Protection of Buildings Against Terrorist Attack," *Journal of Performance of Constructed Facilities*, 22(2) 2008: 117.

39. From the MIPT database of terrorist incidents, calculated as 11 attacks divided by 20 years divided by 4.7 million buildings. We can also restrict our attention to the 108,000 large U.S. commercial buildings that are more than five stories high. For this set of buildings, the attack probability over 20 years (there have been only two attacks) is one in a million or 0.0001 percent per building per year (2 attacks divided by 20 years divided by 108,000 buildings). This is only an order of magnitude estimate, of course, and it could vary significantly because of the highly transient nature of terrorism. However, the results are indicative, and other analysts have come up with similarly low attack probabilities. Bruce R. Ellingwood, "Strategies for Mitigating Risk to Buildings from Abnormal Load Events," *International Journal of Risk Assessment and Management*, 7(6–7) 2007: 828–845; Little 2007. The threat might be higher for targets deemed to be critical by the DHS, and this has led Ellingwood to posit that the minimum attack probability may increase a hundredfold, to 1 in 10,000 per building per year for high-density occupancies, key governmental and international institutions, monumental or iconic buildings, or other critical facilities where there might appear to be a specific threat—although, as discussed in chapter 5, there don't seem to many of these. However, the likelihood that any particular item in that target set will be attacked remains exceedingly low.

40. The annual security cost of hardening the building is $1 million per year, and expected losses are $2 billion.

41. If the attack probability is negligible, there is no net benefit, and the net loss is equal to the cost of the security measures.

42. These include construction, education (universities and school districts), energy (oil, gas, pipelines), financial institutions (banks, insurers, and securities firms), food and beverages, hospitality (hotels, casinos, sporting and arts venues), health care (hospitals), manufacturing, media, public entity (city,

county, and state entities), real estate, retail, technology and telecom, transportation (trucking and bus companies), and utilities (gas, electric, and water).

43. 2004: *MarketWatch: Terrorism Insurance 2005*, Marsh Inc., 6. 2006: MarketWatch; calculated as the median terrorism premium of $18,000 divided by the median insured loss of $388 million. 2007: *U.S. Insurance Market Report 2008*, Marsh Inc., 21. 2009: *The Marsh Report: Terrorism Risk Insurance 2010*, Marsh Inc., 16.

44. The United Kingdom's government terrorism insurance scheme, Pool Re, charges terrorism reinsurance premiums of 0.021 percent to 0.03 percent of the value of the property and business interruption in central London and other major cities and only 0.006 percent elsewhere in the United Kingdom, a premium markedly higher than in the United States but one that is comparable to the mean pricing in Germany of 0.015 percent of total insured value (Erwann Michel-Kerjan and Pedell Burkhard, "How Does the Corporate World Cope with Mega-Terrorism? Puzzling Evidence from Terrorist Insurance Markets," *Journal of Applied Corporate Finance*, 18(4) 2006: 61–75). Yet even these higher premiums suggest the insurers are estimating the yearly likelihood of a successful terrorist attack at only 0.005 percent, or one in 20,000, per building (assuming a premium of 0.025 percent and insured property encompasses five buildings).

45. "Federal Efforts to Strengthen Security Should Be Better Coordinated and Targeted on the Nation's Most Critical Highway Infrastructure," United States Government Accountability Office, Washington, DC, January 2009, 1.

46. From the U.S. National Consortium for the Study of Terrorism and Responses to Terrorism (START).

47. Brian M. Jenkins and Larry N. Gersten, *Protecting Public Surface Transportation against Terrorism and Serious Crime: Continuing Research on Best Security Practices*, Mineta Transportation Institute, San José State University, MTI Report 01–07, September 2001.

48. Smith and Rose 2002.

49. Edward J. Conrath, Ted Krauthammer, Kirk Marchand and Paul Mlakar, *Structural Design for Physical Security: State of the Practice* (Reston, VA: ASCE, 1999).

50. A. K. M. Anwarul Islam and Nur Yazdani, "Blast Capacity and Protection of AASHTO Bridge Girders," *Proceedings of the 2006 Structures Congress*, American Society of Civil Engineers, 2006, CD-ROM. Seible et al. 2008.

51. Barbara Surk, "Truck Bomb Destroys Key Bridge in Western Iraq," *CBN News*, October 17, 2009.

52. Highway Accident Report: Collapse of I-35W Highway Bridge, Minneapolis, Minnesota, August 1, 2007, "Accident Report NTSB/HAR-08/03," National Transportation Safety Board, Washington, D.C., November 14, 2008.

53. Yong Bai, William Burkett, and Phillip Nash, "Lessons Learnt from the Emergency Bridge Replacement Project," *Journal of Construction Engineering and Management*, 132(4) 2006: 338–344.

54. Damaged bridges, Oklahoma bridge replacement: Yong Bai and William Burkett, "Rapid Bridge Replacement: Processes, Techniques, and Needs for Improvements," *Journal of Construction Engineering and Management*, 132(11) 2006: 1139–1147. Los Angeles: Kuprenas et al. 1998. Minneapolis: Jim Foti, "35W Bridge on Pace to Open in September," *Star Tribune*, May 4, 2008.

55. Value of statistical life (VSL) of $6.5 per life saved (in 2010 dollars) as suggested by Robinson et al. 2010.

56. Blue Ribbon Panel 2003. Eric B. Williamson and David Winget, "Risk Management and Design of Critical Bridges for Terrorist Attack," *Journal of Bridge Engineering*, 10(1) 2005: 96–106M. Eric B. Williamson and Kirk Marchand, "Recommendations for Blast-Resistant Design and Retrofit of Typical Highway Bridges," *Proceedings of the 2006 Structures Congress*, American Society of Civil Engineers, CD-ROM.

57. Los Angeles: Seible et al. 2008. Girder bridge: Kuprenas et al. 1998. See also Edward Wang, "Optimizing Bridge Seismic Retrofit Strategy Implementing Bridge Fragility Curves," *Proceedings of the 2006 Structures Congress*, American Society of Civil Engineers, CD-ROM.

58. Assuming a discount rate of 3 percent.

59. Lives saved: attack probability (0.01 percent) × risk reduction (95 percent) × fatalities (20).

60. Eric Lichtblau, "Trucker Sentenced to 20 Years in Plot against Brooklyn Bridge," *New York Times*, October 29, 2003. Mueller 2011.

61. Blue Ribbon Panel 2003, 2.

62. Blue Ribbon Panel 2003, 54.

63. Assuming a discount rate of 3 percent.

64. Luft 2005.

65. Hostile, several days: Kevin Ross and Gary Vogler, "Iraqis Mending Own Pipelines," *Oil & Gas Journal*, 107(7) 2009: 50–53; they note that repair teams suffered 30 deaths between 2003 and 2008. Several weeks: Luft 2005.

66. www.oilrigdisasters.co.uk.

67. *Deterring Terrorism: Aircraft Crash Impact Analyses Demonstrate Nuclear Power Plant's Structural Strength*, Electric Power Research Institute, December 2002. Transporting nuclear fuel is similarly safe: "Extensive analysis, backed by full-scale field tests, show that there is virtually nothing one could do to these shipping casks that would cause a significant public hazard. . . . They are nearly indestructible, having been tested against collisions, explosives, fire, and water. Only the latest antitank artillery could breach them, and then, the result was to scatter a few chunks of spent fuel onto the ground." Douglas M. Chapin, Karl P. Cohen, W. Kenneth Davis, Edwin E. Kintner, Leonard J. Koch, John W. Landis, Milton Levenson, I. Harry Mandil, Zack T. Pate, Theodore Rockwell, Alan Schriesheim, John W. Simpson, Alexander Squire, Chauncey Starr, Henry E. Stone, John J. Taylor, Neil E. Todreas, Bertram Wolfe, and Edwin L. Zebroski, "Nuclear Power Plants and Their Fuel as Terrorist Targets," *Science*, 297(5589) 2002: 1997–1999.

68. Mark Holt and Anthony Andrews, *Nuclear Power Plants: Vulnerability to Terrorist Attack*, CRS Report for Congress, Congressional Research Service, RS21131, August 8, 2007.

69. As an extra precaution for dealing with the potential for increases in thyroid cancer in the event of a radiation release, Belgium, Canada, the Czech Republic, Finland, France, Germany, Luxembourg, Sweden, and Switzerland have predistributed potassium iodine tablets to residents in the vicinity of nuclear reactors ("Decision to Discontinue the Future Distribution of Iodine Tablets,"

Department of Health and Children, Ireland, April 3, 2008). Some U.S. states have done so as well, supplying the tablets to people who live within ten miles of the nuclear power plant at a cost of approximately $22,000 per power plant. Eartha Melzer, "States Offers Potassium Iodide Tablets to People Near Nuke Plants," *Michigan Messenger*, September 8, 2009. This seems a very modest protection cost, and it is effective irrespective of the reason for a radioactive release, whether it derives from an accident, terrorism, or a natural disaster.

70. William Beach, James Carafano, Ariel Cohen, Hopper Smith, Karen Campbell, and David Kreutzer, *The Global Response to a Terror-Generated Energy Crisis* (Washington, DC: Heritage Foundation, November 10, 2008).

71. The worst case would be if there were no credible national and multinational policies to deal with the crises. If this occurs, surmises the Heritage Foundation, "there will be major declines in the economic output of the United States and other industrial countries, as well as rapid impoverishment of developing economies. Without enough energy to maintain current GDP levels, 592,000 workers lose their jobs at the outset and household income falls by $309 billion in the quarter with the lowest income." Whatever the fancifulness, a comparison of these two scenarios does illustrate the potential costliness of overreaction as it compounds the negative effects of terrorism.

72. Potentially relevant here is that Osama bin Laden may have been something of a node fancier. As early as December 2001, even while he was fleeing the American onslaught in Afghanistan, he somehow managed to imagine that United States was then "in retreat by the grace of God Almighty," and he called for "further blows" against it, urging in particular that "the young men need to seek out the nodes of the American economy and strike the enemy's nodes" (Hoffman 2006, 290). Thus far, however, America's nodes (and nonnodes, for that matter) remain unmolested by terrorists.

73. Flynn 2007, 35–36, 93.

74. On the expensive efforts of Augusta, Georgia, to protect its fire hydrants from terrorist molestation, see Corey Pein, "Bin Laden's Next Target? Augusta Is Spending Millions to Guard Its Fire Hydrants from Terrorists. Whatever It Takes to Protect Our Precious Bodily Fluids," *Metro Spirit* (Augusta, GA), May 23–29, 2007. U.S. terrorists: Mueller 2011.

CHAPTER 7: PROTECTING THE AIRLINES

1. National Air Traffic Controllers Association, Media Center, www.natcamember-ship.org/mediacenter/bythenumbers.msp.

2. Domestic flights: *Financial Times*, September 14, 2004, 8. Las Vegas: Clarke 2005, 63; some Las Vegas casinos report that their fourth-quarter earnings in 2001 were about one third of the year earlier. See also Schneier 2003, 235–236.

3. Dean Calbreath, "Attacks to Cost 1.6 Million Jobs," *San Diego Union-Tribune*, January 12, 2002. See also Gordon et al. 2007.

4. "Two arrested in attempted bus hijacking," *Daily Herald* (Utah), October 18, 2001.

5. O'Connor et al. 2008.

6. Joan C. Henderson, *Tourism Crises: Causes, Consequences and Management* (Oxford: Butterworth-Heinemann, 2006).

7. Blalock et al. 2009, 41.
8. Research and Innovative Technology Administration, Bureau of Transportation, TranStats, 2010.
9. International Air Transport Association, "Facts and Figures," Pressroom, March 2, 2010.
10. Artem Fetisov, "On the Mend: Russian Airlines Appear to Have Recovered for a Tough Couple of Years but Still Face Challenges," *Air Transport World*, November 2006, 41.
11. "Airline Fatalities Increase in 2010," *Flight International*, January 6, 2011.
12. Global Terrorism Database.
13. Calculated from 16 terrorist attacks in the 12-year period 1999–2010 (Global Terrorism Database) and using airline flight frequencies from OAG Aviation Solutions, www.oagaviation.com.
14. Fred Bayles, "'Planes Don't Blow Up' Aviation Experts Assert," *International Herald Tribune*, July 24, 1996.
15. Susan Woods, "Crew Tell How They Caught Shoe Bomber," news.scotsman.com, September 2, 2002. Andrew Johnson and Emily Dugan, "Wealthy, Quiet, Unassuming: The Christmas Day Bomb Suspect," *Independent*, December 27, 2009.
16. PETN or Pentaerythritol tetranitrate is one of the strongest known high explosives, and it is also difficult to detect.
17. BBC News, "Boeing 747 Survives Simulated 'Flight 253' Bomb Blast," March 5, 2010. The explosive test was conducted while the aircraft was on the ground. Relevant here is the fact that a terrorist attempted to assassinate a Saudi prince in August 2009 by detonating 100 grams of PETN, which according to some reports was concealed in his underwear, and other reports, his rectum (Peter Bergen, "Saudi Investigation: Would-Be Assassin Hid Bomb in Underwear," CNN, September 20, 2009). A Europol study confirmed that concealment of IEDs in rectal cavities was possible, "but that the body itself would act as a shield for the expansion of the explosive wave, amortising its effects." *The Concealment of Improvised Explosive Devices (IEDs) in Rectal Cavities*, SC5-Counter Terrorism Unit, Europol, The Hague, September 18, 2009, 8. This may explain why the terrorist succeeded in only killing himself, while the Saudi prince who stood close by escaped unharmed. It would seem that a terrorist would need to remove explosives from his underwear for it to be fully effective against a target, an act which will increase the odds of detection.
18. "Southwest to Ground 81 Planes after Hole Prompts Emergency Landing," cnn.com, April 2, 2011.
19. "Depressurisation—475 km north-west of Manila, Philippines—July 25, 2008," ATSB Transport Safety Report, Aviation Occurrence Investigation AO-2008-053 Interim Factual No. 2, Australian Transport Safety Bureau, Australian Government, November 2009.
20. Craig Skehan, "Valve in Oxygen Cylinder the Culprit of 747 Explosion," *Age*, July 29, 2008.
21. Aviation Safety Network, Flight Safety Foundation, www.flightsafety.org.

22. Bryan Walsh, "Why It's Not Easy to Detonate a Bomb on Board," *Time*, December 28, 2009.
23. Chow et al. 2005.
24. Christopher Bolkcom and Bartholomew Elias, *Homeland Security: Protecting Airlines from Terrorist Missiles*, CRS Report for Congress, Congressional Research Service, Washington, DC. Updated February 16, 2006, CRS-9.
25. Bartholomew Elias, *Airport and Aviation Security* (Boca Raton, FL: CRC, 2010), 304. For additional assessments, see Chow et al. 2005, Gordon et al. 2007.
26. C. J. Chivers, "Russians Cite Porous Security in Terror Bombings of 2 Planes," *New York Times*, September 16, 2004.
27. "Budget-in-Brief Fiscal Year 2011," U.S. Department of Homeland Security, Washington, DC, 17.
28. Meckler and Carey 2007.
29. Steve Lord, Testimony before the Subcommittee on Management, Investigations, and Oversight, Committee on Homeland Security, House of Representatives, United States Government Accountability Office, GAO-09-903T, July 23, 2009.
30. Ted Poe, Department of Homeland Security Appropriations Act, 2006: Amendment No. 10, House of Representatives, May 17, 2005. Converted to 2010 dollars.
31. Audrey Hudson, "Flight Marshal Numbers Disputed, Agents Criticize Data 'Padding,'" *Washington Times*, March 3, 2005.
32. Audrey Hudson, "Air Marshals Cover Only a Few Flights," *Washington Times*, August 16, 2004.
33. Brock N. Meeks, "For Air Marshals, Less Equals More," MSNBC, September 15, 2004.
34. Kearney 2005.
35. "FAA Sets New Standards for Cockpit Doors," Federal Aviation Administration Office of Public Affairs Press Release, January 11, 2002.
36. "Airlines Meet FAA's Hardened Cockpit Door Deadline," Federal Aviation Administration Office of Public Affairs Press Release, April 2003. The FAA mandated: "The doors will be designed to resist intrusion by a person who attempts to enter using physical force. This includes the door, its means of attachment to the surrounding structure, and the attachment structure to the bulkhead." The agency also requires that the cockpit doors remain locked and that cockpit access be controlled.
37. Schneier 2003, 4.
38. Mark Kramer, "The Perils of Counterinsurgency: Russia's War in Chechnya," *International Security*, 29(3) 2004: 58.
39. Smith 2007; see also Schneier 2003, 123–124, 247–248; Mueller 2006, 4, 152–135; Banks 2002, 10.
40. Padraic Murphy and Phillip Hudson, "Heroes Foil Qantas Hijack Attack," *Age*, May 30, 2003.
41. Ken Kaye, "More Pilots Bring Guns on Flights," *South Florida Sun-Sentinel*, February 13, 2007.
42. Todd Sandler and Walter Enders, "Transnational Terrorism: An Economic Analysis," in H. W. Richardson, P. Gordon, and J. E. Moore II, eds., *The Economic Impact of Terrorist Attacks* (Cheltenham, UK: Edward Elgar, 2005), 11–34.

43. Seitz 2004. See also Mueller 2002.
44. "Pentagon Repairs to Cost $700 Million," *USA Today,* January 1, 2002.
45. Smith 2007. Similarly, Thomas Kean, chair of the 9/11 Commission, believes that the "best defense is always still going to be the flying public." Comments at the presentation of "Assessing the Terrorist Threat" report, Bipartisan Policy Center, Washington, DC, September 10, 2010. See also Banks 2002, 10; Mueller 2006, 4, 152–153.
46. Kearney 2005.
47. If air marshals were on every flight and all the other security measures were in place as well, we have assumed, then, that the risk reduction is 100 percent— that every attempted hijacking will be foiled. This is a best-case scenario, but there may be circumstances under which hijackings can still occur. Bruce Schneier suggests several: "a plane that's empty enough that the hijackers outnumber the passengers, a hijacker who succeeds in convincing the passengers that he's not suicidal or a terrorist (carrying a baby would go a long way towards calming the passengers), a hijacker who succeeds in taking over a bullet proof cockpit (turning a security countermeasure into a vulnerability), or a hijacker that convinces everyone that he's a sky marshal" (2003, 274). Although none of these scenarios seems to be particularly plausible, there is enough to them to suggest that the effectiveness of the security measures is likely to be overestimated at 100 percent.
48. We deal here with the hijacking of a single aircraft. If multiple hijackings of aircraft are attempted, more detailed system modeling would be required, but the risk reduction will be higher because hijackers would have to overcome all security measures at various airports and aircraft simultaneously. While a single hijacker might be lucky enough to navigate successfully thorough all the security measures, the odds that multiple hijackers could do so would be lower.
49. Following the equation in the text, the net benefit, then, is calculated as (probability of an attack) × (losses sustained in the attack) × (reduction in risk) – (security costs).
50. If we posit that crew and passengers do not resist a hijacking, thereby increasing the risk reduction due to the air marshals to 2.5 percent, the net benefit is still a $950 million loss for a 10 percent attack probability and losses of $100 billion. If we assume that increased expenditures on preboarding security are ineffective, leading to a doubling of FAMS risk reduction to 3.3 percent, the net benefit of the program is still a significant loss of $870 million for a 10 percent attack probability and losses of $100 billion.
51. John R. Lott, Jr., "Marshals Are Good, but Armed Pilots are Better," *Wall Street Journal Europe,* January 2, 2004.
52. It can be even higher in other scenarios. If we assume, as Bruce Schneier does, that the increased expenditure on preboarding security has only been "minimally effective" (2003, 248)—that is, essentially zero—risk reduction for hardened cockpit doors would double to 33.3 percent and the net benefit is $3.3 billion. Quite plausibly, losses could be as low as $1 billion if the aircraft is off target (or misses), damage is localized, and there is not a costly government and public overreaction to the terrorist event. In this case, hardened cockpit doors would need to disrupt an attempted hijacking that would otherwise have

been successful every four years for the measure to be cost-effective. See Stewart 2010 for additional sensitivity analyses.

53. (reduction in risk) = (security cost)/[(probability of an attack) × (losses sustained in the attack)]

54. For example, Schneier 2003, 247–248; Maley 2008.

55. As discussed previously, the effectiveness of combined security measures is likely to be overestimated in our analysis because we assume that the risk of aircraft hijacking is completely eliminated (100 percent risk reduction). There may also be other aviation security measures, such as a secondary barrier to the cockpit, that could further enhance security. If the loss of life due to aircraft hijacking is not completely eliminated or if other security measures are implemented, the percentage risk reductions for hardened cockpit doors and the Federal Air Marshal Service will be less, leading to lower net benefit. Accordingly, the Federal Air Marshal Service would be deemed even less cost-effective. However, even an order of magnitude reduction in the effectiveness of hardened cockpit doors would not change the conclusion that hardening cockpit doors appears to be a cost-effective aviation security measure.

56. Mark G. Stewart and John Mueller, "A Cost-Benefit and Risk Assessment of Australian Aviation Security Measures," *Security Challenges*, 4(3), 2008: 45–61.

57. Hardened cockpit doors may be useful in preventing a direct replication of 9/11, but they contribute little to the prevention or mitigation of other kinds of terrorist acts on airplanes, such as the detonation of explosives. This seems likely to hold for air marshals as well because they are on few flights, are mainly focused on the cabin door, and are unlikely to be near the location in the plane where a bomber attempts to detonate an explosive. However, the other on-flight security measure, the alertness of crew and passengers, may sometimes disrupt other kinds of terrorist efforts besides hijacking as demonstrated with the shoe bomber in 2001 and the underwear bomber in 2009.

58. Lord 2010, 5.

59. Lord 2010.

60. The DHS FY2011 budget request for 500 new AITs includes $214.7 million for their purchase and installation ($430,000 each), $218.9 million for 5,355 new transportation security officers (TSOs) and screen managers to operate the AITs at the checkpoints, and $95.7 million for 255 positions to fund the support and airport management costs associated with the 5,355 new TSOs and screener managers. In addition, this equipment will require maintenance, support, and upgrading.

61. Gale Rossides, "Advanced Imagining Technology—Yes, It's Worth It," The Blog@Homeland Security, April 1, 2010. Actually, the planned 1,800 scanners may still leave 500 airport checkpoints without AITs: A. Halsey, "All Check-Points Won't Get Body Scanners," *Washington Post*, December 2, 2010. If correct, the purchase, operation, and maintenance of additional scanners will add considerably to the costs we have assumed. In addition, scanners may be deployed in foreign airports as well.

62. M. A. Memoli and B. Bettett, "White House Defends Body Scanners and Pat-Downs," *Los Angeles Times*, November 22, 2010.

63. Blalock et al. 2007.
64. Nate Silver, "The Hidden Costs of Extra Airport Security," nytimes.com, November 18, 2010.
65. Chow et al. 2005.
66. Gordon and his colleagues estimate a loss to the airline industry of $420 billion for a scenario, apparently based on the downing of an airliner by a shoulder-fired missile, that entails a shutdown of U.S. airspace for a week. This is more than double the losses experienced as a result of 9/11 and is staggering. Careful scrutiny of the figures, however, reveals an assumption that losses for gifts and shopping would total over $55 billion ($164.29 for domestic travelers and $290.91 for international ones). The assumption, apparently, is that if people do not fly, they pocket the money and do not spend it elsewhere. (The study deals only with the economic impact of a terrorist event on the *commercial airline system* and specifically ignores economic substitution: Gordon et al. 2007, 511). There are also stupendous losses for other sectors of the economy (airline, ground transportation, accommodation, food, amusement). This seems overly conservative. Moreover, adding up individual sectoral losses can lead to double counting, and as Enders and Olsen observe, "Another reason to avoid adding up the sectoral losses is that large scale terrorist attacks cause reallocations of people and resources across sectors. For example, in conjunction with the 9/11-induced decline in air travel, many U.S. tourist destinations experienced increased demand as people took fewer vacations necessitating an airplane flight and more vacations to areas that were within driving distance from their home. . . . The problem, of course, it that it is relatively easy to measure the heavy losses experienced by some areas but very difficult to measure the small indirect gains experienced by thousands of areas." Walter Enders and Eric Olsen, "Measuring the Economic Costs of Terrorism," in M. Garfinkel and S. Skaperdas, eds., *Oxford Handbook of the Economics of Peace and Conflict* (Oxford: Oxford University Press, 2011). Moreover, the downing of an airliner due to a passenger-borne explosive is unlikely to trigger the same response as one caused by a shoulder-fired missile because there are no countermeasures for a missile attack that can be implemented quickly, such as installing laser jammers on each aircraft. On the other hand, a series of measures were implemented quickly following the 9/11 and subsequent attacks. These included the screening of shoes after the 2001 failed attempt by Richard Reid and the banning of liquids in carry-on luggage after the foiled 2006 plot to detonate liquid explosives on transatlantic flights. While the effectiveness of the measures is in doubt, they do provide assurance to the general public that it is safe to fly. By contrast, after an attack involving a shoulder-fired missile, it would be "much more difficult to convince the public that it is safe to fly." Charles Pena, "Flying the Unfriendly Skies: Defending against the Threat of Shoulder Fired Missiles," Policy Analysis, No. 541, Cato Institute, April 19, 2005, 3. The economic costs forecast in the Gordon study assumes a one-week shutdown of U.S. airspace. However, for our scenario of a suicide bomber, a shutdown of a few days would be more reasonable, considering that U.S. airspace was shut down for only three days following 9/11. This

all suggests that the losses forecast for a shoulder-fired missile attack will overestimate losses for our threat scenario.

67. For its part, the OMB recognizes that there are uncertainties in cost-benefit analyses and recommends: "Estimates of benefits and costs are typically uncertain because of imprecision in both underlying data and modelling assumptions. Because such uncertainty is basic to many analyses, its effects should be analyzed and reported. Useful information in such a report would include the key sources of uncertainty; expected value estimates of outcomes; the sensitivity of results to important sources of uncertainty; and where possible, the probability distributions of benefits, costs, and net benefits." "Guidelines and Discount Rates for Benefit-Cost Analysis of Federal Programs (Revised)," Circular No. A-94, October 29, 1992, Office of Management and Budget, Washington, DC. Our full analysis of body scanners includes probabilistic modeling of losses and risk reduction as recommended by OMB. For details, see Stewart and Mueller 2011.

68. Lord 2010.

69. PBS *NewsHour*, November 16, 2010.

70. It has also been suggested that existing screening methods, such as detectors that test swabs wiped on passengers and luggage for traces of explosives, would have detected the explosives. Spencer S. Hsu, "Equipment to Detect Explosives Is Available," *Washington Post*, December 28, 2009.

71. Note that four of the in-flight security measures—air marshals, hardened cockpit door, armed flight crew, and on-board law enforcement officers—are designed to protect against hijackings or replication of a 9/11 style attack. Moreover, since air marshals are on less than 10 percent of aircraft, they are unlikely to be deter, foil, or disrupt a suicide bomber.

72.
$$(airliner\, loss) = \prod_{i=1}^{10} \Pr\left(non\text{-}detection\; for\; pre\text{-}boarding\; security\; measure\; i\right)$$
$$\times \Pr\left(Passengers\,/\,Crew\; non\text{-}detection\right)$$
$$\times \Pr\left(IED\; detonates\; successfully\right)$$
$$\times \Pr\left(aircraft\; downed\; by\; IED\; detonation\right)$$
$$= (0.9)^{10} \times 0.5 \times 0.75 \times 0.75 = 9.8\%$$

73. Larry Greenemeier, "Exposing the Weakest Link: As Airlines Passenger Security Tightens, Bombers Target Cargo Holds," *Scientific American*, November 2, 2010.

74. $9.8\% \times \Pr\left(AITs\; will\; not\; foil,\; det\, er\; or\; disrupt\; an\; IED\; attack\right)$
$$= 9.8\% \times \left[1 - \Pr\left(AIT\; effectiveness\right)\right]^{3}$$

75. If AITs are 100 percent effective, they reduce existing risk to zero and thus risk reduction is 9.8 percent. Because risk reduction is an uncertain variable, and to be consistent with loss estimations, it would be reasonable to assume that risk reduction is normally distributed with a 95 percent confidence interval between 5 percent and 10 percent, resulting in a mean risk reduction that is somewhat lower than this: 7.5 percent. This approach is applied in Stewart and Mueller 2011.

76. Applying the lower, but entirely reasonable, risk estimate of 0.075 rather than 0.086, the annual probability of a successful attack necessary to justify the expenditures comes out to be 61.5 percent.

77. Since there is uncertainty of inputs, there will be uncertainties in the output, which in this case, is the net benefit of full-body scanners, defined as benefit minus the cost of the security measure. Monte Carlo simulation analysis can be used as the computational tool, in which the probability that a security measure is cost-effective is the probability that the net benefit exceeds zero. Applying this approach to the present case determines that if the attack probability is less than 20 percent per year, there is zero likelihood that AITs are cost-effective and 100 percent likelihood of a net loss. If the attack probability exceeds 1,000 percent or ten attacks per year, AITs are certain to be cost-effective. A decision maker may wish the likelihood of cost-effectiveness to be high before investing billions of dollars in a security measure—perhaps to 90 percent—so there is more certainty about a net benefit and small likelihood of a net loss. In this case, the minimum rate of attack needs to exceed 1.62 attacks per year originating from U.S. airports for there to be a 90 percent chance that AITs are cost-effective. Conversely, if the attack probability is less than 37 percent per year, there is only a 10 percent chance of a net benefit and a 90 percent likelihood of a net loss. If opportunity costs are considered, this would increase the threshold attack probabilities. The results are not overly sensitive to the probabilistic models used for loss and risk reduction. While we have tried to err on the generous side—toward determining that full-body scanners are cost-effective— we recognize that the probability estimates for effectiveness of security measures are uncertain and subjective. If we modify the uncertainty models of risk reduction so that their range is 5 percent to 20 percent (as opposed to 5–10 percent as used previously), the attack probability needs to exceed one attack per year for there to be 90 percent confidence that AITs are cost-effective. A break-even 50/50 analysis shows that the attack probability needs to exceed one attack every two years for AITs to be cost-effective. The predicted losses can also be quite uncertain. However, if the upper bound of loss is doubled to $100 billion (as opposed to $2–$50 billion as previously assumed), the attack probability needs to exceed one attack per year for there to be 90 percent confidence that AITs are cost-effective. While doubling risk reduction or losses reduces threshold attack probabilities, they still remain at relatively high levels. For more detail on this, see Stewart and Mueller 2011.

78. Schneier 2003, 247–248. Yates: Maley 2008. See also Gardner 2008, 252. As noted earlier, Edward Smith goes further, arguing that the *only* measure required is crew and passenger resistance.

79. Smith 2007. Banks 2002, 10. See also Mueller 2006, 4, 152–153.

80. Meckler and Carey 2007.

81. James Bovard, "Dead Man Tells No Tales: Media Docility and Another No-Cost Federal Killing," reasononline.com, December 14, 2005.

82. Maley 2008.

83. Marcus Holmes, "Just How Much Does That Cost, Anyway? An Analysis of the Financial Costs and Benefits of the 'No-Fly' List," *Homeland Security Affairs*, 5(1) 2009.

84. National Aviation Policy White Paper, Australian Government, December 2009.

85. Sara Kehaulani Goo, "TSA Would Allow Sharp Objects on Airliners," *Washington Post*, November 30, 2005.

86. Smith 2007.
87. Sara Kehaulani Goo, "Going the Extra Mile," *Washington Post*, April 9, 2004.
88. Sunstein 2003, 132. See also Mueller 2006, 157–159.
89. As noted earlier, one study finds the presence of police officers to enhance feelings of security in banks but to increase feelings of insecurity when apparently focused on terrorism. Grosskopf 2006.
90. Smith 2007.
91. Blalock et al. 2007.
92. Department of Homeland Security Office of Inspector General, "TSA's Role in General Aviation Security," OIG-09–69, May 2009, 1, 16.
93. Spencer S. Hsu, "General-Aviation Security Proposal Is Being Scaled Back," *Washington Post*, February 7, 2010.

CHAPTER 8: ASSESSING POLICING, MITIGATION, RESILIENCE

1. Jeffrey Goldberg, "The Things He Carried," *Atlantic*, December 2008. Schneier: Rosen 2008. See also Mueller 2006, 183–185.
2. It is not clear, however, that massive increases in intelligence spending have been cost-effective overall. See note 13 in table I.2.
3. Office of Management and Budget, 2010 Budget to Prevent and Disrupt Terrorist Attacks.
4. Savage 2011.
5. Dana Priest and William M. Arkin, "A Hidden World, Growing beyond Control," *Washington Post*, July 19, 2010.
6. Dana Priest and William M. Arkin, "Monitoring America," *Washington Post*, December 20, 2010.
7. Mueller 2011.
8. Kevin Strom, John Hollywood, Mark Pope, Garth Weintraub, Crystal Daye, and Don Gemeinhardt, *Building on Clues: Examining Successes and Failures in Detecting U.S. Terrorist Plots,1999–2009*, Institute for Homeland Security Solutions, October 2010, 12.
9. Kurzman 2011.
10. Savage 2011.
11. William Neuman, "In Response to M.T.A.'s 'Say Something' Ads, a Glimpse of Modern Fears," *New York Times*, January 7, 2008.
12. Fernandez 2010.
13. Leinwand 2008.
14. Fernandez 2010.
15. Spencer S. Hsu, "Security Chief Urges 'Collective Fight' against Terrorism," *Washington Post*, July 29, 2009.
16. Dickey 2009, 198, 233–236. See also Brooks 2011.
17. Dina Temple-Raston, *The Jihad Next Door: The Lackawanna Six and Rough Justice in the Age of Terror* (New York: Public Affairs, 2007). Mueller 2011.
18. Lawson 2008.
19. Kareem Fahim, "4 Convicted of Attempting to Blow Up 2 Synagogues," *New York Times*, October 18, 2010.
20. On this issue more generally, see Kenneth L. Wainstein, "Terrorism Prosecution and the Primacy of Prevention since 9/11," in Jeff Grossman, ed., *Terrorism Trial*

Report Card: September 11, 2001–September 11, 2009 (New York: Center on Law and Security, New York University School of Law, 2010), 21–24. See also Jenkins 2010, 10; Brooks 2011; Mueller 2011.

21. On this point, see also Brooks 2011; Lorenzo Vidino, "Homegrown Jihadist Terrorism in the United States: A New and Occasional Phenomenon?" *Studies in Conflict and Terrorism*, 32 2009: 1–17.

22. Jenkins 2010, 10.

23. Rick "Ozzie" Nelson, "Homegrown Terrorism Fact Sheet," January 22, 2010, Center for Strategic and International Studies, Washington, DC. Indeed, the reason about twice as many Muslim Americans as usual were arrested on terrorism charges is because of this cluster of Somalis (for full data, see Kurzman 2011). Overall, it appears that about 30 Somali Americans have gone or sought to go to Somalia over the last few years to fight for al-Shabab, which has been labeled an al-Qaeda affiliate, although much of the recruits' ardor seems to stem from their desire to defend Somalia from invading Ethiopians. Since al-Shabab seems to have more than 10,000 fighters already, it is not clear how their task would be made much easier by a handful of foreign volunteers. It should also be pointed out that the total number of Muslim Americans arrested in a single year is exceedingly low—perhaps some 15 or 20. It doesn't take much to double or triple that number, but the total remains low nonetheless.

24. Jeff Grossman, ed., *Terrorist Trial Report Card: September 11, 2001–September 11, 2010.* (New York: Center for Law and Security, New York University School of Law, 2010), 15.

25. Sheehan 2008, 263.

26. Michael A. Sheehan, "The Terrorist Next Door," *New York Times*, May 4, 2010.

27. Rosen 2008. See also Mueller 2006, 147–148.

28. Furedi 2008, 648.

29. Sam Roggeveen, "Resilience the Key to Fighting Terrorism," *Sydney Morning Herald*, February 24, 2010.

30. Thomas A. Glass and Monica Schoch-Spana, "Bioterrorism and the People: How to Vaccinate a City against Panic," *CID* 34(15) 2002: 217–223.

31. Michael Grimwald and Susan B. Glasser, "Brown's Turf Wars Sapped FEMA's Strength: Director Who Came to Symbolize Incompetence in Katrina Predicted Agency Would Fail," *Washington Post*, December 23, 2005. See also Christopher Cooper and Robert Block, *Disaster: Hurricane Katrina and the Failure of Homeland Security* (New York: Times Books, 2006).

32. For an exception, see William J. Perry, Ashton B. Carter, and Michael M. May, "After the Bomb," *New York Times*, June 12, 2007.

33. Zimmerman and Loeb 2004, 11. Ferguson et al. 2003, 19. G. Allison 2004, 8. See also Rockwell 2003.

34. Recommendation: Rockwell 2003. Baruch Fischhoff, "A Hero in Every Seat," *New York Times*, August 7, 2005. Other specialists: Ferguson and Potter 2005, 335. See also James Glanz and Andrew C. Revkin, "Some See Panic as Main Effect of Dirty Bombs," *New York Times*, March 7, 2002; G. Allison 2004, 8, 59, 220; Dafna Linzer, "Attack with Dirty Bomb More Likely, Officials Say," *Washington Post*, December 29, 2004; Dubay 2010.

35. Zimmerman and Loeb 2004, 10. W. Allison 2009, 176.

36. Gina Kolata, "For Radiation, How Much Is Too Much?" *New York Times*, November 27, 2001. For useful discussions of the debate, see this article and Alok Jha and Sarah Boseley, "Irrational Fears Give Nuclear Power a Bad Name," *Guardian*, January 10, 2010.
37. Zimmerman and Loeb 2004, 8.
38. "Regulatory Guide 8.29: Instruction Concerning Risks from Occupational Exposure," Office of Nuclear Regulatory Research, U.S. Nuclear Regulatory Commission, Revision 1, February 1996.
39. Zimmerman and Loeb 2004, 8. Moving: "Understanding Radiation in Our World," National Safety Council, July 2005.
40. U.S. Nuclear Regulatory Commission, Regulations Title 10, Code of Federal Regulations: Part 20—Standards for Protection Against Radiation, Subpart C—Occupational Dose Limits, May 21, 1991.
41. Matthew L. Wald, "Agency Seeks Broad Standard For 'Dirty Bomb' Exposure," *New York Times*, November 8, 2005; see also Matthew L. Wald, "Proposal on 'Dirty Bomb' Attack Would Accept Higher Exposure," *New York Times*, January 5, 2006. For an excellent discussion of the cleanup problem, see Elizabeth Eraker, "Cleanup after a Radiological Attack: U.S. Prepares Guidance," *Nonproliferation Review* 11(3) 2004: 167–185.
42. Mueller 2006.
43. See note 3 in the introduction
44. Sheehan 2008, 282.
45. Flynn 2004, 20, 33.
46. Warren Rudman, Gary Hart, Leslie H. Gelb, and Stephen Flynn, "'Our Hair Is on Fire,'" *Wall Street Journal*, December 16, 2004.
47. Stephen Flynn, "5 Myths about Keeping American Safe from terrorism," *Washington Post*, January 3, 2010.
48. Clarke 2005.
49. Richard A. Clarke, "The Times Square Bomb Failed. What Will We Do When the Next Bomb Works?" *Washington Post*, May 9, 2010.

CHAPTER 9: CONCLUSIONS AND POLITICAL REALITIES
1. Schneier 2003, 249.
2. Sheehan 2008, 263.
3. Veronique de Rugy, "The Economics of Homeland Security," in Benjamin H. Friedman, Jim Harper, and Christopher A. Preble, eds., *Terrorizing Ourselves: Why U.S. Counterterrorism Policy Is Failing and How to Fix It* (Washington, DC: Cato Institute, 2010), 123.
4. Flynn 2004, 20, 33, 27.
5. Friedman 2008, 35.
6. Rosen 2008.
7. James Fallows, "If the TSA Were Running New York," www.theatlantic.com, May 2010. Sheehan 2008, 7.
8. Speech at the Brookings Institution, June 1, 2006, as televised by C-SPAN.
9. Friedman 2008, 39.
10. Gwynne Dyer, "Politicking Skews Needed Perspective on Terror War," *Columbus Dispatch*, September 6, 2004 (also at www.gwynnedyer.com).

11. Lustick 2006, 115–116.
12. Office of Homeland Security 2002.
13. Gardner 2008, 262.
14. Benjamin Friedman, "Leap before You Look: The Failure of Homeland Security," *Breakthroughs*, Spring 2004, 33.
15. Ridge: Press Office release, Department of Homeland Security, December 21, 2003. Ashcroft: Mueller 2006, 162.
16. Sale 2002.
17. On the media, see Mueller 2006, 39–41; Gardner 2008, ch. 8.
18. Sunstein 2003, 132.
19. Tips: for example, *Consumer Reports*, March 2008, 6. Marc Siegel, *False Alarm: The Truth about the Epidemic of Fear* (New York: Wiley, 2005), 4. Chernobyl: Peter Finn, "Chernobyl's Harm Was Far Less Than Predicted, U.N. Report Says," *Washington Post*, September 6, 2005; W. Allison 2009, 99–109. Posttraumatic stress: Roxane Cohen Silver, E. Alison Holman, Daniel N. McIntosh, Michael Poulin, and Virginia Gil-Rivas, "Nationwide Longitudinal Study of Psychological Responses to September 11," *JAMA*, 288(10) 2002: 1235–1244. Cardiovascular ailments: John Tierney, "Living in Fear and Paying a High Cost in Heart Risk," *New York Times*, January 15, 2008. See also Joanna Bourke, *Fear: A Cultural History* (London: Virago, 2005), 374–391; Mueller 2006, 148–159.
20. Baruch Fischhoff, "Assessing and Communicating the Risks of Terrorism," in Albert H. Teich et al., eds., *Science and Technology in a Vulnerable World* (Washington, DC: American Association for the Advancement of Science, 2002), 63.
21. Chan 2007. One might also want to include a pronouncement in a 2004 book written by Senator John McCain: "Get on the damn elevator! Fly on the damn plane! Calculate the odds of being harmed by a terrorist! It's still about as likely as being swept out to sea by a tidal wave. Watch the terrorist alert and go outside again when it falls below yellow. Suck it up, for crying out loud. You're almost certainly going to be okay. And in the unlikely event you're not, do you really want to spend your last days cowering behind plastic sheets and duct tape? That's not a life worth living, is it?" (John McCain with Mark Salter, *Why Courage Matters: The Way to a Braver Life* [New York: Random House, 2004], 35–36). The inclusion in his peroration of the counsel to go outside when the alert level falls below yellow is, to say the least, odd. The ever-watchful and ever-cautious Department of Homeland Security seems unlikely *ever* to lower the threat level below yellow (or, now, its equivalent), and therefore, McCain's admonition seems effectively to contradict the spirit in the rest of the passage by encouraging everyone to cower inside for the rest of their lives. An e-mail inquiring about the apparent inconsistency was sent to Senator McCain's office in August 2004, but it has yet to generate a reply.
22. As discussed in chapter 7, we calculate that, for the world at large, one airplane flight in 22 million was hijacked or attacked by terrorists in the period from 1999 to 2010.
23. Tenet: *60 Minutes*, CBS, April 29, 2007. Tenet's assertion is strongly contradicted by the testimony of the chief 9/11 planner: "Substitution for the Testimony of Khalid Sheikh Mohammed," www.law.umkc.edu/faculty/projects/ftrials/moussaoui/sheikhstmt.pdf. Chertoff: E. A. Torriero, "U.S.

Security Chief Warns of Rising Risk: Chertoff Cites Worry over Summer Attack," *Chicago Tribune*, July 11, 2007. Lustick 2006, 97. Bart Kosko, "Terror Threat May Be Mostly a Big Bluff," *Los Angeles Times*, September 13, 2004.

24. Banks 2002, 10.

25. Jeffrey D. Simon, *The Terrorist Trap: America's Experience with Terrorism*, 2nd ed. (Bloomington: Indiana University Press, 2001), 227–234.

26. On Canada's notably measured reaction to the 1985 bombing of the Air India airliner that flew out of Toronto, mostly killing Canadian citizens, see Gwynne Dyer, "The International Terrorist Conspiracy," www.gwynnedyer.com, June 3, 2006.

27. It is possible, however, that any effective outrage against Bloomberg's glancing brush with reality was undercut by the fact that his city expends huge resources chasing after terrorists while routinely engaging in some of the most pointless security theater on the planet. For example, New York often extracts police officers from their duties to have them idle around at a sampling of the city's thousands of subway entrances, blandly watching as millions of people wearing backpacks or carrying parcels descend into the system throughout the city— perhaps the ultimate Maginot exercise. And as noted in chapter 8, it is also fond of trumpeting the fact that thousands of people each year call the city's police counterterrorism hotline while managing to neglect to mention that not one of these calls has yet led to a terrorism arrest. It is also possible that Bloomberg's pronouncement was motivated much more by an effort to undercut potential harm to tourism to New York than to responsibly communicate threat.

28. Heda Bayron, "Economic Impact from Bali's Latest Terrorist Bombings May Be Limited," GlobalSecurity.org, October 3, 2005.

29. Statistics Indonesia, Number of Foreign Visitor Arrivals to Indonesia by Port of Entry 1997–2008.

30. James Fallows, "The Evolution of the TSA," www.theatlantic.com, December 8, 2010. Emphasis in the original.

31. Steve Luxenberg, "Bob Woodward Book Details Obama Battles with Advisers over Exit Plan for Afghan War," *Washington Post*, September 22, 2010. See also Woodward 2010, 363.

32. Tammy O. Tengs and John D. Graham, "The Opportunity Costs of Haphazard Social Investments," in R. W. Hahn, ed., *Life-Saving, Risks, Costs, and Lives Saved: Getting Better Results from Regulation* (Washington, DC: American Enterprise Institute, 1996), 167–182.

33. Levitt and Porter 2001.

34. Hansen and Scuffham 1995.

35. Lisa Feuchtbaum and George Cunningham, "Economic Evaluation of Tandem Mass Spectrometry Screening in California," *Pediatrics*, 117(5) 2006: S280–S286.

36. Hansen and Scuffham 1995.

37. Levitt and Porter 2001.

38. "Fire Experience, Smoke Alarms and Sprinklers in Canadian Houses: CMHC Research to 2005," *Research Highlight*, Technical Series 05–107, Canada Mortgage and Housing Corporation, April 2005. Because the annualized cost of

installing a smoke alarm is around $10, installing smoke alarms in 10 million households will cost $100 million and save 50 lives.

39. Kevin M. Simmons and Daniel Sutter, "Direct Estimation of the Cost Effectiveness of Tornado Shelters," *Risk Analysis*, 26(4) 2006: 945–954. This means, for example, $100 million spent on installing tornado shelters in 50,000 mobile homes in Oklahoma would save 17 lives over the life of the shelter.

40. Stephane Hallegatte, "A Cost-Benefit Analysis of the New Orleans Flood Protection System," *AEI-Brookings Joint Center. Regulatory Analysis*, 06–02, 2006.

41. Lomborg 2009, 1.

42. Todd Sandler, Daniel G. Arce, and Walter Enders, "Transnational Terrorism," in Lomborg 2009, 552; they place the value of statistical life at $2 million in their calculations. As it happened, climate change action also ranked very low when compared with other risk-reducing measures. The hazard of global warming ranked a distant 14th for research and development of low-carbon energy technologies, 29th for a mix of R&D and CO_2 mitigation efforts, and 30th (and last) for CO_2 mitigation only. A net present value cost of $800 billion will produce benefit to cost ratios of 2.7 for first of these, 2.1 for the second, and 0.9 for the third. Lomborg 2009, 657.

43. Based on 37,261 traffic fatalities in United States in 2008.

44. Samuel A. Stouffer, *Communism, Conformity, and Civil Liberties* (Garden City, NY: Doubleday, 1955). On this issue, see also Mueller 2006, 87–89.

45. Alexander Stephan, *"Communazis": FBI Surveillance of German Émigré Writers* (New Haven, CT: Yale University Press, 2000), xii.

46. In fact, despite huge anxieties about it at the time, there seem to have been few, if any, instances in which domestic Communists engaged in anything that could be considered espionage after the Second World War. Moreover, at no time did any domestic Communist ever commit anything that could be considered violence in support of the cause. Just about all terrorist violence within the United States since 2001 has taken place on television—most persistently on Fox's *24*—and the same was true about domestic Communist violence during the Cold War. FBI informant Herbert Philbrick's confessional 1952 book, *I Led Three Lives* (New York: Grosset & Dunlap) at no point documents a single instance of Communist violence or planned violence, but violence became a central focus when his story was transmuted into a popular television series.

47. Mike O'Connor, *Crisis, Pursued by Disaster, Followed Closely by Catastrophe: A Memoir of Life on the Run* (New York: Random House, 2007), 278–279.

48. Leinwand 2008. Criticisms of the PATRIOT Act and of the Bush administration's efforts to apprehend prospective terrorists focus almost entirely on civil liberties concerns, worrying that rights for innocent Americans might be trampled in the rush to pursue terrorists. It's a perfectly valid concern, but from time to time, someone might wonder in public a bit about how much money the quest to ferret out terrorists and protect ourselves is costing, as well as how limited the results have been. Thus, in their valuable book, *Less Safe, Less Free* (New York: New Press, 2007), David Cole and Jules Lobel ably detail and critique the process, but, as suggested in their title, the implication

often is that the FBI and other agencies have failed in their well-funded quest to uncover the enemy within, not that the investigators haven't found much of anything because the enemy they are questing after essentially doesn't exist. On this issue, see John Mueller and Mark G. Stewart, "Witches, Communists, and Terrorists: Evaluating the Risks and Tallying the Costs," *ABA Human Rights Magazine*, Spring 2011.

49. H. L. Mencken, *A Mencken Chrestomathy* (New York: Knopf, 1949), 29.

APPENDIX

1. Such as the standard adopted by the International Organization for Standardization, *Risk Management—Principles and Guidelines*, ISO 31000–2009 (Geneva, Switzerland, 2009). The standard was supported by 26 countries (including the United States, United Kingdom, Canada, Australia, and China). Only one country (Italy) voted against it. See also Stewart and Melchers 1997.

REFERENCES

Includes works cited twice or more

Abrahms, Max. 2006. Why Terrorism Does Not Work. *International Security* 31(2) Fall: 42–78.
———. 2008. What Terrorists Really Want: Terrorist Motives and Counterterrorism Strategy. *International Security* 32(4) Spring: 78–105.
Allison, Graham T. 1995. Must We Wait for the Nuclear Morning After? *Washington Post*, April 30.
———. 2004. *Nuclear Terrorism: The Ultimate Preventable Catastrophe*. New York: Times Books.
Allison, Wade. 2009. *Radiation and Reason: The Impact of Science on a Culture of Fear*. York, UK: Wade Allison.
Banks, David L. 2002. Statistics for Homeland Defense. *Chance* 15(1): 8–10.
Bergen, Peter, and Paul Cruickshank. 2007. Self-Fulfilling Prophecy. *Mother Jones*, November–December.
Blalock, Garrick, Vrinda Kadiyali, and Daniel H. Simon. 2007. The Impact of Post-9/11 Airport Security Measures on the Demand for Air Travel. *Journal of Law and Economics* 50(4) November: 731–755.
———. 2009. Driving Fatalities after 9/11: A Hidden Cost of Terrorism. *Applied Economics* 41(14): 1717–1729.
Blue Ribbon Panel on Bridge and Tunnel Security. 2003. *Recommendations for Bridge and Tunnel Security*. Washington, DC: Federal Highway Administration, September.
Brooks, Risa A. 2011. Muslim "Homegrown" Terrorism in the United States: How Serious is the Threat? *International Security*, Fall.
Brown, Vahid. 2010. The Facade of Allegiance: Bin Ladin's Dubious Pledge to Mullah Omar. *CTC Sentinel* 3(1) January: 1–6.
Buesa, Mikel, Aurelia Vilariño, Joost Heijs, Thomas Baumert, and Javier González. 2007. The Economic Cost of March 11: Measuring the Direct Economic Cost of the Terrorist Attack on March 11, 2004 in Madrid. *Terrorism and Political Violence* 19(4): 489–509.
Burke, Jason. 2003. *Al-Qaeda: Casting a Shadow of Terror*. New York: Tauris.
Chan, Sewell. 2007. Buzz over Mayor's "Get a Life" Remark. nytimes.com, June 6, 2007.
Chow, James, James Chiesa, Paul Dreyer, Mel Eisman, Theodore W. Karasik, Joel Kvitky, Sherrill Linge, David Ochmanek, and Chad Shirley. 2005. *Protecting Commercial Aviation against the Shoulder-Fired Missile Threat*. Santa Monica, CA: RAND.

Clarke, Richard A. 2005. Ten Years Later. *Atlantic,* January–February: 61–77.

Daggett, Stephen. 2004. *The U.S. Intelligence Budget: A Basic Overview.* CRS Report for Congress, Congressional Research Service, Washington, DC, September 24.

Department of Homeland Security. 2009. *National Infrastructure Protection Plan: Partnering to Enhance Protection and Resiliency.* Washington, DC: Department of Homeland Security.

Dickey, Christopher. 2009. *Securing the City: Inside American's Best Counterterror Force—the NYPD.* New York: Simon and Schuster.

Dubay, Anthony R. 2010. *Improving Strategies to Prevent and Prepare for Radiological Attack.* Naval Postgraduate School, Monterey, California: Masters Thesis.

Ellig, Jerry, Amos Guiora, and Kyle McKenzie. 2006. *A Framework for Evaluating Counterterrorism Regulations.* Washington, DC: Mercatus Center, George Mason University.

Ervin, Clark Kent. 2006. *Open Target: Where America Is Vulnerable to Attack.* New York: Palgrave Macmillan.

Ferguson, Charles D., Tahseen Kazi, and Judith Perera. 2003. *Commercial Radioactive Sources: Surveying the Security Risks.* Monterey, CA: Center for Nonproliferation Studies, Monterey Institute of International Studies.

Ferguson, Charles D., and William C. Potter. 2005. *The Four Faces of Nuclear Terrorism: Threats and Responses.* New York: Routledge.

Fernandez, Manny. 2010. A Phrase for Safety after 9/11 Goes Global. *New York Times,* May 10.

Flynn, Stephen. 2004. The Neglected Home Front. *Foreign Affairs,* September–October: 20–33.

———. 2007. *The Edge of Disaster.* New York: Random House.

Friedman, Benjamin H. 2008. The Terrible "Ifs." *Regulation,* Winter: 32–40.

Furedi, Frank. 2008. Fear and Security: A Vulnerability-Led Policy Response. *Social Policy and Administration* 42(6) December: 645–661.

Gardner, Daniel. 2008. *The Science of Fear: Why We Fear the Things We Shouldn't—and Put Ourselves in Greater Danger.* New York: Dutton.

Gerges, Fawaz. 2005. *The Far Enemy: Why Jihad Went Global.* New York: Cambridge University Press.

———. 2008. Word on the Street. *Democracyjournal.org,* Summer: 69–76.

Gertz, Bill. 2002. 5,000 in U.S. Suspected of Ties to al Qaeda; Groups Nationwide under Surveillance. *Washington Times,* July 11.

Gilmore Commission (Advisory Panel to Assess Domestic Response Capabilities for Terrorism Involving Weapons of Mass Destruction). 1999. *First Annual Report: Assessing the Threat,* December 15.

Gordon, Peter, James E. Moore II, Ji Y. Pak, and Harry W. Richardson. 2007. The Economic Impacts of a Terrorist Attack on the U.S. Commercial Aviation System. *Risk Analysis* 27(3): 505–512.

Grosskopf, Kevin R. 2006. Evaluating the Societal Response to Antiterrorism Measures. *Journal of Homeland Security and Emergency Management* 3(2).

Gunter, David, I. M. Destler, Ivo H. Daalder, James B. Steinberg, and Michael E. O'Hanlon. 2002. *Protecting the American Homeland: A Preliminary Analysis.* Washington, DC: Brookings Institution Press.

Hansen, Paul, and Paul A. Scuffham. 1995. The Cost-Effectiveness of Compulsory Bicycle Helmets in New Zealand. *Australian Journal of Public Health* 19(5): 450–454.

Hobijn, Bart, and Erick Sager. 2007. What Has Homeland Security Cost? An Assessment: 2001–2005. *Current Issues in Economics and Finance (Federal Reserve Bank of New York)* 13(2): 1–7.

Hoffman, Bruce. 2006. *Inside Terrorism*. Revised and expanded. New York: Columbia University Press.

Hook, Scott. 2008. Assessing Expenditures in Individual Agencies: The Case of the Australian Federal Police. In *Risky Business: Measuring the Costs and Benefits of Counter-Terrorism Spending*, ed. Carl Ungerer, Henry Ergas, Scott Hook, and Mark Stewart. Australian Strategic Policy Institute, 13–18.

Horgan, John. 2009. *Walking Away from Terrorism: Accounts of Disengagement from Radical and Extremist Movements*. London: Routledge.

Jenkins, Brian Michael. 2008. *Will Terrorists Go Nuclear?* Amherst, NY: Prometheus.

———. 2010. *Would-Be Warriors: Incidents of Jihadist Terrorist Radicalization in the United States since September 11, 2001*. Santa Monica, CA: RAND.

Johnson, Kevin. 2009. Weakened al-Qaeda Is Still a Threat. *USA Today*, September 8.

Kean, Thomas H., Chair. 2004. *The 9/11 Commission Report: Final Report of the National Commission on Terrorist Attacks upon the United States*. Washington, DC: U.S. Government Printing Office.

Kearney, Simon. 2005. Air Marshal's Role Now VIP Security. *Australian*, December 9.

Kenney, Michael. 2010a. Beyond the Internet: *Mētis, Techne*, and the Limitations of Online Artifacts for Islamist Terrorists. *Terrorism and Political Violence* 22(2) April: 177–197.

———. 2010b. "Dumb" Yet Deadly: Local Knowledge and Poor Tradecraft among Islamist Militants in Britain and Spain. *Studies in Conflict & Terrorism* 33(10) October: 911–922.

Kuprenas, John A., Farzin Madjidi, Alex Vidaurrazaga, and Chen Lim. 1998. Seismic Retrofit Program for Los Angeles Bridges. *Journal of Infrastructure Systems* 4(4): 185–191.

Kurzman, Charles. 2011. *Muslim-American Terrorist since 9/11: An Accounting*. February 2. Triangle Center on Terrorism and Homeland Security.

Lakamp, David J., and Gill H. McCarthy. 2003. *A Cost-Benefit Analysis of Security at the Naval Postgraduate School*. Naval Postgraduate School, Monterey, California: MBA Professional Report, December.

LaTourrette, Tom, David R. Howell, David E. Mosher, and John MacDonald. 2006. *Reducing Terrorism Risk at Shopping Centers: An Analysis of Potential Security Options*. Technical Report. Santa Monica, CA: RAND.

Lawson, Guy. 2008. The Fear Factory. *Rolling Stone*, February 7.

Leinwand, Donna. 2008. Psst—Leads from Public to FBI Rise. *USA Today*, August 15.

Levi, Michael A. 2007. *On Nuclear Terrorism*. Cambridge, MA: Harvard University Press.

Levitt, Steven D., and Jack Porter. 2001. Sample Selection in the Estimation of Air Bag and Seat Belt Effectiveness. *Review of Economics and Statistics* 83(4): 603–615.

Little, Richard G. 2007. Cost-Effective Strategies to Address Urban Terrorism: A Risk Management Approach. In *The Economic Costs and Consequences of Terrorism*, ed. H. W. Richardson, P. Gordon, and J. E. Moore II. Cheltenham, UK: Edward Elgar, 98–115.

Lomborg, Bjorn. 2009. *Global Crises, Global Solutions*. Cambridge, UK: Cambridge University Press.

London Chamber of Commerce and Industry. 2005. *The Economic Effects of Terrorism in London: Experiences of Firms in London's Business Community, Press and Public Affairs*, August.

Lord, Steve. 2010. Aviation Security: TSA Is Increasing Procurement and Deployment of the Advanced Imaging Technology, but Challenges to This Effort and Areas of Aviation Security Remain. *United States Government Accountability Office*, GAO-10–484T, March 17.

Luft, Gal. 2005. Pipeline Sabotage Is Terrorist's Weapon of Choice. *Pipeline and Gas Journal* 232(2): 42–45.

Lugar, Richard G. 2005. *The Lugar Study on Proliferation Threats and Responses*. Washington, DC: Senate Foreign Relations Committee.

Lustick, Ian S. 2006. *Trapped in the War on Terror*. Philadelphia: University of Pennsylvania Press.

Lynch, Marc. 2006. Al-Qaeda's Media Strategies. *National Interest*, Spring: 50–56.

Mack, Andrew. 2008. Dying to Lose: Explaining the Decline in Global Terrorism. In *Human Security Brief 2007*. Vancouver, BC: Human Security Report Project, School for International Studies, Simon Fraser University, 8–21.

Maley, Paul. 2008. Overhaul Cuts Sky Marshals by a Third. *Australian News*, January 23.

Martonosi, Susan E., David S. Ortiz, and Henry H. Willis. 2007. Evaluating the Viability of 100 Percent Container Inspection at America's Ports. In *The Economic Impacts of Terrorist Attacks*, ed. H. W. Richardson, P. Gordon, and J. E. Moore II. Cheltenham, UK: Edward Elgar, 218–241.

Masse, Todd, Siobhan O'Neil, and John Rollins. 2007. *The Department of Homeland Security's Risk Assessment Methodology: Evolution, Issues, and Options for Congress*. Washington, DC: Congressional Research Service, February 2.

Mayer, Matt A. 2009. *Homeland Security and Federalism: Protecting America from Outside the Beltway*. Santa Barbara, CA: ABC-CLIO.

Meckler, Laura, and Susan Carey. 2007. Sky Patrol: U.S. Air Marshal Service Navigates Turbulent Times. *Wall Street Journal*, February 9.

Mueller, John. 2002. Harbinger or Aberration? A 9/11 Provocation. *National Interest*, Fall: 45–50.

———. 2004. *The Remnants of War*. Ithaca, NY: Cornell University Press.

———. 2006. *Overblown: How Politicians and the Terrorism Industry Inflate National Security Threats, and Why We Believe Them*. New York: Free Press.

———. 2010. *Atomic Obsession: Nuclear Alarmism from Hiroshima to Al Qaeda*. New York: Oxford University Press.

——— (ed.). 2011. *Terrorism since 9/11: The American Cases*. Columbus: Mershon Center, Ohio State University.

National Research Council of the National Academies. 2010. *Review of the Department of Homeland Security's Approach to Risk Analysis*. Washington, DC: National Academies Press.

O'Connor, Noelle, Mary R. Stafford, and Gerry Gallagher. 2008. *A Chronological Review of the Tourism Industry's Reactions to Terrorist Attacks, Using Bali (2002), London (2005), Madrid (2004) and New York (2001) as Case Studies.* EuroCHRIE Conference, The Emirates Academy, Dubai, United Arab Emirates.

Office of Homeland Security. 2002. *National Strategy for Homeland Security,* July.

Office of Inspector General. 2006. *Progress in Developing the National Asset Database.* Washington, DC: Department of Homeland Security.

Paté-Cornell, M. Elisabeth. 1994. Quantitative Safety Goals for Risk Management of Industrial Facilities. *Structural Safety* 13: 145–157.

Pillar, Paul R. 2003. *Terrorism and U.S. Foreign Policy.* Washington, DC: Brookings Institution Press.

Pincus, Walter. 2009. DNI Cites $75 Billion Intelligence Tab. *Washington Post,* September 17.

Porter, Patrick. 2009. Long Wars and Long Telegrams: Containing Al-Qaeda. *International Affairs* 85(2) March: 285–305.

Ripley, Amanda. 2004. How Safe Are We? The Fortification of Wyoming, and Other Strange Tales from the New Front Line. *Time,* March 29.

Robinson, Lisa A., James K. Hammitt, Joseph E. Aldy, Alan Krupnick, and Jennifer Baxter. 2010. Valuing the Risk of Death from Terrorist Attacks. *Journal of Homeland Security and Emergency Management* 7(1).

Rockwell, Theodore. 2003. Radiation Chicken Little. *Washington Post,* September 16.

Rosen, Jeffrey. 2008. Man-Made Disaster. *New Republic,* December 24.

Sageman, Marc. 2004. *Understanding Terror Networks.* Philadelphia: University of Pennsylvania Press.

———. 2008. *Leaderless Jihad.* Philadelphia: University of Pennsylvania Press.

Sale, Richard. 2002. US al Qaida Cells Attacked. UPI, October 31.

Savage, Charlie. 2011. F.B.I. Casts Wide Net Under Relaxed Rules for Terror Inquiries, Data Show. *New York Times,* March 26.

Schneier, Bruce. 2003. *Beyond Fear: Thinking Sensibly about Security in an Uncertain World.* New York: Copernicus.

Seible, Frieder, et al. 2008 Protection of Our Bridge Infrastructure against Man-Made and Natural Hazards. *Structure and Infrastructure Engineering* 4(6): 415–429.

Seitz, Russell. 2004. Weaker Than We Think. *American Conservative,* December 6.

Shapiro, Jeremy. 2007. *Managing Homeland Security: Develop a Threat-Based Strategy.* Opportunity 08 Paper. Washington, DC: Brookings Institution.

Sheehan, Michael A. 2008. *Crush the Cell: How to Defeat Terrorism without Terrorizing Ourselves.* New York: Crown.

Slovic, Paul, Baruch Fischhoff, and Sarah Lichtenstein. 1980. Facts and Fears: Understanding Perceived Risk. In *Societal Risk Assessment: How Safe is Safe Enough?* ed. R. C. Schwing and W. A. Albers. New York: Plenum , 181–216.

Smith, Patrick. 2007. The Airport Security Follies. *nytimes.com,* December 28.

Smith, Peter D., and Timothy A. Rose. 2002. Blast Loading and Building Robustness. *Progress in Structural Engineering and Mechanics* 4: 213–223.

Stenersen, Anne. 2008. The Internet: A Virtual Training Camp? *Terrorism and Political Violence* 20(2): 215–233.

———. 2009. Al-Qaeda's Thinking on CBRN: A Case Study. In *Unconventional Weapons and International Terrorism: Challenges and New Approaches*, ed. Magnus Ranstorp and Magnus Normark. London: Routledge, 50–63.

Stewart, Mark G. 2008. Cost-Effectiveness of Risk Mitigation Strategies for Protection of Buildings against Terrorist Attack. *Journal of Performance of Constructed Facilities* 22(2): 115–120.

———. 2010. Risk-Informed Decision Support for Assessing the Costs and Benefits of Counter-Terrorism Protective Measures for Infrastructure. *International Journal of Critical Infrastructure Protection* 3(1): 29–40.

Stewart, Mark G., and Robert E. Melchers. 1997. *Probabilistic Risk Assessment of Engineering Systems*. London: Chapman & Hall.

Stewart, Mark G., and John Mueller. 2011. Risk and Cost-Benefit Analysis of Advanced Imaging Technology Full Body Scanners for Airline Passenger Security Screening. *Journal of Homeland Security and Emergency Management* (8)1, Article 30.

Stiglitz, Joseph E., and Linda J. Bilmes. 2008. *The Three Trillion Dollar War: The True Cost of the Iraq Conflict*. New York: W. W. Norton.

Sunstein, Cass R. 2003. Terrorism and Probability Neglect. *Journal of Risk and Uncertainty* 26(2–3) March–May: 121–136.

———. 2007. *Worst-Case Scenarios*. Cambridge, MA: Harvard University Press.

Tenet, George, and Bill Harlow. 2007. *At the Center of the Storm: My Years at the CIA*. New York: HarperCollins.

Travis, C. C., S. A. Richter, E. A. C. Crouch, R. Wilson, and E. D. Klema. 1987. Cancer Risk Management: A Review of 132 Federal Regulatory Decisions. *Environmental Science and Technology* 21(5): 415–420.

Treverton, Gregory F., Justin L. Adams, James Dertouzous, Arindam Dutta, Susan F. Everingham, and Eric V. Larson. 2008. The Costs of Responding to the Terrorist Threats. In *Terrorism, Economic Development, and Political Openness*, ed. Philip Keefer and Norman Loayza. New York: Cambridge University Press.

Viscusi, W. Kip. 2000. The Value of Life in Legal Contexts: Survey and Critique. *American Law and Economics Review* 2(1): 195–222.

Warrick, Joby. 2008. U.S. Cites Big Gains against Al-Qaeda. *Washington Post*, May 30.

Wirz, Christoph, and Emmanuel Egger. 2005. Use of Nuclear and Radiological Weapons by Terrorists? *International Review of the Red Cross* 87(859) September: 497–510.

Woodward, Bob. 2010. *Obama's Wars*. New York: Simon and Schuster.

Wright, Lawrence. 2006. *The Looming Tower: Al-Qaeda and the Road to 9/11*. New York: Knopf.

———. 2008. The Rebellion Within. *New Yorker*, June 2.

Younger, Stephen M. 2009. *The Bomb: A New History*. New York: Ecco.

Zakaria, Fareed. 2010. Post-9/11, We're Safer Than We Think. *Washington Post*, September 13.

Zimmerman, Peter D., and Cheryl Loeb. 2004. Dirty Bombs: The Threat Revisited. *Defense Horizons*, January: 1–11.

Zycher, Benjamim. 2003. *A Preliminary Benefit/Cost Framework for Counterterrorism Public Expenditures*. Santa Monica, CA: RAND.

INDEX

air travel (*continued*)
  items that would save more lives at same
    or lower cost than security for, 182–183
  losses sustained in successful airliner
    hijacking, 148–149, 237n66
  losses sustained in successful 9/11-scale
    attack, 142
  9/11's effect on, 133–135
  no successful hijacking since 9/11, 143
  number of terrorist incidents on American
    airliners, 178
  Pan Am Flight 103 bombing, 41, 43, 44,
    135, 136, 154, 180
  plot to blow up ten transatlantic aircraft of
    2006, 212n50
  probability of successful replication of
    9/11, 141–142
  reducing costs for protection of, 154–155
  regulatory expenditure per life saved, 57
  security measures for, 137–138
  "shoe bomber," 46, 79–80, 134, 136, 140,
    147, 152, 237n66
  special impact of airliner destruction,
    132–134
  terrorism fatalities and annual fatality
    risks, 1970–2007, 44
  "underwear bomber," 79–80, 134, 136,
    140, 147, 149, 152, 167, 178
  See also air marshals; airports
AITs. *See* full-body scanners
Allison, Graham, 66, 70, 75, 218n74,
  219n75
Animal Liberation Front, 43
annual fatality risks
  amount of increase for terrorism to
    become unacceptable risk, 53
  comparison of, 52
  for defining acceptable risk, 50, 51
  for terrorism, 43, 51–53
anthrax, 4, 71, 180
Armed Front for National Liberation
  (FALN), 79
Ashcroft, John, 176
atomic terrorism. *See* nuclear terrorism
Aum Shinrikyo, 54–55
Australia
  acceptable risk for hazardous industries
    in, 49
  air marshal service of, 143, 147, 153, 154
  annual fatality risk comparison, 52

attack probabilities for homeland security
  expenditures to be cost-effective in,
  92, 93
hardened cockpit door program of, 147,
  153
hypothetical attack on scale of 2005
  London bombings in, 102
lower homeland security expenditures
  than U.S. in, 11, 179
results of cost-benefit analysis for
  homeland security expenditures in,
  91–92
terrorism fatalities and annual fatality
  risks, 1970–2007, 43, 44, 45
automobile travel
  air travel replaced by, 157
  regulatory expenditure per life saved in, 57
  tolerating risk from, 45, 47–48, 50
  as voluntary risk, 212n56
  See also traffic accidents
aviation. *See* air travel

Bali bombings (2002), 31, 42, 44, 45, 62, 181
Banks, David, 28, 153, 179
Becker, Kurt, 151
benefit of a security measure, 24–25, 76–77,
  84, 117
benzene, 49, 57
Bergen, Peter, 37
Bhopal (India) chemical disaster, 128
bin Laden, Osama
  on attacking nodes of U.S. economy,
    232n72
  on bankrupting U.S., 3, 195n3
  Clinton bombs Afghanistan camps of, 73
  death of, 72, 185
  Muslims turn against terrorism of, 32
  Taliban hostility toward, 33
  threats to U.S. by, 36
biological weapons, 71, 110, 167, 168
Blair, Dennis, 197n13
Bloomberg, Michael, 14, 178, 181, 244n27
break-even approach, 26, 27, 84, 86, 117
bridges, 99–100, 121–126, 131
Brookings Institution, 62–63, 201n15
Brooklyn Bridge, 46, 125, 130
Brown, Michael, 168
buildings. *See* office buildings
Bush, George W.
  accused of shortchanging rural states, 106

and anthrax attacks of 2001, 180
criticism of terrorism policy of, 245n48
9/11 provides occasion to attack Iraq for, 73, 203n21
precautionary principle in, 16
on terrorism in 2004 election campaign, 175, 181
on terrorist threat as existential, 20

Canada
annual fatality risk comparison, 52
attack probabilities for homeland security expenditures to be cost-effective in, 92, 93
concern about closure of U.S. border with, 222n41
lower homeland security expenditures than U.S. in, 11, 179
results of cost-benefit analysis for homeland security expenditures in, 91–92
terrorism fatalities and annual fatality risks, 1970–2007, 43, 44, 45
carcinogens, environmental, 49–50, 51
Carle, Glenn, 34
Chapman, Clark, 20
Chechens, 73, 134, 135, 137
checked luggage, 135, 155
chemical plants, 127–129
chemical weapons, 71, 72, 110
Cheney, Dick, 175, 220n23
Chernobyl nuclear accident, 127, 177
Chertoff, Michael, 3, 15, 20, 168, 175, 178
Chicago
on lists of potential terrorist targets, 105
Sears Tower plot, 46, 212n51
cities
lists of potential terrorist targets, 104–105
See also Chicago; London; Los Angeles; New York City; Oklahoma City bombing (1995); Washington, D.C.
civilian surveillance, 161–163
civil liberties, 187, 245n48
Clark, Helen, 46
Clarke, Richard, 171
climate change action, 245n42
Clinton, Bill, 73, 171, 180, 219n3
Clinton, Hillary, 106
Cohen, David, 34
Cold War, 185–188

Cole, David, 245n48
color-coded alert system, 155, 243n21
Communism, 185–188, 190, 191, 245n46
containers, shipping, 6, 21–22
cost-benefit analysis, 24–26, 76–77
for acceptable risk, 50
for automobile use, 47, 50
benefit as applied to terrorism, 77–80
for bridge protection, 123–126
costs as applied to terrorism, 80–81
evaluations of cost-effectiveness, 92–93
for full-body scanners, 147–152
Government Accountability Office on, 6
for homeland security expenditures, 3, 76–93, 172
list making versus, 107–108
as not sole consideration in public decision making, 27
for office building protection, 114–121
results for Australia, 91–92
results for Canada, 91–92
results for U.K., 87–91
results for U.S., 81–87
for security measures designed to prevent another 9/11, 138–147, 153–154
as standard coin for policy decision making, 9
uncertainties in, 238n67
worst-case thinking and, 15–16
costs
aggregating costs of conventional attacks, 59–65
balancing safety against, 9
of extreme reaction, 72–74
full costs of terrorism, 56–75
of risk reduction measures, 25–26
tendency to neglect, 13, 20–23
of terrorist attack on office building, 115–116
See also cost-benefit analysis
counterterrorism
Australian legislation on, 179
avoiding overreaction as, 170
costs as greater than the security we get in return, 172
gauging impact of, 53–54
governments will not downplay value of, 89
increased spending as greater than for comparable risks, 173

Elias, Bartholomew, 137
Enders, Walter, 60, 142, 237n66
Ervin, Clark Kent, 21
Executive Order 12866, 219n1

Faddis, Charles, 21
Fallows, James, 174, 182, 196n8
falls from buildings, 47
FAMS. *See* Federal Air Marshal Service
    (FAMS)
Faris, Iyman, 46
fatalities, 40–45
    annual from traffic accidents, 45, 47, 48
    from bridge attacks, 122
    compensation for, 58–59
    decline in those from terrorism, 15
    frequency per terrorist attack, 64
    Global Terrorism Database on, 43
    from lightning versus from terrorism, 41,
        178
    number caused by al-Qaeda since 9/11,
        189
    from office building attacks, 115–116,
        116, 228n32
    probability as essentially zero, 14, 181
    probability as low outside war zones, 74,
        176, 189
    small number of people who actually die
        from terrorism, 15
    from typical terrorist act, 63–64
    See also annual fatality risks
FBI (Federal Bureau of Investigation)
    concentrates on terrorism to neglect of
        other kinds of crime, 190
    few terrorists uncovered in U.S. by, 31,
        36, 177
    National Security Agency bombards with
        data, 161
    surveillance of domestic Communists,
        187, 188
    terrorism tips from the public, 162
fears
    continuing fear of terrorism in U.S.,
        189–191
    in definition of terrorism, 42
    health consequences of, 103–104,
        177–178
    homeland security issues as driven by, 5,
        27–28
    internalized, 185–188

    in overreaction, 73
    in willingness to accept risk, 43
Federal Air Marshal Service (FAMS)
    cost-effectiveness of, 144–145, 153–154,
        236n55
    cost of, 139
    free seats for, 4, 139, 203n24
    as in-flight security, 138
    in reduction in risk, 143, 144, 235nn47,
        50
    as security theater, 156
    as unlikely to foil suicide bombers,
        238n71
Federal Bureau of Investigation. *See* FBI
    (Federal Bureau of Investigation)
Federal Emergency Management Agency
    (FEMA), 168
federal flight deck officers, 138, 141
financial markets, 9/11's effects on, 60,
    61
Fischhoff, Baruch, 169, 178
Flynn, Stephen, 129, 171, 173
Fort Dix (New Jersey), 46, 161
Fort Hood (Texas) shootings, 181–182
France, 221n39
Friedman, Benjamin, 174, 175, 176
FTSE 100 Index, 61
full-body scanners, 6, 12, 147–152, 157,
    236n60, 239n77
Furedi, Frank, 103, 167

Gadahn, Adam, 36
Gardner, Daniel, 176, 214n76
Garwin, Richard, 75
gasoline vapor inhalation, 49
Gates, Robert, 67
GDP (gross domestic product), 9/11's effect
    on, 59–60, 61, 149
Gerges, Fawaz, 30–31
Germany, 221n39
Gibson, Charles, 177
Gilmore Commission, 69, 71
Giuliani, Rudy, 1
Glasgow (Scotland) attack (2007), 96, 105
Global Terrorism Database (GTD), 42, 63,
    122
Goldberg, Jeffrey, 160
Golden Gate Bridge, 125, 130
Goldstein, Joshua, 66
Gordon, Peter, 237n66

government
    established regulatory practices regarding
        acceptable risk, 50–51
    military and intelligence agencies created
        in response to 9/11, 161
    public demands substantial response
        from, 14, 74, 179
    regulatory expenditure per life saved,
        57–58
    warning without terrifying as challenge
        for, 14
    will not downplay value of
        counterterrorism, 89
    See also Department of Homeland
        Security (DHS); FBI (Federal Bureau
        of Investigation); homeland security
        expenditures
Government Accountability Office (GAO),
    6, 147, 149
graffiti, 110
Great Britain. *See* United Kingdom
Greenberg, Karen J., 164
Grenier, Robert, 33
Gunter, David, 217n47

Hahn, Robert, 58
hardened cockpit doors, 138, 139, 143–147,
    153, 210n37, 234n36, 235n52, 236n55
hardening buildings, 113–115
Harris, Alan, 20, 41–42
Hawaii, 60
Hayden, Michael, 32
hazardous (toxic) waste, 9, 57, 58
Health and Safety Executive (United
    Kingdom), 47
health consequences of terrorism-induced
    fears, 177–178
Heritage Foundation, 128, 232n71
"high-consequence" events, 15
Hobijn, Bart, 196n1
Hoffman, Bruce, 37
Homeland Security, Department of. *See*
    Department of Homeland Security
    (DHS)
homeland security expenditures
    for air travel protection, 132–158
    cost-benefit analysis applied to, 76–93,
        172
    for critical infrastructure protection,
        109–131

elemental questions about rarely
    answered, 7–9
evaluating, 3–9, 76–93
as focused on low-consequence events, 15
government spending worldwide in 2009,
    195n4
how much are we willing to pay for small
    reduction in probabilities, 1
inflating importance of potential terrorist
    targets in, 18–19
items that would save more lives at same
    or lower cost, 182–185, *184*
massive increase in, 1–4, *4*, 81–82
net benefit for U.K. enhanced
    expenditures of $5 billion per
    year, *90*
net benefit for U.S. enhanced expenditures
    of $75 billion per year, *83*
parameters for protecting potential
    terrorist targets, 94–108
private-sector spending, 4, 82, 201n15
on relative rather than absolute risk
    assessment, 18
results of cost-benefit analysis for
    Australia, 91–92
results of cost-benefit analysis for Canada,
    91–92
results of cost-benefit analysis for U.K.,
    87–91
results of cost-benefit analysis for U.S.,
    81–87
as self-perpetuating, 185–191
sensitivity and break-even analysis for
    enhanced expenditures of $75 billion
    per year, *86*
state and local expenditures, 2, *4*, 81, 82,
    201n14
total and enhanced homeland security
    expenditures by U.S. government,
    2002–2011, 2
United Kingdom dedicated spending on
    counterterrorism, 87–89, *88*
as wildly inefficient, 11
Hook, Scott, 102
Howard, John, 45, 179
human life
    regulatory expenditure per life saved,
        57–58
    terrorism as hazard to, 29–55
    value of, 56–59

valuing equally, 212n54
 See also fatalities
Hurricane Katrina, 168
Hussein, Saddam, 16, 32, 73

Ifill, Gwen, 178
Ignatieff, Michael, 66, 73, 75
improvised explosive devices (IEDs), 111,
 126, 228n32
Indonesia
 Bali bombings of 2002, 31, 42, 44, 45, 62,
 181
 Jakarta hotel bombings of 2009, 100
 Jemaah Islamiyah, 128
informants, 163–164
infrastructure. *See* critical infrastructure
insurance
 life insurance payout per 9/11 victim, 58
 for office buildings, 120–121
 against terrorism, 4, 23–24, 82, 120,
 202n17, 230n44
intelligence gathering
 in homeland security expenditures, 81
 increasing expenditures on, 3
 National Intelligence Program (NIP),
 197n13
 systematic evaluation for, 160–161
Internet, 35, 40
Iraq
 annual fatality risk comparison, 52
 bridge attacks in, 122
 buildings destroyed in, 112
 cause of war in, 72–73
 cost of terrorism-related war in, 4, 72, 82,
 89, 203n21
 fatalities from truck and car bombs in, 63
 oil facility attacks in, 126
 payments to families of soldiers killed in,
 58
 precautionary principle in U.S. invasion of
 2003, 16
 al-Qaeda in, 32–33
Irish Republican Army (IRA), 62, 87, 101,
 122, 133
Israel
 bin Laden on retaliation for support for,
 36
 bombers select other targets when one is
 well protected in, 98
 economic effects of terrorism on, 60

fear of terrorism and health in, 177
 homeland security budget of, 222n45
 Lebanon invasion of 1982 by, 73
 resilience in response to terrorism in, 167
 symbolic targets in, 130

Jakarta (Indonesia) hotel bombings (2009),
 100
Jemaah Islamiyah (JI), 128
Jenkins, Brian, 38, 66, 78–79, 164
Jewish Defense League, 79
Jordan suicide terrorism of 2005, 31–32, 42

Kean, Thomas, 235n45
Kelly, Raymond, 34
Kelsali, Robert, 181
Kenney, Michael, 39–40
Kerry, John, 175, 181
key resources (key assets)
 defined, 19
 parameters for protecting, 94–108
 proportion of homeland security
 expenditures devoted to, 18, 81,
 197nn6, 9
Kosko, Bart, 178
Krauthammer, Charles, 66
Krugman, Paul, 60
Kunreuther, Howard, 1, 3
Kurzman, Charles, 162

Lackawanna Six, 163
Lakamp, David, 111
Laqueur, Walter, 55
Larsen, Randall, 22
Leahy, Pat, 106
Lebanon
 explosion at Marines barracks of 1983,
 111, 113, 180
 Israeli invasion of 1982, 73
Lerhe, Eric, 91
Lewis, James, 99
life, human. *See* human life
lightning
 annual fatality risk comparison, 52
 deaths from international terrorism versus
 from, *41*, 178
 protecting critical infrastructure against,
 109, 129
Little, Richard, 111
Lobel, Jules, 245n48

office buildings (*continued*)
  probability of attack in U.S., 117–119
  progressive collapse of, 226n15
  U.S. Army considers them unsafe, 94
Office of Management and Budget (OMB),
    3, 27, 81, 160, 206n44, 219n1, 238n67
offshore oil and gas platforms, 126
oil and gas refineries, 128
Oklahoma City bombing (1995)
  city added to lists of potential terrorist
    targets, 105
  Clinton's response to, 180
  compensation for families of victims
    of, 58
  fatalities from, 43, *44, 116*
  foiled plots compared with, *46*
  low probability of repetition of, 108
  as one of two significant truck bombings,
    1988–2007, 119
  partial progressive damage in, 113, 115
  people soon reentered office buildings
    after, 133
  seen as harbinger, 54
  target selection in, 97
Olsen, Eric, 237n66
Omagh (Northern Ireland) bombing
    (1998), 43, *44*, 216n34
"one-percent doctrine," 220n23
Oppenheimer, J. Robert, 66, 67, 218n65
opportunity costs
  of counterterrorism efforts, 166
  among elemental questions rarely
    considered, 7
  of full-body scanners, 148
  in full cost of terrorism, 72
  in increase in homeland security
    expenditures since 9/11, 3, *4*
  items that would save more lives at same
    or lower cost, 182–185
  as policy consideration, 104
  in U.S. Naval Postgraduate School security
    process, 115, 227n26
overreaction
  avoiding, 12, 170–171
  as enhancing negative effects of terrorism,
    75
  is it a political imperative, 179–182
  as not inevitable, 74
  opportunity costs of, 72–74
  to port attack, 129

realistic reactions versus, 28, 87
Oxley, Jimmie, 136

Pakistan
  buildings destroyed in, 112
  government on bin Laden's enemies list,
    32
  Marriott Hotel bombing in Islamabad,
    112
  and Mumbai attacks of 2008, 74, 180
  Obama's threat in case of Pakistan-based
    attack on U.S., 218n72
  withdraws support from Taliban, 31
Pan Am Flight 103 (1988), 41, 43, *44*, 135,
    136, 154, 180
Panetta, Leon, 33, 37–38
panic, 169
passenger and crew resistance, 79–80, 138,
    139–141, 143–144, 158, 235n47
Paté-Cornell, Elisabeth, 27–28, 56
PATRIOT Act, 245n48
Pearl Harbor, 224n22
Pentagon
  cost of attack on, 142
  damage as limited at, 100–101
  fatalities from 2001 attack on, *116*
  security measures for preventing attacks
    like that on, 144, 146
  as symbolic target, 130
perimeter security, 116–117
PETN, 136, 233n17
Philbrick, Herbert, 245n46
pipelines, 126
Pistole, John, 149, 196n8
plutonium, 69
policing, 160–166
  apprehension of supporters of terrorism
    abroad, 165
  civilian surveillance, 161–163
  in homeland security expenditures, 81
  international cooperation in, 31
  in inventing terrorists, 163–164
  for nuclear terrorism, 69
  overseas efforts in, 160
  preexisting procedures and capacities of,
    165–166
  versus protection, 95, 99
politics
  concerns as sometimes overwrought, 12
  political realities, 174–182

"shoe bomber," *46*, 79–80, 134, 136, 140, 147, 152, 237n66
shopping centers
  Clarke foresees shootings at, 171
  cost-effective security measures for, 80, 224n27
  protection measures deter customers from entering, 103
  Rockford, Illinois, bombing plot, 38, 96, 163–164
  terrorists in Israel seek other targets, 98
short-haul flying, decline in, 157
Siegel, Marc, 177
Skeptical Inquirer (journal), 20
Skinner, Richard L., 157
Smith, Edward, 157
Smith, Patrick, 140, 153
Somalia, 180
Somali Americans, 241n23
Standard & Poor's 500-stock index, 60
Stenersen, Anne, 40, 72
Stephan, Alexander, 187
Stevens, John Paul, 48, 49
Stevenson, Jonathan, 88
Stouffer, Samuel, 186, 188
Sunstein, Cass, 14, 16, 103, 156, 177
surface-to-air missiles, 136–137
symbolic targets, 130

Taliban, 31, 32, 33, 35
targets. *See* potential terrorist targets
Tenet, George, 67, 178
terrorism
  absorbing, 12, 166–168, 182
  as acceptable risk, 51–53, 74
  adult conversation about, 181
  against air travel, 132–158
  annual fatality risk of, 15, 51–53
  characterization of terrorists, 29, 40, 54
  Communist threat compared with, 185–188, 190, 191
  continuing fear in U.S., 189–191
  against critical infrastructure, 109–131
  deaths from, 40–45
  decline in deaths from, 54
  defined, 42
  direct economic damage from attacks, *65*
  extreme events seen as harbingers, 54–55
  as feature of life, 173
  foiled plots in U.S., 43, 46, 53

frequency and severity of attacks as low, 173
frequency of fatalities per attack, *64*
full costs of, 56–75
future increase seen for, 54–55
as hazard to human life, 29–55
homegrown terrorists, 37–40, 165
inflating terrorist capacities, 19–20
informants and police invent terrorists, 163–164
insurance against, *4*, 23–24, 82, 202n17, 230n44
"lone wolf" terrorists, 37–38
as low-probability event, 77
number of terrorists is small, 96
operatives in the West, 1, 35–40, 209n23
political realities regarding, 12, 174–182
possible future expansion of destruction from, 65–74
pre-9/11 in U.S., 78–79
probability of fatalities low outside war zones, 74, 176, 189
probability of fatality as essentially zero, 14, 181
public demands to "do something" about, 14, 74, 179
resilience regarding, 12, 166–168, 182
risk perceived as higher than it is, 51
seen as criminal problem, 88
terrorists as less clever and diabolical than depicted, 37, 80, 96, 161, 163, 165
transnational, 30–35, 40–41
vandalism compared with, 110
versus war and insurgency, 210n41
See also counterterrorism; nuclear terrorism; potential terrorist targets
Terrorism Risk Insurance Act, 24
Thompson, Bennie, 121
Thomson, James, 3
threats
  Department of Defense approach to, 174
  internalized, 185–188
  plausible, 28
  spectrum of, 16–17
  statistical approaches to predicting, 206n43
  threat-based approach to homeland security, 5
Three Mile Island nuclear accident, 127
TIARA program, 199n

Times Square bombing attempt (2010), 11,
    80, 84, 92–93, 165, 167
Tokyo subway station attack (1995), 55
tourism, 59, 60, 61, 62, 84, 133, 142,
    237n66
toxic (hazardous) waste, 9, 57, 58
traffic accidents
    annual fatalities, 45, 47, 48
    annual fatality risk comparison, 52
    enduring terrorism as we endure, 168
    fatalities between September 11, 2001,
        and October 2003, 134
    knowledge of risk of, 23
Transportation Security Administration
        (TSA)
    budget of, 137
    costs due to enhanced security measures
        of, 202n18
    full-body scanners, 6, 12, 147–152, 157,
        236n60, 239n77
    general aviation requirements, 157
    inbox management approach of, 196n8
    layered approach to airline security of,
        137–138, 158
    "puffers" installed by, 22–23
    railroad security requirements, 5
    resentment against procedures of, 157
    risk reduction target of, 79
Treverton, Gregory, 13–14, 181

"underwear bomber," 79–80, 134, 136, 140,
    147, 149, 152, 167, 178
United Kingdom
    annual fatality risk comparison, 52
    attack probabilities for homeland security
        expenditures to be cost-effective in,
        92, 93
    bridge attacks in, 122
    dedicated spending on counterterrorism
        in, 87–89, 88
    direct economic damage from terrorist
        attacks in, 65
    frequency of fatalities per terrorist attack
        in, 64
    as "frontline state in the campaign against
        terrorism," 87
    Global Terrorism Database analysis of 219
        terrorist attacks in, 63, 216n34
    lower homeland security expenditures
        than U.S. in, 11, 179

net benefit for enhanced homeland
        security expenditures of $5 billion per
        year, 90
Northern Ireland, 43, 44, 52, 88
Pan Am Flight 103, 41, 43, 44, 135, 136,
        154, 180
results of cost-benefit analysis for
        homeland security expenditures in,
        87–91
terrorism fatalities and annual fatality
        risks, 1970–2007, 43, 44
terrorism insurance scheme, 230n44
See also London
United States
    annual fatality risk comparison, 52
    continuing fear of terrorism in, 189–191
    direct economic damage from terrorist
        attacks, 65
    embassy bombings of 1998, 30, 73,
        111–112, 180, 226n13
    foiled terrorism plots in, 43, 46, 53
    frequency of fatalities per terrorist attack
        in, 64
    homegrown terrorists, 37–40
    net benefit for enhanced homeland
        security expenditures of $75 billion per
        year, 83
    no Muslim terrorist has set off bomb for
        more than ten years, 131
    nonimmigrant admissions to, 37, 209n24
    no al-Qaeda attacks since 9/11, 189
    pre-9/11 terrorism in, 78–79
    probability of office building attack in,
        117–119
    al-Qaeda operatives in, 1, 35–37,
        176–177, 178, 209n23
    resilience in response to terrorism in, 167
    results of cost-benefit analysis for
        homeland security expenditures in,
        81–87
    sensitivity and break-even analysis
        for enhanced homeland security
        expenditures of $75 billion per year, 86
    terrorism fatalities and annual fatality
        risks, 1970–2007, 43, 44
    total and enhanced homeland security
        expenditures by U.S. government,
        2002–2011, 2
    See also Chicago; Department of
        Homeland Security (DHS); FBI

John Mueller is Professor and Woody Hayes Chair of National Security Studies at the Mershon Center for International Security Studies and Professor of Political Science at Ohio State University, Columbus, Ohio. He is the author of over a dozen books, several of which have won prizes. Among the most recent of these: *The Remnants of War* (2004), *Overblown* (2006), *Atomic Obsession: Nuclear Alarmism from Hiroshima to Al-Qaeda* (2010), and *War and Ideas* (2011). He has also edited the web book, *Terrorism Since 9/11: The American Cases* (2011). He has published numerous articles in scholarly journals and general magazines and newspapers, is a member of the American Academy of Arts and Sciences, and has been a John Simon Guggenheim Fellow.

Mark G. Stewart is Professor of Civil Engineering and Director of the Centre for Infrastructure Performance and Reliability at The University of Newcastle in Australia. He is co-author of *Probabilistic Risk Assessment of Engineering Systems* (Chapman & Hall, 1997), and has published more than 300 technical papers and reports. He has more than 25 years of experience in probabilistic risk assessment of infrastructure systems that are subject to man-made and natural hazards. Since 2004, Professor Stewart has received extensive Australian Research Council support to develop probabilistic terrorism risk-modeling techniques for buildings subject to explosive blasts and cost-benefit assessments of counterterrorism protective measures for critical infrastructure. In 2011, he received a five-year Australian Professorial Fellowship from the ARC to continue and to extend that work.